Challenging Life on a 1948 Triumph

Daisy's Diaries

Graham Ham

Panther Publishing

Published by Panther Publishing Ltd in 2005

Panther Publishing Ltd
10 Lime Avenue
High Wycombe
Buckinghamshire HP11 1DP
UK

Dedication
For my wife Diane, who's enormous patience and understanding is simply priceless.

Acknowledgements
There are many to thank, not just for their help and support in the creation of this book, but also for being there and supporting me during the events that are described within it. So, in no particular order, the aforementioned thanks go to: my family - mother, father and brothers - all of whom have been wonderfully supportive during the more uncertain moments. The Triumph Owner's Club UK, in particular the Birmingham and Wolves branch, for hosting and supporting the Landmark Challenge and in doing so promoting the use of older motorcycles. Nacelle, the official club Magazine, for printing the original Daisy's Diary short story series. RealClassic magazine deserve a huge thank you, in particular Frank Westworth and Rowena Hoseason for allowing me the chance to develop those early scribbles into the regular monthly series it is now. Rollo Turner of Panther Publishing deserves a medal for turning my scrawls into something resembling English, as does Grandad for his proof reading.

Finally Chris, Chloe and Sheba the dog, for putting up with all this nonsense and sticking with me through thick and thin. This book would not have been possible without them.

ISBN 0954791231

Contents

Prologue

The air is heavy with neglect. Not the deliberate, uncaring neglect of laziness, but the neglect that comes with years of inactivity. Peering into the darkness, I can make out the forlorn shapes of a once proud but now long forgotten machine, wiling away the time under the ever settling dust. It's bright edges have become dulled and lifeless, once slick oil has turned to thick unforgiving toffee, shiny surfaces, once so proudly displayed, fade slowly under the oppressive carpet of grime and time..... which has passed slowly for nearly a decade.

This could be any garage or shed in the country, but it happens to be two hundred yards from my house and suddenly, this small dark corner of the world is flooded, once again, with light. The full sad picture, suddenly exposed, can be seen clearly. But a decade of grime cannot hide the beauty that has rested here, patiently, awaiting a new dawn......

A new owner.....

A new lease of life!

But I digress. This moment is a year away yet, and although it is in many ways the real start of the story, I need to fill in a few of the events that lead up to it. Set the scene so to speak, as there's a story to be told, a story that continues and with luck and good health, will continue into the future.

This book is not just about an old bike and it's travels. It's also about life choices, bucking the trend, breaking the mould and proving some points.

Graham Ham
May 2005

1. The Start of an Obsession

It's a wrench to think back to that day in the early 80's when I parted company with Ruby, the 1955 Triumph Speed Twin that had seen me through courtship, early working life and the arrival of the first of our children. It was time for a car, and finances didn't allow for both, so Ruby had to go!

Both Diane, my wife, and I were more than a little emotional that day, as we watched the new owner take her away after delivering the Renault 14 car, we had swapped for her. But I made a solemn promise there and then - once we had got through the lean years, established our family and achieved financial stability – a Speed Twin would once again become part of our lives. It would be a 1955 just like Ruby, and next time she would be for keeps!

And so life went on. I got over the misery of Ruby's parting, and as is the way of life, the promise was forgotten amidst the hustle and bustle that followed. Another child came; two careers were built and lost; I started a business, which after a hairy first year, grew most satisfactorily; the enlarged family meant a bigger house, bigger car - the dogs and the hamster soon followed. The kids grew, as did the business, the mortgage and the bills. Inevitably, the goalposts moved with them and there were always a hundred and one things to keep my mind occupied and my wallet straining.

And so twenty years passed until March 2000. I was becoming increasingly unhappy with life, as by now the business had pretty much taken over. It had expanded steadily, re-branded, changed direction, re-structured and finally merged with another in Ireland. I found myself totally immersed in a company that I didn't understand any more, employing people I didn't know, supplying customers of whom I'd never heard. I was constantly worrying about seemingly impossible cash-flows, marketing strategies, employment laws and everything in between. I never seemed to be home, but when I was my mind seemed constantly to be churning over events elsewhere.

Attending a board meeting one day, during which I was supposed to give judgements on strategies I couldn't get interested in, so therefore hadn't read, and budgets I didn't understand (and therefore hadn't read either), I realised with a blinding flash that it was all destroying me. Clearly I couldn't continue – the fun had all gone from life and it was time for a change. I resigned the following morning.

I would, I decided, become 'self employed', doing what I chose to do, when I chose to do it and hang the consequences. Friends and family reacted in various ways to this, but the prevailing opinion was clearly 'barking mad'. I didn't care. I was free and intended to make the most of things.

A busy few months saw me settled happily into this new life style. Working from home when I chose, getting out and about when it suited and generally not thinking about anything in advance. Things were looking up. I still had a vague lack of personal direction however and this gnawed away at me in the background. Then it happened. I was browsing the Internet, looking for hotels in Wiltshire in order to attend a family get together. There on the second page of search results was a link entitled 'For Sale, Wiltshire. 1955 Triumph...'

The rest was not displayed, but something, somewhere, stirred in my mind '1955 Triumph' being the obvious trigger of a long forgotten promise. I followed the link and "YES!... it's a Speed Twin." It's for sale and it's a 1955 bike, just like Ruby. I couldn't believe my eyes as I looked at the photograph and remembered the trusty old machine. It was immediately apparent to me that I was going to own this one, today if at all possible, tomorrow at the very latest. No doubts at all. I quickly printed the advert off, and clutching my prize, I slunk down to the kitchen and casually slid the thing into Diane's vision. She looked at it, looked at me, looked back at it and raised an eyebrow in an expression, which said 'is there any point trying to dissuade you?'

That was all the spousal approval I needed, and I hurried back upstairs feeling an almost childish excitement building in me. I reached for the 'phone, all thoughts of the family get together forgotten. I called the number, sweating with anticipation as I asked the dreadful question ...

"Have you still got the Speed Twin?" He did.

"Is it still for sale?" It was. I heard a voice croak "I'll buy it!".

The owner seemed confused at such an outright approval of the deal and began, or so it seemed, to try to persuade me that I might not want it. "It's not in good fettle you know, you'll be wanting to have a look first" and when this didn't dissuade me "It's not original, that's why it's this price. You'll have to do a lot to it" I patiently fended off his concerns - no, I didn't want to see it first, no I didn't care about the bits that weren't original, no I don't care about matching numbers, no I'm NOT a bloody tyre kicker!

Eventually, arrangements and directions were agreed, and early next morning I climbed into the family Espace, freshly stripped of seats, for a long drive down to Wiltshire. I hadn't felt like this for years. I had hardly slept the previous night and now the two and a half hour drive seemed impossibly long to my anticipation-fevered brain. After what seemed an ice age I arrived at the correct address and it was immediately plain why the owner had pressed me on details – what I gazed at was in a sorry state indeed. She was tatty. She was oily. She was a 'bitsa' and the owner seemed keen to point out the wrong tank, forks and front wheel. She was quite simply the most wondrous sight to my otherwise sensible but temporarily crazed, rose tinted eyes. I nodded politely as I was told of the catalogue of things wrong, but I didn't actually listen to any of it. She was about to be mine, and that, really, was that!

I hastily concluded the deal, handing over a pile of the green stuff to the bemused owner (clearly he had expected to haggle), got and checked the log book (I'm not *totally* stupid) and in short order loaded my prize into the Espace via the scaffold plank I had brought with me in an unusual fit of sensible forward thinking. On the way home, I christened her 'Winnie' for reasons which I cannot adequately explain, and therefore won't - but all old machines should, in my view, have a name. I stopped in a lay-by, 'phoned home and issued instructions to my bemused other half. "Get onto the insurers", says I, "get me insured!, "here's the model and registration number – no, stuff the cost, just please make sure there's a cover note on my desk in two hours!!" That done, I peeled off into the nearest town, searching for leathers, helmet and gloves. It's a Harley dealership I find, which means it's expensive. I don't care. Give me that jacket, that helmet, those gloves – thanks and bye bye! I rapidly made my exit, clutching my new prizes and leaving a bemused salesman with a fistful of the folding stuff shaking his head.

As I set off homewards once again, my mind turned over the other issues, MOT? Tax? Stuff it, that can wait - I simply have to, and will, ride her today! Another age passed as I drove home. I kept glancing in the rear view mirror to catch a glimpse of Winnie in the back, and, grinning like an idiot, I wiled away the time trying to remember what Ruby had looked like and planning what I'll need to return Winnie to her true looks. Back at home I couldn't wait to unload her and have my first critical inspection. My family duly gathered in the drive with a mixture of amused expressions as I carefully reversed her down the plank. The looks on their faces as exhibit A, sad, tatty and oily, emerged were a picture - clearly dad had lost his senses and shouldn't be allowed to get excitable or handle sharp objects. Ignoring this I quickly donned my new riding apparel, and with a triumphant grin at the assembled doubters, took my first but long awaited ride. Down the road I went, wobbling slightly, until I reached the first bend and applied the brakes.

The front forks, it transpires, are too short. This becomes evident as the front mudguard jams against the frame, doing something disastrous to the gyroscopic balance, whilst locking the front wheel in an unnatural relationship to the back, resulting in the hair raising experience of carrying straight on when we should be leaning majestically and skilfully into, and thus round, the bend. A very scary experience, very nearly a very painful one and a crushing blow to my immediate plans involving riding without a care into the sunset, collecting flies in my teeth due to the impossibly wide grin that would certainly be fixed to my face. Returning to the house, carefully, the disappointment screaming inside my head is made worse by the obvious amusement of the family. I can feel a tingling flush of embarrassment and shame creeping up my cheeks as, with heads shaking and grins spreading my wife and daughter return to the house. My son completes the misery by sauntering over and saying, "So are you going to get a new one now then?" Before long, I am alone with my misery, and I begin to survey the problem. Measurements are made and telephone calls follow to the first supplier I can find on the Internet.

The problems were quickly identified, as I discussed the machine with a person of superior knowledge, comparing descriptions and measurements. The front forks, wheel, mudguard and tank are all from a later machine of the same model, believed to be a 1958 version, which amongst other things are physically smaller. We surmise that at some point a previous owner had succumbed to a meeting with Mr. Sorry-Mate-I-Didn't-See-You, and in the attempt to fix things had made the common mistake of confusing the two models. .

That initial setback didn't deter me at all. I set to work over the following weeks, scrabbling together all the bits whilst rediscovering some of the long forgotten joys of owning a classic motorcycle. It all came back, the fun of auto-jumbling, the search for those elusive bits and bobs, the thrill of the find, and all along parting with large piles of the green stuff like confetti. By now, the family are exacting enormous entertainment from my predicament, but I am determined to sort things and try to take their scepticism in my stride. The new front end was duly cobbled into place, and the great day arrived in June when I venture forth once more, on a vastly improved machine. How on earth had I given this up – and for so long? How had I come to forget the sheer joy of blasting along on a big twin, throaty roar in my ears, wind in my face, oil on my shoes…! Oil on my shoes? Bugger!

More jumbles, more bits, a re-bore while I'm at it, more of the green-stuff heading for new owners. Oh blimey, a new carburettor as well, and now the tank's sprung a leak. Ah … the joys of classic motorcycling! Seven months, and the wrong end of £1,200 later, including the forks and tyres, she's right. Oh yes she is! Even the family have stopped giggling into their dinner, and are queuing up for a ride on the back! I settle down to a daily routine, and we start to clock up the miles, do Winnie and I. But I wasn't to know that this was just the beginning of what would become a far greater passion in my life and I had no inkling of the quirky event that waited, literally just around the corner.

A regularly used classic bike attracts quite a bit of attention, and I was getting used to strangers accosting me on a regular basis to regale me with their own tales from distant times and places. But I wasn't quite prepared for the chap who turned up in June 2001, who had noticed Winnie on her daily rounds and was about to place me in a real quandary! On returning home one day from work I found this particular person in my porch, peering through my letterbox. I approached with caution and from a safe distance enquired as to whether I might assist him.

The poor man nearly jumped out of his skin, but, recovering magnificently, he pointed at Winnie and asked "Is that yours then?" Ah, another one of these.

"Yes" says I, relaxing a little since he doesn't appear to be holding an axe, "Why?"

"Well" he says, "Do you want another one? Only I live just down the road, and well, I've got one just like this. It's years since I've ridden it, but I'm sure you would soon get it running, and you'd make a good owner for the old girl!"

I ran his statement around in my mind for a few seconds. I blinked and looked away. I looked back – he's still there – so he must be real. Resisting the temptation to pinch myself, I recover my wits and respond in a clear, off-hand, don't really care sort of way…. "Wah?" I squawk.

It's a bit surreal this, as I walk down the road, all of three hundred yards to his garage. We're back where we came in at the beginning of this story as he opens his garage door and light floods in to reveal a 1948 Speed Twin, differing from Ruby and Winnie in that it was made in the last year before Triumph's famous nacelle became standard. This one sports a separate headlamp, a quaint instrument panel in the tank and no conventional suspension. Instead I was delighted to see that most infamous of Edward Turner's less celebrated designs – the Mk1 Sprung Hub. She seems to be all original and complete and the owner is telling me all about her, but I'm not really listening. I catch bits, like "last run nine years ago" and "too old to ride" but it's just background noise because I'm absolutely and hopelessly Smitten (note the capital 'S'). Despite the layers of grime she is, I am thinking, the prettiest thing I've ever set eyes on. I determine there and then that she's going to be mine. He names his price and I agree, I think, without even listening. She's been waiting patiently in the dark all that time (for today – for me!) and I am going to pay whatever this dear man wants.

We concluded the deal and I left with a promise to return in short order with the agreed sum. But as I walked the three hundred yards home an urgent and worrying thought niggles at me - the fact that after Winnie and her fettling costs, I had absolutely promised Diane that no more money would go on bikes until I had furnished her with a new bathroom. The funds for this currently nestle in the building society and represent all available capital. I knew that if I asked first, the answer would be the wrong one but I equally understood that Fate had delivered to me this opportunity and who could argue with Fate? It was immediately clear to me that the best thing to do would be to buy the bike, say nothing, sneak the new arrival up the drive, park it just so and then go indoors and wait for an opportune moment to look meaningfully out of the window and pronounce something like "Isn't she pretty!?" whilst adopting some form of pathetic "don't be cruel to me I'm a helpless fluffy animal" type of expression. I felt absolutely sure that Diane couldn't fail to agree and that common sense would prevail.

I won't go into the messy details here, but four years on I am still paying the price for that rash leap of faith! Anyway, Daisy came into my life. Daisy? Well it's appropriate, as it's a good name for a cow. You work it out. After a good few attempts, she cleaned up just fine and I was delighted to discover that underneath the patina of neglect was a very tidy machine indeed. Her engine however, was in poor condition. Not so bad that she didn't run, so I set about fettling her as best I could and then started using her. Daisy oozed character and charm, and if I was smitten when I first saw her I quite simply fell in love once I started using her!

With my life-style fundamentally changed, I had time on my hands to set about enjoying myself a bit and the acquisition of a pair of Speed Twins was a big step towards that ideal. I had found that 'missing bit' and quite simply, life had never been so good. With my old interest in the classic scene rekindled, I began visiting an increasing number of shows and auto-jumbles, swapping yarns with fellow enthusiasts, making new friends and generally feeling happy that all the effort had been worthwhile. Next I re-joined the Triumph Owners' Club, decided that I would be an active member and, in short order I signed up for a number of rallies. This attracted the immediate attention of both Chris and Chloe, my children, as it would involve camping. Camping indeed – when was the last time I had been camping?

Little was I to know that one of these events would sow the seeds of an irresistible challenge that would lead me in pursuit of adventure and discovery with the old Triumph, and for those who know me, confirm beyond doubt that I had truly lost any remaining marbles.

The real story begins here.

2. The Landmark Challenge – and into the Fens

"Are you really, really sure about this?" That was my wife, some time after my impromptu announcement that I intend to 'do' the Triumph Owners' Club's Landmark Challenge. On Daisy in fact, and not only do it, but hopefully land the Individual Gold Award. And yes … I *am* sure about this. In fact I have thought of almost nothing else since being captivated by the large colourful display in the Triumph Owners' marquee at a Northampton show, which explained the challenge and told the story of the previous year's winner, accompanied by numerous photographs. Something stirs deep inside me as I gaze in awe at this heroic adventurer posing with his machine at a variety of exotic, historic and far-flung destinations. I have ridden Daisy up to this event in response to a plea from the club for owners of older machines to bring them for display. Being 1948, she is in fact the oldest machine on show and they have accordingly given her pride of place in the marquee, parked beneath the Landmark display. It is here that a fellow owner helps make up my mind to mount an assault on the challenge, when he interrupts my daydreaming with a comment that provokes the bulldog spirit in me.

"You wouldn't be wanting to do that on your old nail." I turn to study the source of this declaration and note the broad grin of a friendly but clearly mischievous fellow clubman.

"Oh, you don't reckon?" says I.

"Nah. Not practical mate. Even if the bike survived it, I doubt *you* would eh?"

I look at Daisy, then at my provocateur who, as a small audience begins to form, feels he needs to embellish his reasoning.

"Well, I mean, it's 1948 innit? No suspension, ancient electrics, cruising speed of what?…60 mph if you're lucky? It'd take you a year! You'd have to be mad to try it!" His audience seems to agree with him, but riding home, I find myself fighting an irrational urge to prove them all wrong.

Why couldn't I do it? People have scaled Everest, explored just about every nook and cranny on Earth and, when we get right down to it, even landed on the moon! This is just a paltry collection of 50 Ordnance Survey map references, each with a cryptic clue to identify the Landmark residing there, and you have a riding season, January up to December each year, to solve and visit them, collecting photographic evidence of your visits as you go. Couldn't be that hard surely?

There is a range of awards from bronze to gold, depending on how many of the 50 Landmarks you manage. The Individual Gold, a spangly great trophy by all accounts, and one which I am steadily convincing myself will be mine, goes to the oldest machine that completes all 50. That'll be Daisy then, and I waste no time once home digging out the published list of the current year's challenge before retiring to my computer where I spend the evening feeding map references into the thing.

Take a large map of the United Kingdom. The largest you can find. Spread it out on the floor. Take 50 coloured map pins, cup them between both hands and then stand over your map and throw the pins up into the air letting them cascade down. What you're now looking at is a good representation of the Landmark Challenge. Note the random pattern, and particularly note that no remote corner is left without a pin. The size of the task becomes apparent but being a man of firm resolve, I press on with the planning by attempting to carve up the map into manageable portions which can be picked off as individual sorties. Next I had to decide whether to try and identify the Landmarks in advance, or whether to just wing it on the day each time and hope something obvious presented itself. Two evenings of research on the good old Internet had most of them identified, with only a few that were not clear. They ranged from interesting historical sites such as standing stones or castles, through windmills, viaducts and interesting bridges to stadiums, famous sites such as theatres and a smattering of various museums or public interest sites thrown in.

So the task is now clear, and I reckon that if I'm to do something this stupid, it really should be for charity and once you've said that to a few people, particularly in the local, there's *no* turning back. Within a month helpful associates have chosen the John Jackson Youth Scholarship for me, they've agreed and are eager to publicize it. Before I know what's happening the charity have arranged (with the help of aforementioned associates) to come down in order to meet me, take photo's and tell me all about their work. The Scholarship scheme, named after that famous Jazz musician, is run and supported by a bunch of professional musicians with the aim of assisting underprivileged youngsters with a possible flair for the art to develop their skills. They do this by providing both financial support and, of course, their own skills, running a series of residential workshops through the year as well as festival activities and personal support. Pretty soon I've got lots of sponsors queuing up – again thanks to those mischievous associates, and that's that - I've *got* to do it now.

Having carved up the map in order to attack it in chunks, a plan emerges that'll see me picking off everything roughly south of Birmingham over a number of weekends, some of which will need to be of the long variety. Now that I am my own master, I can take 11 days out of what would have been work, which will give me the required 15 days to do the Northern, Welsh and Scottish bits. It's also clear that I need to be half sensible and choose a more central geographic location from which each foray will commence and finish, due to the mildly inconvenient fact that I live in the furthest south east corner of Kent. There are two fairly straightforward reasons for this and I make no apology! First, there is only one real road out of the far southeast corner of England, which during this particular summer is undergoing major, major road works. No fun at all on a machine this old and due to the nature, length and disposition of the project, nowhere to go if disaster strikes! Second, it actually takes an hour and a half just to reach South London from this corner, where I will then be presented, for my pleasure and enjoyment, with the M25! I can't get enough time off to do that each time and I have no inclination whatsoever to take Daisy round the M25. After some deliberation I choose Cambridge as my starting point for all forays.

With all the necessary preparation done, and with the first months of the year already gone, it's decision time. We'll make a start by attacking the east first –

Cambridge, Suffolk, Norfolk and Lincolnshire. There is a total of six Landmarks awaiting me in these fair counties and the choice of east as the first full weekend sortie is not without reason. For all my blind faith, Daisy is truly untested in terms of reliability, durability and general fettle. I also have the niggling worry that she has spent nine years standing in that dark garage and the potential for problems with bearings, magneto windings and the like is far from certain. So this is an easy option designed to find out the stark truth, for better or for worse. From our chosen start point at Cambridge, an anti-clockwise route has been plotted that should see the six Landmarks found and recorded and have me arrive back at the start again some three hundred miles later - whilst never actually taking me more than sixty miles away in real terms. This means that any disastrous occurrences will allow me to get recovered in a timely fashion.

As the days tick past, I am left with one further task. In typically cavalier fashion I had thrown myself into the few rallies attended thus far with a minimum of actual thought or preparation, and I had learnt very quickly that camping without suitable equipment is not fun. I had bought the cheapest tent I could find, and hadn't bothered with any supporting infrastructure such as panniers, cooking and eating utensils, kettle, stove or indeed a light. I had reasoned that rallies were organised events and as such would supply all the necessary, surely? Wrong. Even if that was true, the Landmark is a different bag of onions entirely and therefore a pilgrimage to the local outdoor activities store is absolutely necessary.

So off I go, armed with a list of the required (or so I thought) items. The kindly proprietor takes pity on me and is good enough to spend nearly an hour putting me right on a number of things. He even takes the pain to go out and check Daisy over before making recommendations. I return some hours later with a full set of the necessary paraphernalia, which the kids and I then set about trying to fit together in the garden. They are keen to test out this fabulous array of explorer's tackle, so spend the night out there, pronouncing everything in order the next day. We then set about trying to hang it all on Daisy and after a number of scenarios with only a mild bout of buffoonery, we settle on a configuration that looks like it might stay on after the first ten miles. New throw-over panniers are sourced to finish off the whole thing, and I declare Daisy, and myself, finally ready for the great adventures ahead.

Unloading Daisy and camping gear at a convenient lay-by on the A428 west of Cambridge from the back of the Espace, I have a sense of great adventure about to commence out there on the open road. Although this is a mere taster for the far greater distances that will be traversed later on in the year, I'm fairly confident that if we can get through this weekend without mishaps then the rest is just more of the same for longer, surely, albeit with different scenery. And another heartening fact is that I'm not alone as I thought I would be. Both of the young Ham brood have enthusiastically signed up for the challenge in turns and I have Chris, my son, riding shotgun on this first foray. He has no idea what he's getting himself into, but the exuberance of youth has left him enthusiastically ready for anything.

It's four o'clock on that Saturday afternoon and we're off, but unfortunately the weather hasn't responded kindly to the great occasion as it's grey and overcast as far as the eye can see, with a fine drizzle drifting across the landscape. The first

Landmark is only a few miles from our start point, and it's something I've never had experience of before, a military cemetery. It's a strangely sobering, unsettling experience and I feel slightly uncomfortable taking photographs of Daisy at the entrance. There is nothing quite like a field full of white crosses to focus the mind and our mood becomes somewhat contemplative as we move off into afternoon traffic.

We now have to ride through Cambridge in order to head east into Suffolk. As it's approaching rush hour this proves not to be much fun - I've learnt that Daisy hates stop-start traffic. It's not long before she overheats and I struggle to keep her running at each of a seemingly endless string of red traffic lights. I finally lose the unequal struggle as she stops on the ring road somewhere in the northwest suburbs. Fine, I have been here many times before and I know the drill, which simply entails waiting for the poor old thing to cool down. Twenty minutes is normal, so we park her up and watch the choking traffic rumble on by whilst listening to Daisy making 'tinc, tinc' noises as she cools down.

Finally she's ready and starts without fuss, so we get back underway and manage to free ourselves from the nightmare Cambridge circular, heading out east towards Newmarket. We head along the A14 and our spirits lift as the drizzle eases. Newmarket comes and goes and we continue on into the evening, getting dry in the wind. The countryside is beginning to open-up as we cross into Suffolk, heading for Bury St. Edmunds. With the rain giving way to broken cloud, through which the sun makes an occasional glorious appearance, we begin to enjoy the ride. Daisy is content to rumble along at a steady sixty mph, with her deep burbling exhaust note like music in my ears. I turn to look over my shoulder at Chris, and the big grin he displays says it all. It's not too long before Daisy's 1940's seating arrangements make their presence felt, and after an hour we both need to take a break. We stop at a lay-by in order to rest the nether regions and do a map check. We both agree that life really couldn't get much better than this as the last of the clouds finally clears to the west and the glorious late afternoon sun bathes us in it's warmth.

Motorcyclists are nothing if not a communal breed, sharing a comradely spirit and it is gratifying that within minutes of our stopping a chap on a big shiny BMW pulls in to ask what the problem is and whether there is anything he can do. This happens to me a lot as I amble my way through life on Daisy. Explanations follow, and as we describe our mission I can see he clearly thinks we're certifiable but is too polite to say so. Directions are checked and after another incredulous look at Daisy off he goes, followed by us a few minutes later. After a while we leave the A14 as it begins to head south and take the A1120 at Stowmarket. This is where we can really begin to enjoy things as the road heads off east again into the sticks. Evening is drawing in and I reckon it's about fifteen to twenty miles to the next Landmark. We need to get a shove on as the sun is sinking steadily and Daisy's not blessed with stunning lighting abilities. This road's fantastic though, and as it twists and turns into the hazy Suffolk countryside a light mist begins to hang around the fields. We have to find a post mill, according to my detective work earlier, and we are getting pressed for time because we also need to find somewhere to camp.

As we pull up for a map check, It dawns on me that I really should have planned the camping, rather than trust to luck that I'd find somewhere just when needed. I also realised with a feeling of desperation that my economy map, being a large-scale thing covering half of Britain, doesn't actually show the little roads we are now heading into. Just how stupid a mistake this is comes home in spades as we realise that we are looking for a fairly small Landmark in roughly 100 square miles of blank paper.

Placing the mark on the map at home had seemed all too straightforward at the time. We had no idea of the reality that a myriad of little country roads all heading for uncharted places would bring. What to do? Chris expresses an opinion that we should just camp in the nearest field, as he's tired and hungry, but we can't find anywhere that's suitable. By now, we are thoroughly lost and, as the light is going fast, we both begin to feel desperate. Suddenly, rounding a hedge lined bend, we stumble across the post mill, almost by accident. This is a huge relief because I can at least tell where on the blank bit of map we now are. We quickly get our photograph and set off in earnest looking for camping. As the last light fades I turn the ancient switch on Daisy's tank panel but the resulting orange glow from her headlamp fails to help.

Things are getting fairly desperate but as if by divine intervention, we spy a B&B sign emerging from the gloom, and I decide to shell out the readies if they have a vacancy. What luck we have too, because at the end of the lane is a big country inn, and yes they do indeed have a vacancy. The room turns out to be a delightful bed-sitter situated in what were clearly the stables in by-gone years when this very inn served as a vital safe haven for the stagecoach of an evening. With no further ado we book in and the landlord insists that Daisy be bedded down for the night in his garage. That done, we look forward to a few beers (coke for Chris), some good old country home cooking and a comfortable bed. The locals are very friendly, and want to know what we're up to on such an old bike, this far from civilization. As the tale is told we find ourselves at the centre of a small gathering and by closing time we feel as if we've known these people for a lifetime.

We're up early the next morning, and it's gloriously sunny. After a hearty breakfast we are pleasantly surprised when the landlord insists on only charging half his normal fee because, he informs us, he rather liked the story we told him the previous evening. What a nice man, and the gesture leaves us both feeling remarkably content with the world as we set off again, heading north. I know we are heading north because I have about my person a small, but rather splendid, plastic compass, which I had got from a Christmas cracker that year. But there's trouble ahead as we soon become hopelessly lost in the tiny back roads that still don't show on my map. Most of them refuse to behave themselves and take us north as we require, preferring instead to change direction every hundred yards or so and head off anywhere but north. Daisy, sensing our vulnerability, suddenly decides to start mucking about. We press on with an intermittent misfire jarring what would otherwise be a splendid ride, and as the miles pass it gets steadily worse.

After an hour, I can't believe that I still can't locate us on the map, which doesn't even contain reference to the numerous villages that we've passed through, but this train of thought is summarily halted as Daisy decides she's had enough for the time being, thank you, stopping ceremoniously with an impressive backfire. We coast to a stop, dismount and take a five minute rest while a slightly panicked Chris grills me about what was that bang, what has happened, what we can do about it and how do we get home? Very good questions indeed, I consider, as I ditch the riding gear and crouch down to start the process familiar to all classic motorcyclists - the application of skill, luck or miracle, to coax life back into the old girl.

So here we are, on the first of our forays in pursuit of the Landmark Challenge Individual Gold Award. We've managed two Landmarks only, and less than one hundred miles. To add to our misery it starts raining again, we're cold, we're lost somewhere in Suffolk with a map that may as well detail Mars, and we no longer have a working motorbike. Chris has remembered that we have breakdown cover and suggests rather persistently that calling those fine people is the only sensible option. "Certainly not" I say, being very reluctant to surrender so quickly, although it is dawning on me that we are an awfully long way from home. Determined to show young Chris that where there is a will there is a way, I begin to prod optimistically at the BTH magneto in the vain hope of finding the problem. The usual drill then suggests itself and I take the plugs out, kick, kick, kick. There are good sparks. I give them a good clean and put them back in, before trying to start her again. Kick, kick, kick, BANG! I had to stop myself laughing out loud as Chris jumped about three feet in the air and ran for it. He's not used to this sort of thing at all, and tells me from his new, safer position what he thinks about it and that in his view it's all over. We should go home. I suggest that whilst the situation is not good, certainly, I am confident there is a simple explanation. He does not look at all convinced.

That sort of backfire really isn't good it is true, especially if you notice, as Chris has, the apparently impressive long finger of flame that issued forth and is the cause of his rapid retreat. I start to suspect she has shredded the magneto pinion, that feeble fibre thing so popular with Joe Lucas, or that at the very least it has slipped, which would of course completely throw the ignition timing. Worse still is the thought that a valve is stuck open. Mind ticking busily, I decide to try the cylinders one at a time and discover that the left one is in fact fine and running evenly. The right one causes the backfire.

At this point Chris has clearly decided that Daisy may spontaneously combust at any minute and retreats even further down the road, with his fingers jammed firmly in his ears. His face tells me that he's not at all impressed with this suddenly nerve racking game, and that we should jolly well stop playing silly buggers and call the nice breakdown man. Undeterred, I quickly check the valve clearances, and find all in order so I convince Chris that having one cylinder running smoothly is good news, as it means that nothing fundamental is broken. All we have to do, I explain confidently, is find out what's causing the problem with the other one. Daisy is a simple soul in that respect and with no coil, rectifier or battery in the circuit, there are only so many things it can be! This is of course so much bunk, but I start by pulling the points to bits, cleaning and re-assembling. Then I pull the HT leads off and clean everything, put it all back and get ready to try her again. Chris, who has slowly crept back to watch, takes his cue and all but sprints away down the road, fingers back in ears, but he needn't have worried because she's fine! We don't know exactly what the cause of the mystery backfire was, but now she is thump-thump-thumping away in a steady and even tickover. Chris returns slowly, tensed and ready to bolt at the first sign of danger but eventually and reluctantly agrees that we can get underway again.

We consult the map. We don't know why we do this, other than a vague hope that it has undergone a metamorphosis into something useful. Alas it hasn't and we've lost nearly an hour and a half, with the amount of distance covered so far woefully inadequate. If we're to have any chance of meeting our target of six Landmarks this weekend we must press on and ride Daisy that much harder. We miraculously manage, after only mild clownery in the navigation department, to blunder into the A144, which actually exists on my novelty map. Turning north, Daisy settles down to a steady 65 mph, with no sign at all of her earlier problems, and pretty soon we're passing through Bungay and heading for Norwich on a lovely rustic 'B' road of the sort that probably made up the main roads back in Daisy's younger days. Riding a classic motorcycle on such a road is an experience guaranteed to warm the soul. Unfortunately it seems like no time at all before we are forced onto dual carriageway around Norwich itself and on into Norfolk to reach the Coast and the next Landmark. The Holt Steam Railway connects the little town of Holt to the holiday resort of Cromer, and is a popular attraction judging by the packed car park and picnic area, Daisy obviously feels that it's time to wake Chris up again as we pull in, letting off a loud backfire just as we stop.

This time though, it's not just Chris she upsets, as all hell breaks loose around us with a cacophony of car alarms immediately springing to life, followed by a whole concert party of babies suddenly wailing their hearts out, jerked unceremoniously as they were from their slumbers! I feel the red flush of embarrassment creeping up my neck and cheeks as seemingly the entire population of Holt turn to stare in hostile demeanour at these hoodlums who have barged in here in their leather jackets and destroyed the peaceful tranquillity with their nasty, noisy motorbike. We quickly take our photograph then scuttle into the shop, buy some coke and crisps, and as quickly as possible push Daisy out to the road, as the stares continue to bore into us like lasers. Once out of view, we both see the funny side and have a good chuckle as we eat and drink. Nervous about the backfire however, I start Daisy just to be sure that the problems have not reappeared and I grin to myself as she bursts into life. I turn to Chris to reassure him that all's fine, only to see him down the road again, with his back to me, fingers firmly in his ears!

It's time to turn west now, and before long we have picked up the A148 heading across Norfolk without further incident, lovely roads for Daisy, and the sun has come out too. Things are clearly looking up, but we're increasingly against the clock with something like one hundred and fifty miles still to do and three Landmarks to find. We haven't stopped much in last few hours so we're feeling it. We stop at King's Lynn for a late lunch, a country pub that used to be a water mill serves the purpose nicely, and after a pleasant hour watching ducks and dragonflies busy themselves along the banks of the adjoining stream, we're off again towards the Wash and our next Landmark The Sutton Bridge, an old iron bridge that spans the border between Norfolk and Lincolnshire. Arriving here Daisy displays the same bad manners as earlier, letting off a ripping backfire that extracts a "Woaaagh" from Chris and makes me jump too.

With the photograph taken, we attempt to get underway again but Daisy has other ideas. After several minutes of trying, the best she manages is a loud spit through the carburettor as the kick-start rebounds violently against its stop. Chris begins his by now familiar retreat and I decide to give it a rest for ten minutes or so, not least because my kicking leg is now so much jelly after the exertions. As we sit in the lay-by we can see the intense heat radiating from Daisy's engine in the harsh sunshine and Chris begins his litany of doubt, checking that I've still got the breakdown number. Oh he of little faith! It then dawns on me that we actually have the makings of a brew in Chris's rucksack, a fine idea we both agree, and pretty soon we have a bubbling kettle hissing away on the little primus stove as we wait for Daisy to cool off in the Saharan sun.

It is thirty minutes before Daisy would play again and enable us to set off west into the fine summer backdrop of Lincolnshire. We really must investigate this overheating back at home, preferably before our next foray, but for now We've got two Landmarks still to get, one of which is away to the north nestling amid the Fens. Time's running away from us but strangely such worries dissolve into insignificance because it's hard not to enjoy this now.

It's turned into a scorching afternoon, the roads we've chosen are fantastic, as is the countryside we're riding through and Daisy's settled down again nicely out on the open road. Landmark number five, a tropical forest of all things, is knocked off in short order and after only the shortest of stops for the photograph, we're away for the final one of this foray some twenty five miles to the north of us. Our comedy map is actually of some use here, as it shows some very clear routes up to where we need to be. We choose a 'B' road which seems to take us most of the way. This turns out to be the pick of day, as with the sun off to our left bathing us in glorious late afternoon warmth we pick our way along an alternately wooded, river hugging road which is virtually dead straight, but undulates lazily like a shallow roller coaster as far as the eye can see. We truly can't believe how picturesque this road turns out to be, and suddenly it doesn't matter about time anymore, or anything else for that matter. It turns out that this wonderful road takes us to within five miles of the air museum that is the last Landmark, and with that done, we head back south the way we came, stunned at the beauty of the wonderful sunset across the fields to our right.

Daisy however, has begun to show signs of upset at low revs, with the symptoms particularly showing up at junctions where we have to slow right down or stop. Whatever problem she's been having these past few days is clearly getting worse, and I find myself willing her not to let us down with only sixty odd miles to go. I ease back on the throttle, to cruise along at fifty, and conduct a conference with Chris over my shoulder. We agree that we dare not stop now, however many aches develop in the nether regions, for fear that Daisy will call it a day and spoil our achievement so we press on ever southwards. As we approach Cambridge once again both of us are reduced to desperate fidgeting in an attempt to ease the increasing pain in both legs and backside or at least to move it around a bit. When we finally arrive back at the car, which mercifully still has all of its wheels and indeed windows, it is eight in the evening.

With the last light dying, I reflect that I doubt we could have gone another five miles. Nor would Daisy, it seems, because as we pull into our lay-by, she refuses to tick over at all, finally succumbing to whatever gremlins have infested her with a loud spit and an amusing 'pop'. As for us, we're tired, aching and my backside has gone on strike but we congratulate ourselves on the fact that we've done the first six Landmarks and we're on our way.

3. Back to the Drawing Board

Sitting at home the following weekend, I perform a mental post-mortem on the first of our Landmark forays. It is abundantly clear that I had made several large errors of judgement. First and foremost is the pressing issue of Daisy. She had not let us down on that first trip out, certainly, but those niggling worries I had harboured about her general mechanical state are looking like far more of a reality. Her final few miles were a struggle, and the way she had stopped when finally arriving back in the lay-by at the end of the tour was distinctly unsettling. I chide myself for being so foolish - what did I honestly expect after nine years of dormancy? I had been rash to expect any different, and an urgent investigation to ascertain the extent of the deterioration is called for before any further jollies can be considered.

Secondly, I had learned that my usual approach to adventure, a mixture of maximum impatience with minimum preparation, was possibly not the right approach to the Landmark. If I were to succeed on the much longer wanderings in pursuit of the other forty-four Landmarks I would be an idiot not to actually investigate the positions of such vital things as campsites. It simply hadn't struck me as being an issue, but once out there in the wilds it had become startlingly apparent that campsites are not around every other corner when you need one. The Landmark, obviously, is a very different situation to say, attending a rally, where you are heading for a single gathering place and on arrival, expect the organisers to have thought of such things as where to throw the tents up.

This self-critical train of thought led to a sharp reminder about maps. Maps, when you are lost in the bush, so to speak, are a fundamentally vital bit of kit. Possessing a map, which for example, fails to show eighty percent of the roads or villages that one is actually travelling on or through, is at best ill advised and actually, in the cold light of day pretty damn stupid. I know this now as I find myself thinking back to that post mill, and just how lucky we had actually been to stumble across the thing at all. Equally, Daisy's shenanigans in Norfolk and Suffolk had focused my attention on the very real need for more than just a plug spanner and a penknife, shoved hastily in pockets almost as an afterthought. What, I demand of myself, would I have done if something more serious had occurred – if a vital banjo, for example, had actually worked loose and began spouting oil? I would have been utterly ill prepared to deal with that or worse, given that I had neglected to take even a most basic selection of spanners.

None of these fine and sensible thoughts had occurred to me at all, back when I was in the grip of the rabid enthusiasm and blind optimism that had led me to take up the challenge. But apparently, a good experience is that which leaves one intact to fight another day, better informed, better prepared and indeed better organised. The first foray was therefore clearly a good experience, I decided, and after all was I not right now applying the lessons learned in my planning and preparation for the next sortie? Also on the plus side, we had six Landmarks in the bag and had in theory proved that the thing, if broken down into bits, can be done with relative ease.

We have also made some new friends out there in the boonies and most importantly we have enjoyed ourselves. Finally I also consider that this type of adventuring could not possibly be anything other than valuable life experience for the young Ham brood, of a sort which they would definitely not get from almost any other activity. Chris has certainly had his moments of doubt, particularly when Daisy was at her most troublesome, but he had perked up considerably coming home in the car. Things always look remarkably different once the immediate threat that they bring with them is past, and Chris has managed to turn most of the mishaps into talking points rather than negative memories. We laugh at our luck in finding the mill, agree that the chap running the big pub B&B was a jolly decent fellow, laugh harder at the memory of the Holt car park and picnic area, where Daisy had left such an impression and finally agree that far from being at all discouraged by her antics, we can discuss with pride her achievement in making it back in one piece, still running, despite clearly having an engine that is well past it's sell-by date.

All in all then, we're not at all put off and from the safe surroundings of home we set about enthusiastically listing the things we need to do before the next foray. The biggest of these is to urgently make an attempt to sort out Daisy herself. The following day, being a Sunday, I am free to make a start. But where exactly does one start when there is no clear idea of what's actually wrong? There are many obvious things that can cause problems with a machine of this age, especially when the history is unclear, but there are only so many things that can give the overheating and general misbehaving that had dogged us on our first trip. These mostly revolve around the peripheral parts such as magneto, carburettor or top end (pistons, bore, valves and cylinder head) and so these are the things that will receive my immediate focus.

As I unbolt the carburettor, it is apparent that the studs that hold it on have not been disturbed for many, many years and this leads me to thinking about Daisy's past life. What *did* I actually know about her? When, for example, was the last time someone had undone these self same nuts, and what exactly had been done? How long had this collection of parts that made up her engine unit actually been together? Could it even be possible that they are all in fact, the original components that left the factory as a working motorcycle way back in 1948? There is no way of knowing, but I find the thought rather appealing and not a little romantic. As the carburettor comes free this thought is reinforced after only the briefest inspection: it is absolutely worn out and actually has a crack in it, underneath where the flange meets the manifold of the cylinder head. I marvel that Daisy has managed to run at all, let alone in traffic and heat, but at least this quickly gives the answer to those niggling problems because a cracked manifold can only lead to a weak mixture, which in turn leads to heat and of course aids the vaporization problems that make a hot engine almost impossible to start.

If the carburettor was that worn, I reason, then the engine itself must be in equally poor shape, so I carry right on with the spanners in order to lift off the cylinder head and have a peek at the general condition of valves, bore and pistons. It is fortuitous that I do so, because what I find in there is truly shocking. The head itself is also cracked, again in a place between the cylinders that is almost impossible to see with the thing in place. All of the valves are badly worn and badly burnt, but what really shocks, and indeed, fascinates me is the state of the actual piston crown surfaces. Take a telescope on a clear summer evening, and wait for the moon to rise. Focus in on the thing, and imagine it being a different colour, not dissimilar to say, a piston crown. What you are looking at is a fairly good representation of Daisy's right hand piston, which indeed looks as if a passing meteor shower has come a bit too close and left a number of it's constituent parts embedded therein for eternity. On closer inspection, there also appears to be a fair sized chunk missing from the top edge of the piston.

These discoveries do absolutely nothing to convince me that the rest of the engine will be able to endure the adventures I have planned. With a feeling of resignation, I accept that the rest will have to come apart in order that I can investigate further. The thought of stripping an engine is often too much for many owners, but it's actually not at all difficult. Meccano for adults is probably a good way of thinking about it, and I was not at all afraid to wield the spanners further in my quest for mechanical surety. The barrels came off next, revealing further woes when the majority of the piston rings, freed from their entrapment, fall apart with a disdainful clinketty-clink and decorate the workshop floor. Except, that is, the top ring on the right piston. This one appears to have burnt itself into its groove, and looks like an un-mined coal seam running round the top of the piston. It is here that the piece of crown has also disappeared, leaving an ugly scar that joins the coal seam. This would explain the moonscape piston then, and I imagine that piece, together with several bits of compression ring, bouncing around the combustion chamber causing merry havoc.

I began to wonder with no small sense of awe how Daisy has actually run at all, let alone conveyed Chris and myself all round Suffolk, Norfolk and Lincolnshire, but at the same time I have to admit to a growing respect for a design that can continue on after such a clear disintegration of what I have always thought of as vital parts. Having got this far and finding nothing good, the inevitable question is whether the internals are any better. Removing the pistons, I tenderly test the big ends by grasping the con rod firmly and easing up and down to feel for play. What I find is not what I expect, surprisingly there is no big-end wear that I can detect, but something far more sinister becomes apparent. The whole crankshaft assembly moves from side to side instead. I sit and fiddle with this new discovery, fascinated at the sheer amount of lateral movement I am able to effect, whilst contemplating it's meaning. What it means is that the engine has to come out altogether in order to split the crankcases and sort out the obviously totally worn-out main bearings.

This leads to another jolting revelation, which is a far scarier one than the mechanical challenges facing me – cost. Clearly none of this is going to come free, and having already spent the bathroom fund once on Daisy, how on earth am I to break the news to Diane that the same Daisy now requires yet more of our hard earned funds before she can take to the highways again? It was fairly obvious to me that this will be a very tricky situation indeed, and my mind begins working on the best way to introduce the subject in such a way that the conclusion would be favourable. I retire to the local hostelry in the evening and try out various approaches in my head, but none of them seem likely to obtain the result required. In fact, the more I think about the whole thing, it seems increasingly likely that far from receiving spousal support, I will, in contrast, face a harsh inquisition during which I will be asked to explain just how I had come to exchange a sizeable slice of our worldly wealth for a barely disguised pile of scrap. I have to admit that there is no ready answer to this, or at least, not one that doesn't invite a swift dink round the ear with the frying pan.

To add to my mental woes, there is also the almost unbearable shame that would inevitably come from failure. The charity will be less than brimming with gratitude at my consummate lack of success. The sponsors will have to be told why they can hold onto their money and all those associates who have so enthusiastically pushed me headlong into backing up my mouth with action, will be contemptuous to say the least. And that smug git that had started all this, back in the TOMCC tent that day will be proved right. It is all unthinkable, and if I can not find a way to get Daisy back into action, pretty damn soon, I feel that the only option will be to quietly emigrate, or do a Reggie Perrin and simply disappear.

With nothing better to do, I continue with the dismantling, all the time thinking of ways and ruses to acquire the necessary funds to put things right. It strikes me that at least a proportion of the required bits could be 'borrowed' from my other machine, Winnie, but even this has it's difficulties as she was now in the possession of my father. With the arrival of Winnie and then Daisy, my father has found his own interest in classic motorcycles re-kindled. I am besotted with Daisy now, and anyway I can't ride both at once, so it seemed sensible to allow him to indulge his renewed desires. It would surely be churlish in the least to ask for her back, merely to rob parts in order to indulge my own pleasures. There was also the age difference between the two machines, some eight years, during which a number of significant design changes had been introduced meaning that I can only use top end components such as barrels, pistons and valves on Daisy anyway. As I think it through, it is obvious that Winnie only represents an absolutely last resort and I put that desperate kind of thinking to the back of my mind for the time being. In the mean time, I dismantle Daisy's entire engine and there is no getting away from the fact that it would need just about everything fixed or renewed. Bearings, bushes, a re-bore, new pistons, cylinder head, valves, carburettor ... the list seems to be endless and the cost will be truly frightening. The weeks are sliding past as well. Things are starting to look fairly dim on the Landmark front!

Another week goes past, with no clear inspiration, and I begin to face up to the reality that it is game over for this year, after only a paltry few miles and a handful of Landmarks. I had just decided that I will have to come clean with everyone when I suddenly hit upon a wizard ruse. It was cheeky, and it was a bit outrageous, but these facts only serve to convince me that it is therefore, a particularly fine ruse indeed. I will go and see my old colleague, Steve Williams, with whom I had founded the company from which I have recently resigned, and see if I can persuade him to stump up some company funds in order to assist Daisy back onto the road to glory. This, I feel has a fairly good chance of succeeding, due to the fact that he was the 'associate' who organised the initial contact with the charity I am allegedly in the process of supporting, and is in fact very involved with the trustees! I am sure he will not want to see things come to such a pitiful halt so early in the challenge, and will no doubt feel almost duty bound to offer assistance. I go down to my old offices the next day, casually like, and soon find myself sipping a coffee in the boardroom where, until only recently, I was numbered amongst those that wielded executive power. But you don't work as closely as I have with Steve for twelve years without getting to know him quite well, and vice versa.

Steve quickly decides that I am here, in his words, 'on the scrounge' and just as quickly guesses that all is not well on the Daisy front.

"Crashed it then, have you?"

"No I bloody haven't!" I shoot back, "but, well, now you mention it, there has been a teensy bit of a set-back..."

I don't get the chance to explain, as Steve is well ahead of me.

"So it's blown up then, and now you're here on the scrounge, like I said." Before I can conjure up any clever responses to this he continues "How much?"

Suddenly, it seems, this is going awfully well, and experience has taught me that there's no point in being shy in such circumstances. I pull a number out of the air, to see what sort of response might be forthcoming. I can not quite bring myself to maintain eye contact as I do this, choosing instead to stare over Steve's shoulder whilst adopting a nonchalant air.

"Shouldn't be more than a grand" I hear myself mutter "which of course I haven't got on account of being unemployed."

This I know is dodgy territory. Steve is one of the people firmly in the camp that thinks I am stark-staring mad to resign my position. He has felt a little betrayed as well, I guess and we have stayed well clear of the subject ever since on the few occasions we have met up. I do not expect any kind of sympathetic response, and I am not disappointed.

"An unemployed twat, is what you mean, and you've got some bloody neck coming out with that argument, if you don't mind me saying."

Ah, not going so awfully well then. But his next statement just as quickly cuts off this thought.

"Eight hundred is all I'll put up, although Christ knows why I should. And this is a one-off. Oh and you'd bloody well better win this thing if I do!"

And that is that. Eight hundred pounds, just like that! Problem solved. I am free to go out and get it all sorted! I thank Steve profusely for his generous offer, receiving only mild insults for my trouble.

I hurry back home from the meeting to begin the search for parts. It is vital to get this underway as soon as possible, due to the obvious challenge involved in finding all the required bits for a 1948 engine. I am sure that this will prove interesting at the very least, but a solid morning's furtive research (courtesy of various offerings in a well known newsagent's) provides me with a number of possibilities which, I am sure, will at least get the ball rolling. I make the telephone calls and began to tot up the damage as bit by bit I find suppliers for what I need. Several calls lead to the taking down of further numbers, which themselves lead to yet more numbers until, by the end of the afternoon, my desk is awash with hastily scribbled details of various specialist engineers, bearing stockists, carburettor outlets and general parts dealers.

That evening I take stock of my progress. The re-bore, with new pistons to match, is no problem. All I have to do is take the barrels and old pistons up to Essex, an hour and a half's drive, where an old style engineer will work his magic. Bearings and crankshaft fettling is also easy, with an engineering supplier in Dover able to deliver the required expertise and parts. Gaskets, seals and perfunctory bits and pieces as may be necessary are all available mail order from Devon. Things were looking up but I still have two very clear problems, for which none of the calls have provided an answer. The carburettor on Daisy, although a thing of beautiful antiquity, is not an easy thing to replace or get fixed. Known as the pre-monobloc, production came to a halt in the early fifties with the introduction of the much improved monobloc version that superseded it.

As the name suggests, the later carburettor is a one-piece design, incorporating all of the necessary gubbins into one casting. Daisy's has a rather quaint separate float-bowl, which stands upright and proud to the side of the carburettor body and is attached by a flange and banjo at the bottom. The resulting assembled appendage is delightful to look at and probably remarkably inefficient, but it is an essential part of the character of the machine. I therefore decline the numerous suggestions to just 'throw it away and fit the later one' although I have to quietly accept that it might come to this given the time frame I am working to. The second challenge is sourcing a replacement for the old cast iron cylinder head. These are quite common, when you don't actually need one of the things. Go to any auto jumble if you want the proof, happy in the knowledge that of all the things you may wish to find, a Triumph cylinder head isn't one of them. I guarantee that packs of the things will follow you round the place, peeping from every other box. Of course, if I were to attend the same jumble, wanting nothing else but a Triumph cylinder head, they will have magically disappeared before I get there. Strange but true.

I decide to get the engineering works under way, and whilst waiting for those jobs to be completed, I will resume the search for the more elusive parts. A further week drags past and despite collecting an ever-increasing list of numbers where 'I might get lucky', I havn't so far. I am beginning to feel enormously frustrated, but I console myself with the thought that having received the cheque from Steve during the week, at least I am able to take the barrels to Essex and the crankshaft to Dover this weekend. In the event, a chance conversation renders all such plans unnecessary, and it happens this Friday evening in, of course, the pub. I am drowning my sorrows, as one does at such times, in the company of a fellow Triumph owner. I describe to him the challenges of the week just past and moan that it is going to be weeks or even months before I find the correct parts to finish Daisy, and that by then I will have no time left for the Landmark Challenge, at which point failure will have to be conceded and I will have to give the engine money back whilst bathing in a spotlight of shame.

Or something like that. I probably even affect a nasal whine as I bend his ear, but far from tipping his beer over my head and telling me to snap out of it, he does something far more dramatic.

"I know where there's a complete engine for your bike, recently rebuilt and ready to run" he says. He had of course let me ramble on, enjoying my misery, before telling me this but he isn't joking it turns out. The following day I make the call and am able to secure the apparently reconditioned lump, complete with magneto and dynamo. There is a catch – I will have to collect the thing from Manchester, which is a good five hours away but this seems a small inconvenience compared to the alternative of a soul-destroying search for individual parts.

I am left with only the carburettor to find then, but it seems that luck is now firmly on my side as I continue to make calls to my list of potential saviours. I hit gold dust when I speak to a company who not only agree that they can help, but unveil the fact that they actually have genuine, brand new Amal pre-monobloc carburettors, in the original box and wrappings. Do they have the right one for Daisy? They do, and yes I can, if I am prepared to hand over a hundred and sixty five quid. Ouch! This is a shock to say the least, representing rather more than I have left over in the Daisy fund after the engine acquisition, which has set me back nearly all of the eight hundred pounds donated. But there is nothing else for it, and I agree to buy one there and then, reasoning that I will only get a minor beating about the ears, if I take care to pick my moment to come clean with Diane.

It is only a matter of days before I am happily settled back in the garage, with my new treasures, ready to put it all together and launch Daisy once more on the trail of adventure. The engine slots in with almost no clownery at all and only minor blood loss to my fingers, primary drive, clutch and casings follow in short order and finally I take the superb shiny new carburettor reverentially from it's wrappings. A thing of beauty indeed, but it's got a serious purpose so on it goes. A test ride round the block sees me grinning like an idiot – she is perfect. Better than perfect, but more to the point, ready for the Landmark challenge once more.

Running about locally with a refurbished Daisy bedding in, I start thinking that the fitting of an engine of unknown provenance is a bit risky in the cold light of day. After all, it may look shiny and new but I have no idea how well, or not, the engine has been built. Has the builder used good quality components? Were the tolerances and fit of things like bushes and bearings properly checked and adhered to? How much of the thing has actually been reconditioned?

Of course, in my haste to find a solution, I have utterly failed to ask all of these pressing questions or request evidence of components fitted or cost. Neither have I actually checked things over before chucking the thing into Daisy's waiting frame. We will find out soon enough, and it is high time that we get back on the Landmark trail again, so it is back to the maps in order to choose some 'safe distance' forays that can be taken at a leisurely pace whilst everything beds in. Unfortunately, there are not that many Landmarks particularly close, and the list of 'local' sites is only four long. One of these is very close, the South Foreland lighthouse down here on the south coast, near Dover. Being just twenty miles each way with plenty of green lane routes to choose from it seems an ideal starter for the 'new' engine. Setting off one afternoon, in lovely weather, it is fantastic to be back on the open road, even after only a short break. We meander across the Sandwich marshes heading vaguely west, Daisy purring along as I gently coax her on through winding lanes and pretty little villages.

But it isn't long before I am jerked back to reality, receiving an almighty shock as suddenly I catch a strong whiff of burning oil. I look down past my leg to see the black stuff everywhere. Bucket loads it seems, absolutely covering Daisy's timing side, my shoe, my leg and all over her exhaust. Pulling up rapidly in a blind panic, I get off and survey the mess, as oil-smoke boils up from under the tank engulfing me in a sulphurous cloud. Anyone used to riding or working with classic machinery will know that a small amount of hot oil can look like a gallon once it escapes the confines of the engine and spreads. What I am looking at here however, is not a small amount of oil. It covers every surface of the timing side, has coated the gearbox, smothered the oil tank and toolbox, and is boiling away on most of the exhaust system. The stuff is dripping in great glops from the underside of her petrol tank, before cascading in an almost surreal waterfall effect down her engine fins where it adds to the general mess underneath.

What on earth has happened? Nothing good clearly, and I have that awful sinking feeling as I crouch down to take a closer look under the tank. It is difficult to see amidst the carnage of all that oil, but it doesn't seem as though anything has a large hole in it. There are only two other possibilities I can immediately think of, those being that there is a leak in the oil feed to the rocker boxes or the oil feed to the oil pressure gauge, mounted rather cutely in the tank itself, in a panel which also holds ammeter, light switch and a rather neat lead-light.

As it is clear that most of the oil is indeed cascading down from that tank recess, I groan inwardly at the thought of attempting to get the panel off, with it's nightmare of wiring lurking inside the diamond shaped hollow that it covers.

And that thought leads to my next problem. I have failed to learn from earlier escapades, and still only have a paltry few tools stuffed in various pockets about my person. None of these is the little eight-millimetre socket required to remove the panel securing bolt. Cursing my own stupidity once again I sit heavily on the grass verge and glory be! I can see the problem clear as day, right there in front of my eyes. Daisy has a rather quaint copper pipe, feeding off a banjo down on the timing chest and connecting to the oil pressure gauge. Under the dynamo it goes, before running round in a gentle curve, following the dynamo's contour, and finally straight up in front of the push rod tube, where, just before the tank recess, it joins onto a flexible rubber pipe. This joint is firmly held together with a stout hose-clip. Or rather, in this particular instance, it is *not* firmly held together with a hose-clip.

The pipe is waving about in the air, pointing straight up under the tank, and has clearly been pumping the black stuff merrily at some forty pounds per square inch. I shuffle closer and peer up between the exhausts, and there is the rubber hose, dangling innocently and uselessly. I grasp hold of the thing, and realise with deep shame that the whole mess is a self induced event, resulting from sloppy workmanship on my part – the hose-clip was not tightened when I put it all back together leading to the inevitable result that it has blown off under the pressure. I am able to reconnect it with no problems, and scrabble about in my pockets for a screwdriver with which to do up the clip. The rest of the journey is completed to the accompaniment of a constant, thick and acrid smoke, which boils up and engulfs me at every stop. I am also attracting amazed stares from onlookers who clearly view what they see with deep distaste or, in some cases, outright amusement.

Back at home, I set about the tiresome task of cleaning up the mess, which is actually almost impossible with the bike in one piece. The stuff has worked its way into every nook, cranny and crevice and every ride for a week afterwards is rewarded with yet more of it creeping from unknown hiding places to drip or dribble onto engine, exhausts or the floor. That fairly short ride has also caused the expected bedding down of new gaskets and the loosening off of nuts and bolts just about everywhere, so a good hour with the sockets and spanners is spent getting everything just so again, once the basic clean up has been completed. I console myself with the fact that the mishap has been entirely my own fault, and therefore does not constitute an ongoing problem. Quite the reverse, Daisy feels much more settled and responsive to ride, cruising along easily at the 55mph running in speed on almost no throttle at all. She sounds beautiful as we potter around the local streets on our daily business and shows far less inclination to get hot and bothered.

4. *Diversion to Le Mans*

The unexpected telephone call that was to change my plans for the coming month came on the following Tuesday. Long before I had made the decision to start and build a business, I had, like most people, held a steady and settled career job. The last few years of that part of my life had been spent in the role of Port Services Manager at the freight terminal in Ramsgate, but it's never that simple and I had also inherited a few additional 'hats' along the way, one of which was the esteemed post of Liaison Officer to Her Majesty's Customs and Excise. Those stout gentlemen, by necessity, tend to operate at odds with the rest of the Port Community in that their very role requires them to actually interfere with the normal, smooth running of the operation. Their frequent desire, for example, to take the wheels off trucks in order to look for some substance or other tends to be a bit of a disruption, and of course the owners of the truck in question were invariably not impressed. A Liaison Officer's job was to attempt to work out best practice between these parties of opposed interests, smoothing over ruffles here, looking for compromises there, but in general getting kicked from both sides and being used as the communal punch-bag. In any such position though, one tends to meet and become friends with certain of the characters involved and one of these was Dave. We'll simply call him a senior Government employee for the purposes of this story, and during the two years of my tenure in that position we became very firm friends both in and out of the official environment. This was helped along immeasurably by the fact that Dave kept a 'bottom drawer' from which, in times of stress, he would produce a variety of decent whiskies to aid the process of diplomatic negotiation.

That was all in the distant past, but this was Dave on the telephone now. I hadn't seen or spoken with him for well over a year and it is great to hear from him, but it gets better when I hear what he is calling about. He opens the conversation with "Is that right you're retarded!" booming into my ear. Before I can respond to that, "Sorry *retired*... My mistake!" He hasn't changed then, I think, as I explain that whilst certainly I am not employed these days, I am keeping myself busy on and off, with my own choice of work.

"Always were a skiving bugger" he offers "And that's why I'm calling – you ever been to Le Mans?" A pause, whilst I try to catch up with the sudden change of tack. I explain that no, I never have been there – but why is he calling to ask such a strange question? As usual with Dave the answer isn't a straight one, instead he answers with another question "Do you remember Tim?"

He goes on to explain, after I ask what on earth he's jabbering on about, that he has got into the habit of going to Le Mans for the 24 hour endurance race that the circuit is famous for hosting. He has been making the pilgrimage every year for the past seven or so, with his sons, a few friends and Tim, one of his colleagues from the Service. I had met and dealt with Tim on many occasions, and had got on well with him I recall, but what did all this have to do with me exactly? I ask the obvious question and Dave explains that due to unforeseen circumstances, two of the group booked this year have had to drop out, and therefore he, Dave, is in possession of two very hard to come by tickets with camping, going cheap. "Would

I be up for it?" he asks. I am taken aback a bit at this point. Why on earth did my name come to mind? I've never had any interest in racing, and certainly even less interest in *car* racing. Why ask me?

I ask this question as well, and after a short pause the booming reply clarifies things "You're missing the point old mate!" he declares. "It's not about the bloody *racing*, it's about the camping, the beer, the eating and partying! I can't think of a better bloke to ask!" he adds. I say nothing, so he continues "You *do* realise that there's a big classic scene down there, don't you! You'd be in your element." I still say nothing, but Dave is, if nothing else, tenacious and knows which buttons to press "Hey! Why don't you trailer that old thing of yours down there! It would be a hoot!" He carries on for a while, passionately describing the thing in such a way that I have to admit it sounds like fun. But I don't know… I'll have to think about it and give him a call back. In fact, he's convinced me, but I'm wondering how on earth I would broach the subject of yet another non-earning fun-jaunt, which again doesn't involve my long-suffering wife. Diane has been awfully good, and unbelievably understanding so far, as she watched me dump a career and then drift into this almost nomadic and quite possibly menopausal hobby at the expense of much of our leisure time together. But I suspect that there are limits to her patience and it's very obvious to me that suggesting I should be allowed to flit off for a week's boozing in France could well be the trigger that invites an almighty explosion especially in the middle of the already time-consuming Landmark challenge. No, I'll definitely need to think about this, but I promise Dave that I'll call him back soon. "Better be bloody soon matey," he says "We leave on the evening sailing next Tuesday!"

As I replace the receiver, it's clear that I won't be going. Given some time to work up to it with Diane, I *might* be able to construct a persuasive argument. Or at least work out a good bribe that from my perspective would see the correct spousal response. But next week? Absolutely no chance. I'd be a suicidal fool to even suggest such a thing and I decide that I might as well just ring Dave straight back and tell him the truth. I will be declared a lightweight, no doubt, but I would explain about the Landmark and hide behind that for a reasonable excuse.

I reach for the telephone again when Chris, who unbeknown to me has heard the whole conversation, or at least my end of it, pipes up. "Are we going to go Dad?" I stop and turn to face him.

"What's this 'we' business" I ask "and you're not supposed to eavesdrop on other people's telephone calls!" I add, exasperated as I realise that this is what he's done.

"I didn't deliberately" he protests his innocence "I was in the hall cleaning my shoes – like you told me to! Its not my fault you shout down the 'phone!" I back off, having no intention of being embroiled in a petty argument with a teenager right now, thank you.

"We can't go unfortunately." I explain "Your mother would go ballistic if I even suggested it, and you've got school anyway!" He doesn't respond, but there is a huge look of disappointment on his face and with that, I wander off to the kitchen to search the 'fridge for beer. I know how wheedling and persuasive both kids can be when they really want something, and I can see Chris is scheming up some kind of logical argument which I have no intention of getting sucked into. I completely forget to telephone Dave.

I run a bath shortly after, and when I have floated around soaking for about an hour, I return downstairs to where the family are watching television. But as soon as I enter Chris pipes up with "Mum says it's OK for you to go, but that I'll have to get permission from school" I stare at him for a split second, and then cast a fearful look at Diane, only to be met with a face that in all but actual words is saying "This is going to cost you – dearly". And it didn't take long to discover what scheming had been going on in the last hour, as the girls present the details of a deal that would see Chris and I in Le Mans next week, whilst they, at my expense apparently, go to London for a show, a hotel stay and of course, shopping in Oxford Street on the Saturday. I try to do the mental arithmetic, but give up at the thought of mother and daughter let loose in London, armed with funds. I concentrate instead on the thought of father and son set loose in France, armed with a tent and an old motorcycle. I quickly agree to the blackmail and retire to make the call to Dave accepting his kind offer. I tell him that I am going to ride Daisy to Le Mans and not trailer her as he had suggested. He expresses an opinion that I am, in fact, barking mad, but I explain that there are two very good reasons for my decision. One, the weather forecast is good and the ride will be fantastic. Two, I don't posses a trailer or for that matter, even have a tow-bar on the car!

I meet up with Dave on the Monday, in order to hand over our camping gear, spare clothes and other paraphernalia, which he had offered to take down for us in his car. He has Tim with him, and we retire for several pints in the local pub, where the pair regale me with tales from previous Le Mans expeditions. We part company that afternoon having agreed that Dave, his two boys and Tim would be the advanced party, leaving on Tuesday evening and driving down overnight and we'll make our own way down and meet up with them on the Wednesday. If all goes to plan Chris and I will get an early ferry and be at the site late afternoon. Packing Daisy is much easier now that the bulky gear has gone on ahead, and I choose to use the space for some more sensible precautions against the unknown. A full set of tools, plug spanner, spare inner tube, some gasket goo, spare bulbs and some spare chain links. This is more than I've ever had the space to carry before, and confidence is high for a successful trip come what may.

Wednesday morning, six o'clock, and it's raining. In fact, it is stair-rodding down outside and I've been caught out yet again in the planning department because we still don't posses any sensible waterproof riding gear. Our total protective kit still consists of a pair of thin nylon water resistant trousers each and little else. We both put on extra layers under our jackets, and I pack a pair of spare gloves into Daisy's tank bag, knowing from experience that my first pair will get saturated after a while. With that we venture out into the thoroughly grey and miserable morning and set off towards Folkestone and the Channel Tunnel. Once out on the open roads, we are subjected to a buffeting wind which whisks the ragged black clouds across our heads and throws the rain harshly at us in great sweeping waves. By the time we have covered the thirty or so miles to Cheriton, we are not only thoroughly soaked through but uncomfortably cold. As we pull up under the harsh bright lighting to check-in for our crossing, I can see that my entire body surface is glistening and shiny with water. My teeth begin chattering as I attempt to converse with the patient stewardess, and I mentally shrivel when I insert my hand into the damp clammy pocket of my jacket to retrieve the tickets. There is nothing quite so distasteful as a waterlogged leather jacket, I think, but that thought soon changes as I try to insert my hand back into the equally waterlogged glove. I give up, stuff the thing into my teeth, and head off towards the terminal building which looks warm and inviting but most importantly, dry.

Pulling up as close as possible to the main entrance, I kill Daisy's engine and brace myself for the horrible moment when I'll have to get off. Anyone who has been soaked over a fair distance, due to inadequate precautions, will know exactly what I mean. I had settled into a fixed slouch, where most of my joints had got at least half rigid and whatever moisture had seeped through the leather and nylon (and there was quite a lot) had at least been warmed marginally with body heat. In short, I had settled into a cocoon of semi optimised misery and the awful moment of actually moving and standing up will shatter all that and allow a myriad of new and cold leaks to work their horrors on me, whilst the act of dismounting and walking will cause the soaked jacket to transmit the most unpleasant clammy sensations. I am also waiting for the inevitable grumps from Chris, who is doubtless wishing he had stayed home in bed, and will probably start suggesting that we give up any minute now. As we walk into the blissful warmth, my spirit is further dragged down by the squelching and squishing coming from my shoes, which, it is now plainly obvious, are full of water. I curse myself yet again that I still have not got round to buying any boots. Chris is at least luckier in that department as we had recently picked up some ex-para boots for him at an Army & Navy store, but none were to be had in my size. I squish my way miserably to the nearest table, sit down, remove the things and pour about a pint of water into a large indoor tub, complete with small tree, nearby.

Chris is having no such problems, and it appears that he is not remotely bothered by the conditions. He even offers to go and get coffee for us both, and as he cheerfully heads off to the cafeteria I ponder the fact that I will probably never get the hang of teenagers. Or is it possible that the experiences he is having on these adventures is paying dividends, and he's far more prepared to go with the flow? I don't know the answer, but it's a pleasing thought and I begin to feel my mood lighten as I go through the motions of removing all the wet gear and hang it around the place in a vain attempt to at least dry it a little bit. Chris returns with two large steaming styrofoam cups and as we sit and drink I surreptitiously remove my socks, one at a time, and wring them out in the tub. Chris is appalled by this apparent delinquent behaviour, and tells me to stop as I'm embarrassing him. Twenty minutes later our train is announced and we are called for loading, which means climbing back into all the clammy damp gear again, a truly distasteful experience, but there's nothing for it so on it all goes, and out we go into the waterfall once more. We have to stop at Passport Control, whilst I scrabble about in the tank bag looking for the things, then we're through and being flagged over at the security checkpoint. They want me to pull into a side-lane for a check. I just want to get on the train and get out of this damp gear, but there's no point arguing, and over we go to the checkpoint where we are subjected to a sweep with some kind of device that I presume is 'sniffing' for explosives or some such. Finally we're allowed forward, but as we head up and over to the loading platforms the sky opens up it's sluice gates and we are caught in a fierce cloudburst that soaks us more thoroughly than anything has this morning.

On the train at last, we have a whole compartment to ourselves. The Euro tunnel or 'Le Shuttle' trains are a fascinating design and the operation is actually very smooth. Unlike ferries, travellers stay in their car in large airy compartments and although it is possible to get out and wander around, there is nothing really to see. There are no facilities other than airline style toilets. If, like us, you are travelling with a motorcycle, you literally just park in the compartment and sit on the floor! On this occasion, we have draped various wet and soggy clothing over just about anything that will hold it, and the venting system is at least blowing warm air onto it all. I chat to Chris about the appalling weather, and we both fervently hope that France will offer an improvement. The thought of more of the same makes me shudder, because we have some three hundred and twenty miles to cover the other side and here we are after only thirty, thoroughly soaked, bedraggled and not very warm. Daisy is also looking rather bedraggled, and as the water drips off her to form an expanding puddle, decorated with a psychedelic rainbow of colours, I think that she won't cut much of a dash in Le Mans. She is spattered with mud and road dirt, and has that smudgy brown/grey residue smeared over most exposed surfaces – she looks a mess. I cheer myself slightly with the thought that at least the camping gear and spare clothes went ahead in a dry car. The black square that is the window suddenly flashes into daylight once more and within minutes the PA system announces arrival in Calais, urging all drivers to return to their vehicles. For us this means climbing back into that damp gear once again and I steel myself for what's about to come.

Once you're wet you're wet, and we are soon seriously wet. I don't really mind being wet, as such, but being wet and cold is just pants. I am wet and cold now, as we sit under a bridge and watch the maelstrom of wind and rain that we have just escaped. This is not helped by the lorries that sweep past at some 70mph, engulfing us in a blast of air, spray and dirt. We have managed no more than fifty miles and it has been nothing short of torture. I haven't even managed to maintain a decent speed, due to my open faced helmet, which allows the hammering rain to batter my face and make my vision seriously deficient. And this is hard rain, stinging like needle points as it hits. Thankfully, French roads have wide hard shoulders, in which I am able to position Daisy, well out of the way of those barrelling trucks, in an effort to survive at the 40mph we are forced to ride. This is the fourth bridge we've sheltered under and Chris is getting fractious about the number of stops we're making, but I am just not able to carry on in the current downpour and I explain to him that it's bloody dangerous to try. I feel sorry for the lad though, as I reflect that this great adventure is turning into a miserable and, for him, boring endurance. We climb up the sloping concrete foundation and sit high up to get out of the spray from those trucks, and I almost laugh as I look at Chris who has a little river running off his helmet, onto his nose, where the water gathers in drips before falling. He ignores this and sits hunched looking out at the rubbish we've been riding through. I try to roll a cigarette, but abandon the attempt as futile after wasting three papers. Chris voices his own feelings, "This is crap!" I couldn't agree more and I want to go home, I decide, but I'm not going to be the one to suggest it hoping that Chris will and should he voice any such thoughts I will readily agree. He's not about to though, instead he offers a different approach – "Can't we find a services, and then we can wait until it stops," he says, "at least we can get food then" he adds.

The services are a good twenty miles, it turns out, and when we finally get there I am on the edge of losing the will to live. We pull into the place and ride right up to the entrance of the cafeteria, where there is a cover, lurch to a stop and almost collapse in a heap right there. I have never been wetter or colder in my entire life. I put Daisy on the stand, and marvel at the cloud of steam coming off her. She looks a complete state, and an observer could be forgiven for thinking that we'd just ridden her through a series of increasingly muddy fields. I can't be bothered to worry about that though, I am just desperate to get inside and warm up. Chris has beaten me to it and has already disappeared into the place, and I follow *toute-suite*. We look at each other as an alarming puddle spreads around our feet, Chris struggles out of his jacket, pulls off his helmet gives his head a good scratch and exclaims "Thank God for that!" before heading straight over to the food counter where he critically inspects the offerings. I get my own gear off more slowly – my jacket seems to weigh three times it's normal amount, the gloves feel like a pair of sodden turfs and my shoes are full of water again. My shirt and fleece have both succumbed to leakage and are damp all around the chest and arms. The nylon trousers have given up any attempt at resisting the rain some time ago and my jeans now sport a big dark patch around crotch and knees. I stand there feeling relieved at least to be rid of it all and I turn to survey the food counter.

Chris is coming back from his inspection and as I turn he clocks that big dark stain and bursts out laughing as he speaks "Dad! – You've peed yourself!" is the unhelpful exclamation.

"Yes...very bloody funny" I mutter, not a little amazed at his continued good spirits. "It's all right for you, you're sheltered behind me," I add.

"Yeah right!" comes the sarcastic response. He points at the counter area, makes the simple statement "food" and smiles happily. We go and get a tray, and in short order we are sitting with large sausages, large coffees and giggling like a couple of schoolgirls at the state we've got ourselves in. There's nothing like food and warmth to restore some semblance of spirit, but we're soon talking about what we should do now. Chris still hasn't even begun to look like he's ready to quit and in that way of blind optimism he occasionally shows, he assures me that it's just a matter of waiting. I fail to see the logic of this but one thing I do agree about, is that we're not going to go out in this rubbish again, and in the meantime I decide to teach young Chris a trick or two in the survival department.

"Get your gloves and jacket," says I "and follow me". For an instant, I think Chris believes that I have lost my senses and am about to go back out. Instead, I head for the gents toilet, carrying my jacket, gloves and shoes.

Inside, I see what I was hoping for, but first I lay the stuff out on the washbasins, and wring it all out in the sink before grabbing a handful of paper towels, which I proceed to stuff up sleeves, in shoes and inside gloves.

"What are you doing?" enquires Chris.

"Trust me, and do the same" I say, reaching for his gloves and stuffing them with towels.

"What for?" he's not convinced at all "I'm not doing that – it's stupid" he adds. I can't be bothered to argue and simply leave it, saying,

"OK, suit yourself, but just watch and you'll learn something and probably be much drier!"

As he slouches by the basins, looking as cynical as can be, I reflect that it may seem to him that I've lost my marbles. Clearly all that water has addled my brain, but as I squeeze and squish the arms of my jacket and my gloves, then pull the saturated towels out and re-charge with fresh ones, he can clearly see the merit of my actions. Of course, being a teenager, he's not about to admit anything, but he does grab a handful of the things and begin shoving them in his own jacket. He manages to convey a clear message - 'I'm only doing this to humour you' and I smile to myself in that way that only a parent of teenagers understands. After three refills I am feeling a bit guilty for wasting the towels, but needs must when the devil drives and I go for one final stuffing. Now it's time for the warm-air hand dryer, and I demonstrate to Chris how to thread the sleeve end over the thing and allow the lovely drying air-rush to do it's stuff. It's tedious this, but quite effective, with even Chris quickly seeing the merits of the operation and doing the same on another dryer. We're there for over half an hour, swapping sleeves, gloves and shoes until everything is at least only damp rather than sopping wet as it was when we started. Miraculously, when we finally exit, we see through the windows that it has actually stopped raining. On the minus side, we are now being scrutinized by the counter attendant, who is clearly wondering what on earth we've been up to in the Gents for nearly forty minutes and has equally clearly convinced himself of an answer that definitely doesn't meet with his approval. I wonder whether the gendarmes might show up before we leave!

We go outside and have a look around at the sky. It is definitely brightening and the rain has stopped for sure so we decide to make a go of it, helped by the fact that I am not about to go and face the attendant, with his withering glare and ask for more coffee. We get ourselves togged up again, only wincing slightly at the horrible sensation of warm, damp clothing, which I know from experience, will rapidly become cold clammy clothing once outside and we exit under the continued suspicious glare of the Frenchman inside. Helmet on, only shuddering slightly as the wet earpieces slide damply over my ears and the clammy strap tightens. Gloves on, ditto the horrible sensation, climb onto Daisy and fire her up. Nothing happens. Another kick, then another and another. Nothing. Not even a pop. I lean under the tank and tickle her up again, flooding the remote float well and truly. Ease over compression and then a big heave on the kick-start –still nothing, not a sausage. I immediately reach an all time low for the day and slump in the seat to stare into oblivion. "Don't do this to me Daisy, not here, not now!" I'm thinking, and Chris, bang on cue, mutters "Oh great!" I dismount, remove helmet and gloves, scrabble about in the tank bag for a plug spanner, and proceed to remove a plug for inspection and a spark test. It is soaked with petrol, indicating that Daisy has succumbed to the Prince of Darkness' famous weakness in the wet. Attaching the plug to it's HT lead, I ask Chris to hold it against the cylinder while I kick, but he's gathered a small knowledge of the workings and quickly backs away muttering "No way". We bicker for a few seconds, but he's adamant and I can't be bothered, so I do it the hard way, holding the thing myself whilst trying to kick and squint down to see if there's a spark. I already knew the answer I suppose, but confirmation follows. Not a sausage. Bugger.

Squatting down on the cold wet concrete is horrible, but there is no choice, as I struggle to get at the magneto. Everything under there is coated with filth, so I revisit the tank bag for some Kleenex, wipe the worst of it away, and then remove both HT connectors from the Magneto body. These are full of water but that's easy to sort out by making little twisted sausages from Kleenex, shoving them into the pick-up and wiggling around. I hold my lighter under each one, being careful not to melt the things, until I'm happy that they are good and dry. I give the same treatment to the HT lead ends themselves, before reassembling it all and trying the kick-starter once more. Daisy is still sulking, producing no hint of the healthy blue spark I was expecting. I curse virulently, look at Chris, shrug, and head back down behind the engine. This time I remove, after a Herculean struggle, the screw on end-cap behind which live the points. It's possible I reason, that water has got into this part of the magneto, and a set of damp or wet points will easily cause a lack of sparking action. As the cap comes off, I am amazed as something like an eggcup full of water pours out and dribbles down my hand. Clearly this would cause the problem, but I can't think how it got into the cavity which is, after all, a sealed unit to all intents and purposes. I spend a good five minutes dabbing the Kleenex in there and by now Chris is looking over my shoulder wanting to know what's going on, and I explain about the water in everything and how that effects the electrical connections, causing the lack of sparks.

Having dried things as best I can, we try again but after several hefty kicks I am no further forward. Still no sparks. Crouching once more, I mutter about the difficulty of getting the points and their assembly dry and Chris asks why I don't do the same trick with the lighter. I explain that the ancient carburettor, with its leaky float chamber which has been freshly flooded, is directly above the magneto, dripping petrol. It would be pretty dodgy holding a naked flame under that, I suggest, and he gets the point. What we can do though, I suddenly realise, is take the end plate and points off and take them inside to the hand dryer which would surely do the trick. A few minutes later I have them off, but as we head back inside, it occurs to me that the French gentleman, already highly suspicious of our earlier long absence in the gents, must now be absolutely convinced of wrongdoing as he watches us both disappear back into them once more. I avoid eye contact, and hurry into the place, eager to get this done and get out again as quickly as possible, but it takes nearly ten minutes under the dryer before all the bits seem thoroughly dry. We scuttle back out again, under the continuing steely glare, and I have to resist the urge to stop and try and explain. It would only confirm the man's suspicions I'm sure. At last I have everything re-fitted, and once again straddle Daisy. The underside of my foot is already painful, with the beginnings of a mighty blister I think, from the earlier kicking, and I wince as I heave the thing once more. Not only does Daisy spark, but she also starts on the one cylinder that still has its plug in place. Hurrah! What a relief.

Every cloud has a silver lining. We have lost another half an hour, but by the time I've finished mucking about and we're ready to go, the weather has improved further. It hasn't rained for nearly half an hour, the tarmac is beginning to dry up and there are even breaks beginning to show up amongst the clouds in the otherwise grey leaden sky. With Daisy now ticking over sweetly beneath us, I look over my shoulder and hail Chris, "Ready then?" I ask. "I was ready an hour ago" he quips, but there's a grudging half smile there so I take that as a positive as I let out the clutch and we thread our way through the service area and out onto the road once more. We're heading for Rouen first, taking the long coastal dual-carriageway that connects Calais, Boulogne and Le Havre and this turns out to be a sore test for Daisy as the road undulates like a roller coaster between a number of fairly severe inclines. Down into the dips we build up a head of steam before turning up at the bottom and facing the long steep climb up the other side of each, testing Daisy to the full and causing me to work the gearbox several times in order to keep the poor girl moving without strain. And so it goes, until eventually Rouen is behind us and we get onto the smaller road that takes us across country to Alencon, then Le Mans. There is evidence of a new motorway under construction, but this existing road is far more suitable for Daisy's abilities, sweeping along between sleepy little towns alternating with woodland or heath, with the bright yellow gorse bushes bordering the tarmac. The air has got steadily warmer as we continue south, and the sky is increasingly becoming lighter with more and more breaks through which patches of blue sky show. We stop in a lay-by and look back along the incredibly straight stretch of road and can see the dark clouds, almost black, that we have left behind us. A cricket strikes up a tune off to our left, and there is no traffic in sight at all. The road stretches ahead, empty of traffic and the only sound is a light wind in the trees.

Reaching Alencon, we avoid the new motorway to Le Mans, this section of which is freshly open, and take the smaller route that takes us through some delightful little villages as it meanders south. We have something like 30 miles left and I stop after a while to make a telephone call to Dave. He seems surprised that we are so late, and I am shocked on checking my watch to find that the time really has been tramping on – it's nearly 7.30 in the evening, and I tell Dave that we'll give him the full story on arrival, over a few beers. He gives me directions to what he refers to as 'the pub', which is apparently opposite our campsite, and armed with that we get under way for the last leg of our journey. We are soon on the outskirts of the town, which is a fairly sizeable place, and pick up the ring road following signs to the red camping zone, our base for the week. Although it's early in the week, it is obvious that already there are a fairly large number of visitors here from the UK, judging by the number of GB-plated cars we encounter. And what cars – MGs, Bentleys, TVRs, Porsches, you name it there's an abundance of them. The racing set is here in force, sporting their own road versions. Daisy is attracting a lot of appreciation as we continue round the ring road and we get honked, tooted and waved at numerous times before we find the red sign off to our right and turn off. And the roads here are very, very busy, with the whole area around the racetrack and the camping zones completely grid-locked. There are Gendarmes at every junction, doing their best to keep things moving, but they're fighting a losing battle I reckon. It's even difficult to filter through the mayhem with Daisy, and before long she's getting hot, bothered and temperamental. Fifteen minutes later however, we finally find the junction across from which is the entrance to our campsite, turn left as Dave had instructed, and there at last is the big pub.

The road leads down a long slope to the main stadium and circuit, but half way up is this large bar. It has a sizeable forecourt sloping sharply down to the road, and is itself built on a platform with a large veranda. The net effect is to give patrons a very good vantage point, looking down on the main drag to the circuit and the sprawling campsite opposite. The place is absolutely heaving with happy souls enjoying what has become a sunny evening, and as we ride down the hill to the forecourt, and pull up on the apron, a loud cheer goes up from the veranda. We thread slowly up through the crowd, in an attempt to park Daisy somewhere close, and I suddenly become aware that we've picked up a following of about four happily drunken admirers. Another one decides to assist, and pushes ahead of us yelling "mind y' backs!" and using his arms like a snowplough. We stop under the veranda, the crowd pushes in around us, and before I have even turned off Daisy's overheating engine, someone is pushing a pint of beer at me! Several more are patting me on the back, Chris is receiving the same welcome and I am overwhelmed by the sheer bonhomie and almost Mardi Gras atmosphere. Helpful hands reach out to steady Daisy as Chris and I dismount amongst the jostling crowd, and by the time I have managed to remove helmet and gloves and get her on the stand, I am the proud owner of two pints of beer, with several more on offer. Marvellous.

We dump the helmets in a flower bed just by the pub entrance, stretch, and both find ourselves fending off a barrage of questions "What is it?" "How old is she?", "Have we ridden her all the way?", "Which ferry did we catch", "What? All the way from Calais?", "Wanna beer?" And in the middle of all this, Chris is standing nine-feet tall with pride, enthusiastically regaling his new friends with the stories from our recent trials and troubles. He's got a beer too, I notice – I'd better keep an eye on him. Over the hubbub I hear my name being called and looking around I see Dave and the rest of our party up on the veranda. Excusing myself from my new found mates, I make my way through the crowd towards the steps, but Chris is having far too much fun telling stories to follow me at the moment and I go up to meet Dave on my own. There is more beer waiting at their table and I realise I'll have to watch myself as well as Chris, although there is no more riding to be done today what with the entrance to our campsite being directly opposite. I gratefully take the offered chair that they've kept for me, and finally sit to soak up the surprisingly warm evening sunshine and atmosphere. As I chat to Tim and Dave, they give me a run down on the layout and what's in store for the week.

This whole area, the campsite and the pub, are at the centre of what has become, unofficially, the British sector of race week. The Brit contingent to the Le Mans 24 hour race is about 80,000 although they tend to be spread across a number of large campsites around the central stadium. The one we're staying in is fairly small and is actually a cattle market where you can camp under the tin roofed stalls, which I imagine normally are filled with next week's dinner. Crowds of Brits, in party mood, gather here at the pub to watch the steady arrival of various owner's clubs and tasty machinery. And this is one of the real attractions of Le Mans week – it has a huge classic following, albeit the four wheeled variety, and Dave's enthusiasm is infectious as he rattles off the marques to look out for. You have, he tells me, the AC Cobras, the vintage Bentleys, MGBs, Jaguars (E, S and even C types in abundance he says), Ferraris, Morgans and everything in between. "Oh, and you get the odd crappy old bike turning up as well." This is Tim's contribution. This reminds me to check on Chris, and I stand to peer over the balcony to see him still holding court. He seems to have acquired another beer, and is earnestly discussing some finer point of Daisy's design with a man who seems to be fascinated with the sprung hub. They're both crouched down and peering at the back wheel, and I wonder just what Chris is telling the guy. But he's happy, so I decide to leave him to it. When I go back to our table, more beer has appeared, and I realise that this could turn into a bit of a session and before that happens I need to get Daisy parked up, and more to the point, get something to eat.

Dave agrees. He despatches his boys Dan and Mitch to go and get the food started – "They're doing us a Spag Bol" he declares. The beers are consumed whilst we idly chat about the week ahead and eventually we all get up to go across to the camp. Pushing back through the crowd, I find Chris still burbling away, helped I'm sure by two pints of ale he's not used to and tell him it's dinner time. As we retrieve our gear, Dave sets off across the road and the crowd gives us space to turn round ready to leave. I think about pushing her, but the track up to the campsite is on a steep incline. We'll ride.

Daisy starts first kick, and another huge cheer goes up from the veranda. I look up and there is a crowd of happy alcoholic grins looking back at me. I nearly fall off laughing as we slowly pull off the forecourt, the crowd has burst into and impromptu rendition of the theme tune to 'The Great Escape' in which Steve McQueen made at least one bit of his escape bid on a pre-unit Triumph. British 'off the cuff' humour at it's best and I have a suspicion that this will happen to us numerous times as we visit this bar through the week! We settle down at camp, enjoying the huge tub of Spaghetti the lads have produced and sitting outside the tents watching the last of the sun's rays dying on the Western horizon. Chris has been sensible and moved onto coke but Dave, Tim and Myself, renewing our friendship after more than a year's gap, indulge a bit too much. At some point in the evening, Dave's chair collapses under him, a result of leaning back too far, and he promptly goes over backwards into the little half-tent serving as food and beer store, demolishing the thing. The lads, who have been watching us, collapse into laughter but Dave seems to find his new position just as comfortable as his chair was, and carries on regardless. All around us, across the site, the party is in full swing, with music, laughter and the odd firework going off, but the long day is catching up with us and we retire, some of us distinctly unsteadily, to bed.

There is nothing major to do until Friday evening when the real events linked to the racing begin to take place, starting with practice and qualifying. The party atmosphere is certain to continue building steadily, and we decide to spend Thursday and Friday exploring all the roads around Le Mans and the surrounding villages. We start by following the others through the lanes to the local town of Arnage, (the place after which the recent Bentley model was named), where we'll get breakfast. The sun has come out in force this morning, and at 8.30 it's already hot. The others tell me that it is likely to get much hotter through the day, but right now, sitting at a table under large umbrellas, waiting for the French version of bacon and eggs, it's almost ideal. We're right by the main road (it's actually quaint and picturesque) through the town, and passing us by is a constant stream of very extravagant cars which excite Dave, Tim and the lads, whilst for me there are also some fantastic classics mixed in with them. By nine o'clock the pavement cafés along the entire street are absolutely packed with people and there is nowhere to sit. One gets the impression that they're here for a reason, and it's not long before I understand. It's customary it seems, when driving through such places, to stop by any of the crowded pavement cafés and to a count down from the boisterous patrons produce a display of 'smoking tyres'. The more smoke, the louder the praise and applause. It's fascinating to sit there and just watch this spectacle going on, and I marvel that the local people completely ignore it all. I guess that they're used to it, and certainly they must welcome this annual boost to the local economy. This tolerance of what would probably be deemed completely unacceptable anywhere else, is underlined by the Gendarmes. It appears to be a bit of a game – the tyre smoking happening spontaneously at whichever café is furthest from the Gendarmes, who are moving around the whole time. Occasionally one will appear from nowhere and catch someone in the act, but a wagging finger and a cynical raised eyebrow tends to be the only reprimand to most.

We split up after breakfast, with Chris and I deciding to take a ride round the surrounding area using the roads for the circuit where possible, large parts of which are on public roads. These will be closed for the racing but are open until this evening when practice starts. On race day, it will be necessary to go out into the surrounding lanes and cut across country in order to get to some of the viewing areas, such as the Arnage bend, or the Mulsanne straight, so this recce should come in handy. By lunch time we have worked out how to get around, and have marked various short cuts and routes that we can use when it all gets shut off, using a map of the circuit and surrounding roads supplied by Dave. By now, the heat is intense to say the least so returning to the camp site we meet up with the others once more and agree that lunch in Arnage is the thing to do. Traffic is getting pretty nasty and it seems that half the circuit is in gridlock, all heading for the outlying villages with the same plan as us. Chris and I filter past the long queues and go on ahead in an attempt to secure a table at one of the pavement café's. We're lucky, securing what we need as the village rapidly fills to bursting point. The others take nearly half an hour to join us, but then we all sit there in the glorious weather and watch a repeat performance of the endless line of tasty machinery filing past. There is a noticeably larger Gendarme attendance now however.

After lunch, it's back to the site, and time to park Daisy up for the day. We spend the afternoon wandering around, visiting the circuit, the Le Mans museum and finally the big pub, before meeting up once again with the others and heading back to enjoy an evening in the sun and a large barbecue. From our position above the surrounding area, we can look down on the airfield that is adjacent to the circuit, watching an endless line of private jets and helicopters shuttling the corporate VIPs in and out. The evening is finished off by a walk down to the circuit, where there is a funfair in full swing, a number of bars, shops and a plethora of little stalls selling various offerings to eat, if one dares. A final visit to the pub on the way home rounds the day off nicely and it's bedtime. It's wise, apparently, to get a good night's sleep today, as precious little will be had from now on as the huge gathering swings fully into party mood. Bizarrely, there is a group of Danes camped next to us who, as a way of getting themselves into the right frame of mind for the big race, have a tape of racing cars variously accelerating at full chat, or crashing through gears at some hairpin or other. They play this at full volume continuously and it makes sleeping almost impossible. After a while it grates seriously on the nerves, but thankfully someone else feels the same and a harsh verbal altercation eventually takes place, after which the Danes, protesting loudly, turn the thing off. Further attempts to sleep are only occasionally disrupted by the odd firework or burst of noise or laughter from one or other of the group camps nearby. There is no denying however, that it's a great atmosphere, and as I drift off I wonder what tomorrow, which I'm assured is when the *real* party begins, will be like.

Friday dawns, and we are awoken by a loud murmuring nearby. As I slowly become conscious, Chris stirs too, and we both lie listening to a seemingly one-sided conversation that is clearly not English, or French. It's Dutch, I think, as I turn over and try to get back to sleep, but the monotonous monologue continues. Chris mutters something about wishing they'd shut up and somebody else obviously agrees because a very belligerent English voice yells out "Oi! It's bloody six o'clock. Some of us are trying to sleep so will you shut up about your sodding tulips!" Chris spontaneously starts giggling, which starts me off, and we both listen hard to see what comes next. But the Dutchman has got the message and we dose off again in the early light and don't come round again until nearly ten o'clock. We stumble blearily out into the bright sunshine, finding most of the others in the act of brewing up the morning tea, and stumble off to the ablutions block to freshen up before breakfast, which apparently is best had at a little café about half a mile up the road, towards the town. Being in a car, Dave, Tim and the boys decide to walk up as there will be no place to park, they say. Chris and I are going to have a ride down past the circuit and around the campsites first, and agree to meet up with them all at the café. The airfield is already busy, we notice, as is the general area at the entrance to the stadium and track. Traffic is murderous at the junction there, with many a Gendarme attempting to keep things moving, but once past it we can stretch Daisy's legs down the long straight road, past the campsites on the right and down to the end of the enclosed part of the track.

As we continue to thread our way along we can tell from the building atmosphere that this is going to be a great fun day. This is still largely the British sector and It is clear from the now packed fields that most of the visitors have arrived, set up camp and are killing time till the race in that peculiarly British way – by consuming vast amounts of ale! Already they're lining the roads, sitting on the grassy banks or fences watching all the tasty cars go by. Daisy attracts a number of cheers or shouted compliments, and at regular intervals Chris, who has never before experienced such a gathering, leans over my shoulder to exclaim his amazement at the scenes. We head round in a large circle, back towards our own site and that appointment with breakfast, arriving just in time to see the others filing in. There's no menu, breakfast is a large bowl of coffee, bread, butter and fried eggs. That's it. If you don't like eggs you're out of luck. We do, and as we eat, Chris enthusiastically tells the gathering about the scenes down towards the track. "That's nothing," he is told by those who have been before "They're just waking up at the moment. Wait until later, when they've had a shed-load of beer. You will be amazed at what goes on!" We all discuss the day's plans, and we are told that we must make sure that we're back at the site by eight o'clock. We're to be taken 'to a restaurant the likes of which you will never see anywhere else' but they won't tell us any more. It sounds intriguing, and knowing Dave as I do, it must be something pretty out of the ordinary. Great, something to look forward to, but for now it's back to the site for a while, freshen up and then off around the area again to see what transpires. We have booked a lunch table at Arnage again, and as Chris and I get ready to leave, we all agree to meet up there later.

Now, it's a tradition in Le Mans that on the Friday, various parts of the roads around the circuit become unofficial 'checkpoints'. Unofficial because it is manned, not by French Gendarmes as you might expect, but drunken Englishmen. When passing one of these 'checkpoints' you will be stopped and asked to provide 'smoking tyres' up the road for the entertainment of the crowd lining both sides of the road for about 200 yards. It doesn't matter what you're driving or riding, but the more extravagant your wheels, the more insistent the crowd are that you must please. If you decline, your attention is drawn once again to that long line of happily drunken spectators and you may now notice, possibly for the first time, that they are armed with big plastic water cannons! You can expect loud derision and a thoroughly good soaking if you try to escape without making the effort. Occasionally a few Gendarmes will show themselves, just to make sure that things are not getting out of hand, and it's a piece of pantomime second to none. It's also great fun to watch, as Chris and I discover when we stop at the big pub for a couple of cokes.

There are two chaps 'manning' this checkpoint. The pub forecourt is absolutely packed, as is the road on both sides, and *everything* is getting stopped. Those that think they're safe behind wound up windows, and therefore able to ignore the challenge laid down, find that they really should have locked their doors. More than one local French family, and indeed incidental visitor, declining to put on the required show, found all four doors suddenly opened and half a dozen water canons spoiling their day.

The best part for us was seeing the occasional unknowing *poseur* in their open topped TVRs or Ferraris, clearly caught out and more than a bit rattled as they try to decide between whether to abuse their expensive tyres or have their pride and joy (and themselves) thoroughly soaked inside and out! Some simply tried to push their way through without stopping. Oh Dear! While we watch the fun and games Daisy is attracting more than a little attention, and Chris, the duty hero, gladly talks with any who wish to. My attention is distracted however, as down at the checkpoint a motorcyclist on a modern street-fighter style machine has been stopped. As the crowd cheer, jeer and cajole, this chap removes helmet and gloves, hands them to the guy that has stopped him, and settling down in the saddle once more gives his throttle a number of almighty blips. He studies the crowd. The crowd roar a cheer and egg him on. He sits back, cups his ear up towards the pub, as if to say 'What?' He gets a louder roar, and, with a couple more blips and a quick check to make sure the way is clear, he's off popping a wheelie right up through the cheering crowd. He gets huge applause as he comes down at the end and stops. He turns, facing down the hill now, and cups his ear again. Another huge roar, and down he comes, slowly, grinning at the crowd. He stands up on his pegs now, and as he gets to the pub, he hits the front brake, bringing his rear wheel up to head height – a 'stoppie'. He hangs there, rear wheel waving around in the air, and then working the crowd for all they're worth, he proceeds to bounce up and down on his front wheel, like a pogo stick. Up and down he goes, pulling these and various other stunts to ever more enthusiastic applause.

Chris is mesmerized by this display, quite forgetting his own audience, and particularly when this guy does his grand finale. He dons his helmet and gloves once more, takes a bow to the crowd and waves. The crowd cheers, but he cups his ear again and gets a much louder one. He sits and blips but then, doesn't just pull away, but shuffles up to sit on his tank, pulls hard on his front brake, winds up his throttle and dumps the clutch. His rear tyre spins wildly on the tarmac and rapidly starts to burn, a huge plume of smoke is soon billowing from it as his front forks depress to their maximum. He stays on the spot, seemingly forever, engine revving madly and wheel spinning wildly. The smoke now obscures most of the audience and just as I wonder in amazement that he has any rubber left at all, he's off, to a wild standing ovation from the highly appreciate crowd. Smoke hangs thickly in the air, and a buzz runs through the crowd on the forecourt. They are having a seriously good time.

Next up is a Citroen 2CV, and the crowd go wild as the driver grins at all and sundry and gives it the rev treatment. Dumping the clutch, the 2CV bounds like a Kangaroo on its springy suspension and promptly stalls. Another wild cheer, but the guy stays dry as he sheepishly starts his engine again and slinks normally up the road. And so it goes, all afternoon until, deciding to move on and see what's going on elsewhere, Chris and I find ourselves stopped on Daisy as we try to leave. But luckily the bare chested drunkard peers through his alcoholic haze taking in the antique look, the tank top instruments, the sprung hub, exposed battery holder and mercifully realises that here is a machine that it would simply be a waste of time trying to wheel-spin or wheelie. He lets us off with a theatrical "Nah!" to the crowd, and a signal from him seems to excuse us the ordeal, we get a cheer anyway, as we head up the corridor of water canon, and not a drop is aimed our way – but I am staggered and ridiculously flattered that instead, another drunken whistled rendition of 'The Great Escape' goes up all around us. Although this happened earlier, I didn't realise that Chris doesn't get the joke, but this time he's clicked that it's aimed at us and I find myself having to explain about Steve McQueen and the film.

We head on down to the bottom fields by the track again, and as we're filtering through all the traffic I am amazed, and indeed heartened, to be buzzed by a little moped. Chris is horrified, but I am laughing, as this little machine and it's rider pull up alongside and we're offered that universal 'give it some' gesture of the throttle hand. Chris's horror comes from the simple fact that the rider is not wearing a single stitch of clothing. We accelerate away, leaving the streaker to entertain the crowds, but the muttering from Chris suggests that he has actually just been shocked by the close encounter. I'm still chuckling as we do a long circuit that takes us round to our lunchtime rendezvous, where we find Dave, Tim and the crew relaxing in the early afternoon sun. Having stayed clear of the stuff all morning, I grab a beer, and we settle down to swap stories from our morning's meandering, whilst the street show continues unabated. Dave now tells us of the treat we are to experience later. The Mulsanne straight, he tells us, is one of the public sections in normal life, but the fastest, longest straight in the race. It has, he tells me, a lovely little Chinese Restaurant half way down, which although cordoned off for the race, can be accessed via some back lanes and a couple of fields. The owners have an arrangement with the local farmer, and we are booked for a meal there this evening. Dave explains that the very fast straight on the circuit goes past literally five feet outside the restaurant windows, and goes on to promise us a meal the like of which we have never experienced before. He wasn't kidding.

Getting to the place is entertaining in the least, and this restaurant must be one of the best kept secrets in Le Mans. You simply wouldn't find the thing unless somebody in the know had showed you, which is how Dave had discovered it several years ago. Bumping across the field behind it, we park at the rear and can now see that the normal entrance from the road has been blocked by crash barriers. It is possible to look over these, just, and see up the road to the bend at the top. With the exception of the restaurant front it looks for all the world like a section of Silverstone or some other such pure racing track. The practice sessions are due to start in a while, and our table, right by the windows at the front, is ready. We order a right old mixture to share amongst us all, and as the starter dishes arrive, we hear the first car going down through the gears rapidly approaching the bend at the top of the straight, before accelerating hard up through them again as it hits the straight. The noise builds rapidly to a crescendo as the thing howls past us, less than twenty feet the other side of the windows, which vibrate. "Woooaah!" exclaims Chris, shocked at the ear splitting din. Several cars later, it's interesting to note just how different they sound, and Dave, Tim and the others have fun trying to guess what each car is by it's engine sound.

Dave certainly wasn't wrong when he told us this would be a meal like no other we have experienced, but even so, nothing has prepared me for what comes next. We hear a gaggle of rapidly decelerating engines approach the bend, sounding like angry wasps in the distance, and I can count about four, I think, as they come round to the straight and hit the pedal. There is obviously a fight for position here and as the cars hurtle past the restaurant on their way down the straight, they are bunched neck and neck. The noise is indescribable, but what's more startling is that not only do the windows vibrate this time, but the table we are sitting at is shaking, all the cutlery is rattling and I watch in fascination as ripples spread across my beer. Another bunch tear past shortly after, with the same effect, and when I look up, Chris has his fingers jammed in his ears, and a startled look on his face. Small particles of dust are also dropping from the overheat lighting, and I can't help but think of the marvellous dining room scene from the film 'Carry on up the Khyber' where the British Embassy staff stoically work their way through four courses as the room disintegrates around them from the battle raging outside. It is impossible to actually hold a conversation now, as the full compliment of cars is on the track, relentlessly hammering past time and time again. Quite an experience, and certainly one which it would be hard to repeat anywhere else.

After the meal, ears and nerves shot, we walk out with the last of the suns rays dying over the western horizon; the plan now is to carry on round the back roads to some of the marshalled viewing points scattered around the circuit. The Arnage corner is, I am told, a great place to go, but as we thread our way towards it the roads become gridlocked with like minded souls attempting the same. Eventually we get there, park in an adjacent field and walk up the large bank overlooking the bend and approach, and here we spend half an hour watching the cars, lights blazing, gears crashing, exhausts screaming and spitting fire. Wonderful, if a tad heavy on the eardrums.

Back at the campsite there is an almighty party going on, and the pub across the road is absolutely heaving. The Gendarmes have brought the daytime activities on the road to a halt, and are now keeping a steady presence to ensure that they stay that way. We wander across for a few beers before settling back at camp to just relax and listen to the cacophony of noise all around us. Chris and Mitch go off down to the circuit, where they intend to wander around various vantage points and watch the last practice session until midnight. As they come back, a while after the end, the first of what is to be an ongoing barrage of fireworks go off somewhere in the middle of the site. This seems to be a signal, and before long there are rockets flaring all around us, detonations abound and we sit transfixed, listening to the debris landing on the roofs of the cattle sheds in a continuous pinging noise. And so eventually we head off to bed, leaving the younger lads to sit about chatting and enjoying the experience to the full. They're allowed a beer each to be going on with. Most of us won't get much sleep, but it's fine just lying there listening to mayhem going on outside.

Race day dawns with a blazing sun and clear blue skies. I have abandoned any attempt at personal protection and have resorted to riding around in shorts and sandals. It's just too damned hot for anything else but I will take extra care. For Dave and the rest, racing buffs that they are, today will be spent entirely at the circuit but Chris and I plan to continue to sample the villages and roads all around Le Mans. We decide to start with breakfast of croissants and coffee in Arnage, and although it's only two miles away, the roads are so congested that it takes nearly twenty minutes to get there. Daisy is overheating pretty badly under these conditions and I can feel the intense heat radiating off her engine and cooking my bare legs. The village is as busy as ever, although once again the street show has been suppressed by a visible police presence all along the main street. We sit in the early morning sun, talking about the highlights of the previous evening. Chris burbles on about the restaurant and the all-night firework party, admitting that he hadn't gone to bed until after three in the morning. But we are delightfully sidetracked by the arrival of the Bentley Owners' Club – complete with no less than six of the big 3 litre classics. They park in lines on both sides of the road and I can't resist placing Daisy in front to get some photographs of this rare sight.

After breakfast, the traffic is that bad we decide it's time to lay Daisy up for the day and head on foot down to the circuit where they have a Classic race which precedes the main event. It's something else to watch, as the cars are lined up along the side of the track with the drivers on the opposite side. When the gun fires the drivers run to their cars and must start them before pulling out and away. It's a real treat to watch those old bygone racers giving it their all around this famous circuit, and one of the drivers taking part this year is Stirling Moss. We take a wander around the track, with it's myriad of corporate stands, food stalls, beer tents and the posh exhibition-style offerings by most of the big names that are actually racing. Audi, Bentley, MG, Ferrari and Porsche all have large representations and we spend a fair while browsing the displays.

The main event starts at four pm, and, courtesy of Dave we have grandstand tickets to watch the start. The place is crammed full, and from our high seats we look down on a sea of bright banners depicting support for the carriers' favoured marques. It's like cup final day at Wembley, and the tension builds as the cars finally form up and head off behind the pace car for the warm up lap. They're gone for a while, but a buzz goes up through the crowd as in the distance we see them approaching once more, still at sedate speed. Just before the grandstand, the pace car peels off up the pit lane and the racers floor their accelerators and come screaming past for the first lap of this long twenty-four hour endurance race. The noise from both cars and crowd is absolutely eardrum splitting but soon they're all past and a strange quiet settles on the place. We stay for the first few laps, but then we're off bimbling around the circuit to various vantage points until the evening. As it gets dark, the thing to do is sit on the grass banks by one of the chicanes, and watch the cars come screaming down the straight, lights blazing before crashing down through the gears and hitting the anchors hard. The disks on the brakes glow bright red in the dark, and as the cars accelerate away, spitting flame, the noise is indescribable! Then it's over to the funfair in the middle of the entire stadium area where we go up the big wheel for a panoramic view of the whole circuit. We pause at the very top, and it's great to just sit there looking down at the heaving crowds, the cars hurtling round in a blaze of light from their multiple rally spots, before finally coming slowly down to earth and wandering from there up to the pub. It's about midnight, and us old un's agree that it's almost certainly time to partake of a final few pints of giggle-juice. The lads wander off again, to pursue their own enjoyment back down at the circuit, as the rest of us wander back to the thriving campsite and eventually off to bed.

We awake to the heartening news that the British Bentleys are out in front, and Dave insists that we must join him for what he says is a traditional wander around the campsite to find the biggest beer-bottle-pyramid. These have slowly taken shape over the week as each group consume their stock and place the empties in an ever-expanding construction by their tents. We reckon the Morgan owner's have it this year, having built a truly impressive wall of empty bottles stretching some ten feet long by more than six feet tall. We decide to have our final breakfast in Arnage again, returning via some circuitous country roads to break camp for the long haul home. We agree to meet up with Dave later in the week to retrieve our gear and then, waving further spirited goodbyes in response to the numerous farewells yelled at us we thread our way through the site.

We're on the road once more and heading out towards Alencon and it's not long before the tide of Brits going home begin to start passing us. This is another memorable thing about Le Mans week – the procession home up the long straight roads between Le Mans and Rouen is conducted in something like carnival atmosphere. The local French population comes out in force to line the roads, lay-bys and roundabouts, eager to witness the constant stream of interesting and rare cars, the like of which are probably never seen in such concentration anywhere else.

For many it is an event for the entire family. They set up picnic tables, deck-chairs and barbecues and make it a big occasion. Again, for Chris and me this is an entirely new and not unrewarding experience. When we saw the first of these family groups, happily ensconced in the middle of one of the roundabouts just outside Le Mans, Chris was bewildered. "What are they doing?" He asked, but no answer was necessary - it became obvious as they all waved at us and called out some encouragement or other. As we progress further, the gatherings increase in intensity and many of them wave the Union Jack or the flag of Saint George, cheering, waving or offering up their glasses (red wine, of course) in a toast. We respond in kind to each, and by the time we reach Alencon my arm is tired from all the waving back. The downside to being a part of this parade however is the stream of maniacs in the TVRs, Jags, Porsches and everything in between, who feel that they must perform for the crowds and are, it would seem, hell bent on wrapping their kidneys round the nearest tree. The problem is there is every chance that one of them will take us with them as they frequently pass us at ridiculous speeds. Before long though, the Gendarmes are out in force with their radars and we get entertained by the regular sight of the French version of 'you're nicked Sonny Jim!' being played out in numerous lay-bys.

But it's impossible not to feel good about it all: a feeling of bonhomie buoys the spirits, as the journey, free of the normal emptiness of the miles, flees past. The more modern of our sports car escorts have long since departed to the horizon, but as we progress steadily north, the older examples begin to pass but much more slowly. We are treated to a mixture of the fairly common Morgans, MGBs and older Jags, interspersed amongst which are some real treasures such as AC Cobra's, Lagondas and the like. The occupants of these more sedate sportsters, obviously having a bent for the classic era, nearly all slow down to inspect Daisy, the appropriately ancient bike, and now we find ourselves waving back at these as they toot, hoot or yell encouragement as they pass. All in all it's a hell of a pleasant experience and a thoroughly nice way to end what for us has been an enjoyable and certainly different week.

We maintain a leisurely fifty-five to sixty mph and although it's murderously warm, Daisy takes the return trip in her stride, burbling along beneath us with ease and I reflect happily that she has conducted herself flawlessly the whole week. Some nine hours after leaving we land back in Blighty without incident, and as we complete the final thirty miles I enthusiastically remind Chris that that's another eight hundred odd miles behind us, incident free, and that the Scottish leg of the Landmark should be no problem at all to such seasoned adventurers! He mumbles something along the lines of me being a bit silly, but I can see he's proud of himself, and I suspect, of Daisy. This is confirmed to me in no uncertain terms, over dinner that evening as Chris, brimming with enthusiasm, recounts to his sister the things that we did and saw through the week, the crowds, the sights, the high-jinks, culminating in an awestruck account of the return trip home. Diane raises her eyes to the ceiling as she looks over at me, the unspoken question, "What on earth have you started here?" clear on her face. We'll put this one down as a success then, I smugly tell myself.

It is time to extend the range of our forays once again and it has come to my notice that there is a weekend rally being held within sensible striking distance, in an area near Hastings.

There are two Landmarks down thereabouts, which will be fairly easy to knock off with a good day's ride out from the rally campsite but on announcing this, I have an immediate problem - Chris and Chloe both want to go. This is going to be tricky, as although it was Chloe's 'turn', this one involves a new experience, the rally, which neither of them had ever had or indeed, wanted to miss. Chloe's claim to this trip becomes far more pronounced when she hears that it is in fact the Rabbit Rally, clearly conjuring up visions of the fluffy animals in her mind rather than a field full of old bikes and tents. Salvation and a solution come when I find myself explaining my latest plan at a dinner with my parents that weekend. My father, (universally known as Grandad) decides that he will join us on the other Speed Twin, and do the full camp and Landmark thing with us.

That solves the pillion problem outright as one of the kids can go on his machine, and it will be a right merry family adventure. Suddenly the plan has taken on a far more enjoyable facet. Grandad seems to have an extra spring in his step as the great day comes closer, bringing with it the need to plan and get organised. It soon became apparent that he is woefully ill equipped for such things as we survey his stock of camping necessities. He has a stove. That's it, if you discount the enormous ten-year-old sleeping bag, which with the best will in the world will simply not fit on a motorcycle. We therefore take another trip to the camping shop in order to fit him out with the necessary tackle.

Here's a thing; everything these days comes in ever smaller, more compact, and infinitely better designs. We choose a two-man tent, laughing at the fact that it is smaller, when packed, than his old sleeping bag. We add a bedroll, compact inflatable mattress, sleeping bag, a gas light and a little folding stool – Grandad is nearly seventy, and a few home comforts will be vital if we are to drag him from his crypt and force the great outdoors on him! Next, we have to sort out the loading of Winnie, his machine, in order to make sure that he is comfortable with everything bungeed in place. This is proven by the simple expedient of taking a local ride around the nearby countryside, with all the gear and a willing participant pillion, Chloe. Grandad declares everything to be good, so we are ready for the next stage of our adventure this coming weekend, and another one hundred and fifty miles will be put under Daisy's wheels, taking her running in period ever closer to completion ready for the much longer forays that will follow.

5. *Practising on Rabbits*

The Rabbit Rally is hosted by the Triumph Owners' Club's Rother branch in Sussex, and hopefully this will be a stroll in the park for the freshly refurbished Daisy. It's only seventy-five miles away from home, along the coast to the West, and our route is one of my favourite weekend rides. There is no need for a dawn parade, either, and we can safely leave in the afternoon of the Friday, and have plenty of time to get there, set up camp and find the bar before the sun sets. Chloe is riding pillion on Daisy's little pad this time, whilst Chris mounts up behind Grandad, with the luxury of all the mod cons that the later 1955 machine has to offer by way of suspension at the rear and a large comfortable dual seat. Both kids have full rucksacks, carrying spare clothes and some of the camping paraphernalia we'll be needing.

It's four o'clock, and all's well – and it really is a glorious balmy afternoon - we can't wait to get out on the green lanes that make up almost the entire route. Out of Ramsgate, through the school traffic, we're soon on the back-roads between the ancient towns of Sandwich and Canterbury. After thirty minutes or so we cross the old Dover road, and cut across country through the Barham woods where the canopy of trees makes a refreshingly cool contrast to the blazing sunshine as we thread our way through the network of single track roads, and duly arrive at the quaint country pub that we have earmarked in the sleepy little village of Stelling Minnis. We've had a gentle ride and are still fresh, but a refreshing drink is in order, so we sample a half pint of Olde Badger's Scrotum or some-such brew, whilst the kids settle for coke, before heading off again. Half a mile later, we connect with Ye Olde Roman Road of Stone Street, which is a gloriously humpty, bumpty but fairly straight route that takes us down to Lympne, on the edge of the Romney Marshes.

This is classic biking at it's best, with a maze of tiny unmarked roads that meander across the marshes, heavy with the heady scents of the summer countryside, little hamlets, lambs gambolling in the fields, hawks hovering in the sky, small country inns, fantastically old, nestling quietly in chocolate box surroundings…You get the picture – Ye Garden of Olde England at its grandest. Some of the roads here have those very high hedgerows at each side, and as they snake along with 'S' bend after 'S' bend, we rarely get out of second gear. We cautiously ease our way along waiting to meet the inevitable caravan or tractor that seem to be so carefully placed by the Gods at such times in the worst possible places just to test us. No such bad luck presents itself on this occasion however, and our progress remains steady and undisturbed. This is official, unadulterated 'Bimbling' – note the capital 'B'. It's that good!

But enough of this nonsense, we eventually, and not a little reluctantly, find our way out of the marshes, just east of the ancient fishing town of Rye, and after threading our way through the town, past the tidal harbour with it's parking plot so beloved of motorcyclists as a gathering place on those long summer evenings, proceed in a leisurely fashion westwards, through Winchelsea, with it's rather amusing hairpin-bended hill, up and over, and without further ado, we pull up after a few more miles at the Rally site. They've got this well sorted too, the rally being in the field behind a large country Inn just outside the village of Icklesham (The Robin

Hood), which boasts a well appointed beer garden backing onto the camping site. This will be the focus for grub and beer then! We check in, proceed to the corner of the field closest to the bar, unload Daisy and Winnie, and set about making camp. But at this point the first jarring note of the weekend makes itself known. Winnie is displaying a distinctly oily patina, with a liberal coating round the top end of her engine, which is dripping down to make a nice mess of her otherwise shiny chaincase. Investigation shows that she has lost a rocker cap, leaving her right hand exhaust valve free to spray the stuff liberally through the resulting hole.

I get out the Kleenex, and clean up her dribbles, before throwing up the tents. Grandad is chewing his blanket by now, however, over what to do about the problem with his bike, so we amble over to the welcome tent to enquire about rocker caps for pre-units, and the likelihood of being able to find one hereabouts (after all, this is a Triumph rally, so surely someone will have one in their pocket?). A quick conference reminds us that there is a fine establishment, the Miller emporium, in St Leonard's, Hastings, where all things classic Triumph can be had in exchange for some coin of the realm. It's only ten miles away, so we agree to make that the first stop next day, before we go Landmark hunting for the rest of the day.

The weather has settled to deliver a glorious evening, and despite the oil problem with Winnie we decide on a leisurely ride down to Winchelsea beach as the sun sets, and are absolutely captivated as we watch a near full moon rising magically over the sea. A truly stunning sight, which causes us to loiter for nearly an hour before heading back to camp to spend the rest of the first evening watching late arrivals, whilst sipping a glass of the finest mental sledgehammer the Robin Hood's cellars could offer. In due course some lads that I had partied with recently, at a little rally in Belgium, appear and as greetings are exchanged we agree to share some fluid refreshers later on. By now the last of the sunlight finally gives way completely, but in the moonlight Chloe is delighted to note the emergence of a plethora of bunnies in the next field, and she sets off to stalk them as I reflect that the 'Rabbit Rally' is just that. She spends an age, down on all fours, in the dark, creeping ever-so-slowly towards her targets and manages to get within thirty odd feet eventually, before they decide that's quite enough of that thank you and vamoos in all directions. She comes back flushed with happiness, and settles down to wait eagerly for them to return, in order to repeat the whole exercise again.

The evening passes slowly by, but Grandad retires early (poor old thing, combined age of him and Winnie is 120 years!). Chloe finds some friends in the beer garden, and with nothing pressing to do I wander up to the pub where I settle down in the cosy bar to swap yarns and imbibe with the lads, before turning in at 11.30 or so feeling very satisfied and content, which is the whole point of these rallies, after all.

We're all up by seven thirty and already it's getting hot. As we brew some tea, the talk turns to the choice of routes to the Landmarks we intend to find, and how lucky we are that the day is set to be a classic scorcher. Looking at the rally agenda, we note that breakfast will not be available until nine, so we decide to forego that, finish the brew and hit the road. There are two Landmarks within a leisurely day's striking distance, but first it's down to St Leonard's to Mr Miller. We get underway shortly after eight, which brings us into Hastings too early, so we hunt down a café, where breakfast is duly dispatched, before presenting ourselves to the Miller establishment to obtain the vital cap. Winnie is soon kitted out with a shiny new one, at a cost of three pounds, but the shop is such a fascinating Jackdaw's nest of treasures that it's fully ten thirty or so by the time we finally say goodbye and thread our way out of Hastings, heading west. The first Landmark is about forty-five miles away, on the edge of the South Downs behind Brighton. It's lovely geography is this, if you choose wisely, and we deliberately plot a 'rural' route that takes us across country, including a number of inviting single-track roads, if the map is to be believed.

Riding at leisurely pace it's not long before I notice that Winnie, despite the shiny new rocker cap, is busily producing another Herculean oil slick all over her top end. I pull ahead of Grandad, and at the first opportunity we pull into a lay-by where more Kleenex is brought to bear. It's not obvious where the problem is but it needs investigation, so I get Grandad to start and run her whilst I peer under the tank. Aha! It becomes clear immediately that she's actually blowing oil out of the rocker box gasket, where it joins the cylinder head, and had fooled us with the missing cap! I explain to the others, and suggest that we should attempt to sort the problem, so it's out with the spanners, in order check all the nuts and bolts that hold the thing down. They all seem good and solid which suggests closer inspection is called for, and in due course it transpires that the gasket is actually a very poor fit. I suggest that we undo the bolts, and lift the rocker box in order to attempt to straighten things up, which we do, putting it all back as best we can and setting off again half an hour later fervently hoping it's better.

No such luck, is the answer to that hope, as we stop for lunch at a little country inn, strangely situated *inside* a chalk pit! It's immediately apparent that Winnie, far from being fixed, is settling down to be a royal pain – she's managed to cover herself with more oil than ever and as she stands in the hot sun, a gentle cloud of oily smoke drifts from under the tank, whilst hot oil drips down her barrel fins and makes a nice mess of her chaincase.

Bugger.

Further incensed prodding around reveals that not only have we failed to make the gasket fit better, but a half inch piece has now come out altogether. There's a nice little gap in the rocker seal, bubbling straight to atmosphere! We don't have any gasket stuff with us, so we adopt one of those desperate bodges that keep you going until proper repairs can be carried out at home – we stuffed Kleenex in the gap, and wedged more Kleenex tightly into the head fins under the rocker box to catch the dribbles. Not ideal, and certainly not pretty, but we hope that it would do the job. Pausing only to visit the gents, in the vain hope of removing some of the oil which is now ingrained on fingers and palms, we order a pub ploughman's each for lunch before setting off on the remaining short stretch to our first Landmark, which is one of the few that I have been unable to identify in advance.

The clue is simply 'strange noises from the basement in this house' and we are guessing that it is maybe a water mill, an interesting haunted pub or something of that order. On arriving at the spot marked 'X' nothing seems to present itself, and in fact the only structure of any sort in view is a bridge over a railway cutting. There is nothing strange about the bridge, certainly nothing that would match the clue. I re-check the map reference that has been supplied, but this only confirms that we are supposedly in the right place so we decide to cross over the bridge and ferret about on the other side. And there it is – as we cross, we can see that the railway disappears into a hill about two hundred yards up the cutting, and there, projecting from the hillside, is a house built over the tunnel entrance. After getting the photo of this bizarre structure, we check Winnie over, and decide to change her nappy - the bodge is working but the Kleenex has become saturated. That done we strike out west again to the next one, which is about twenty miles across country. We choose to stick to the tiny back-roads, and with Winnie's incontinence plugged we are really enjoying things in the near perfect weather.

We reach the Landmark, a roman villa nestled amidst the South Downs, without incident, but we don't have time to go in, so we take a short rest, get our photo, change Winnie's nappy again before considering a route back to the Rally. On the map, we notice that we're close to Bignor Hill, a fairly well known National Trust beauty spot, which I've heard of but not been up. We decide that as we're here, we will indeed, and pretty soon we're on a long rough uphill ride through thick woods, twisting and turning, dodging the ruts and holes, until we emerge from the trees on the top of the hill, where the road promptly stops. The view is stunning, and we pull up and get off in order to enjoy the moment.

Picture the scene; two classic motorcycles, in perfect weather, parked on the top of the South Downs, surrounded by grandiose views. Before we know it, Grandad has picked up an admirer (I'm far more experienced, saw him coming, and took evasive action!) and is basking in his audience's admiration, whilst he talks expansively about the bikes. Without warning, Winnie delivers him a shocking blow – her side stand bolt snaps and she promptly falls over with a mind-juddering CRASH!

I think I might have died laughing, but the immediate concern for the fuel spilling everywhere and the possible damage that the rocky surface might have inflicted galvanised me into action. As it was I still couldn't help but snigger as we scramble to pick her up. I'm actually almost in tears and desperately trying not to laugh out loud, but poor Grandad is clearly hugely embarrassed and his audience is no longer quite so full of admiration.

You had to be there. …but it's a memory etched on my mind for eternity.

I soon stopped laughing as I survey the damage though. The fall has bent her handlebars, crushed the nacelle headlamp trim and taken a nice few lumps out of her paintwork on the stony surface. Grandad's all upset, but I settle him down with assurances that this is 'campaign damage' – you have to expect it if you use the thing, and anything that is bent or chipped can, with some effort, be fixed! After ensuring that everything's as straight as we can make it, we stuff Winnie's defunct stand into Chloe's back-pack and head back towards camp, still sticking where possible to back-roads. Unfortunately it soon becomes apparent that Grandad and Winnie are not keeping up. I stop and he explains that there's a drumming noise coming from the tank that gets louder with speed. Where she's gone over earlier, she's dislodged the padding in the tank recess. So, at the expense of more time, we loosen off the tank, sort out the padding and put it all back together. She's fine now and we set off again, in earnest, looking forward to grub, beer and in Chloe's case, more bunnies.

But the day has one more nasty surprise in store for us yet. As we bowl along a delightful wooded back-road, easing down a gear to sweep round a tight corner, we come face to face with a full grown stag! Huge and majestic it certainly is, but nevertheless standing in the middle of the road! I have no idea to this day how we missed the thing, and my memory is scratchy as to what happened next, but somehow we come to a sliding, panicked halt, diagonally across the road, and the stag has gone. Just like that, off into the trees so fast that I sometimes wonder if I'd dreamed the whole thing. Sadly, Chloe has missed it altogether, being behind Grandad and looking in the wrong direction at the time. Back at the Rally site that evening, it all makes for a good yarn, and I promise Winnie a smacked bum when we get home!

As the evening gets into full swing, it's apparent that TOMCC Rother know how to lay on a good do. Food is available at the pub, beer is despatched in satisfactory quantities, everyone's in good spirits, the band, '90% Proof' eventually gets underway, and prove to be excellent entertainers. The weather's fantastic, and as our hosts fire up the biggest spit roast I've ever seen at the bottom of the field, a full moon rises over the sea. Chloe goes bunny hunting again and, much later, as the pub closes, another fully equipped (if you like lager or bitter) bar opens up in the field. Eventually we all end up around the midnight bonfire. Absolutely brilliant! Chloe and Grandad turn in shortly after, both utterly exhausted, but I stay watching the fire burn down, nattering to various people and drinking the last of the beer. The last of us stumble off to bed at around 3.00 am. Good people, good venue, good beer and well, just a damn good do all round. Now we're ready for the big ones.

6. Heading West

Daisy has settled down rather nicely, with no further dramas and she is also definitely run-in now so we can cast our eyes further a field. The kids have debated who's to do what in terms of sharing the pillion duty. Chloe has opted for the two shorter forays of the West country and Wales, while Chris has gone for the long haul north and into Scotland on what will be at least a week's worth of camping. With a day's holiday looming at her school and Chloe keen as mustard since the Rabbit, we decide to tackle Devon, Cornwall and thereabouts next. With a brother, Colin, able to offer a very well placed overnight stop in Bournemouth, we begin to plan our strategy.

A study of our Landmark map reveals that from Ramsgate it's about 175 miles to Colin's house and then we've got a 600 mile round trip, encompassing seven Landmarks. That's 800 odd miles total, which on a sprung hub, I suspect, is going to hurt. Nevertheless an optimistic plan emerges which has us leaving for Bournemouth on the Saturday afternoon where we plan to go out for a meal with 'Uncle' Colin. After a hopefully relaxed evening we will set off early on the Sunday and get as far as we can. Monday is going to be the tough one, and will see us hopefully completing a big loop ending back home, sometime in the evening. Marvellous. A plan with no downsides I reckoned and Chloe, in her matter of fact way, agrees wholeheartedly.

Saturday arrives and off we go, loaded up for a full weekend of camping and fun, but the weather has decided to do it's best to make us suffer for our small pleasures. It's a fine afternoon - of drizzle, mist and grey stuff. We're absolutely soaked through after an hour and have to stop because I'm having real trouble with the mist. I stop for what seems like the fifteenth time to wipe the lenses of the sunglasses I wear with the open face helmet, but I can't see a thing again after two minutes riding as the glasses yet again collect a fine layer of condensation. Constant wiping with the finger is required to keep even a rudimentary window on the world open. Worse than that my beard, obviously feeling left out, starts dribbling a persistent little funnel of water straight down my neck.

The beard had seemed like a good idea at the time. I hadn't had one before the bikes came, but the planned miles left me with the idea that the thing would offer some protection in the sun, equally it would keep the wind and any rain from chaffing my face and although it managed all this magnificently, I had not reckoned with it's funnelling effects. In short, this is a miserable experience, with neither of us having any fun at all. Before too long we're stopping under yet another bridge to get out of the misery, and stamp about trying to get the worst of the wet stuff off and get a little circulation going. Despite the conditions Chloe seems to be in remarkably good spirits. She's had the benefit of being behind me, certainly, which has kept her largely dry but I'm sure she can't be having much of a good time. "You alright then?" I enquire, and the smile she flashes at me as water drips from her helmet seems to defy logic as she responds with the single word. "Yep!"

We can't stop for long because progress has been inordinately slow and time is increasingly against us as the grey afternoon begins to give way to a sullen, murky evening. Daisy is blessed with electrical apparatus in keeping with her years, supplied by the Prince of Darkness himself, and I am further depressed at the thought of the next stage of our journey, which will, for our comfort and convenience, put us on the south section of that blighted carbuncle of a road, the dreaded M25. From Ramsgate to anywhere there's just no way of avoiding the damn thing, and in the type of weather we're currently enjoying it is sure to be a challenge. This belief is reinforced as we head down the slip road into a vast cloud of spray, whipped into a frenzy by the endless line of heavy goods vehicles sweeping along at barely diminished speeds in the gloom.

We are buffeted repeatedly as the maelstrom engulfs us from all sides, and the only thing to do is hunker down in a miserable squat, chin pressed as far as possible into chest, peering from under the lip of the helmet while I desperately count off the miles to the blessed exit that will take us southwest. After half an hour of torture and misery and with huge relief, we peel off onto the A3 – much more suitable for Daisy once past the initial six lane stretch to Guildford, as from there it stretches and winds up across the Hog's Back, round the lip of the Devil's Punch Bowl, a huge prehistoric crater miles across, before dropping down to the coastal plain around Portsmouth and Southampton. We stop at the first available place for a rest and general wringing out, during which Chloe continues to display a cheerful disposition entirely out of keeping with current circumstances. That girl is beginning to worry me! Ten minutes later, during which I had utterly failed to roll myself a cigarette due to the impossibility of completing the task with damp trembling fingers, we're off again towards our rendezvous with Colin in Bournemouth.

We must have looked a pretty picture, judging by Colin's face on our arrival at his house – our blessed shelter for the night. He's not a motorcyclist and considers such activity to be, at best, a misguided attempt to achieve a second youth (unsuccessfully in his view). As we divest ourselves of sopping wet garments, which we hang over the bath, I can see that nothing about the current scene is changing his opinion in much of a hurry. But he soon makes with the teapot and while he and I catch up with family, careers and generally set the world to rights, Chloe heads off for a long soak, still insanely happy. I suspect that the promise of pizza in town, later in the evening, has more to do with that than anything else. Two hours later, we are ensconced in a rather pleasant Italian restaurant, poring over the large-scale map, on which I've marked the Landmarks in felt-tip. Chloe, embracing the idea that big roads are bad, small roads are good, spends a long time tracing various routes with her fingertip, and is full of enthusiasm each time she manages to make a 'complete' connection between two marks without resorting to green or blue roads. Even Colin gets the bug now, as we ponder various undoubtedly picturesque options, whilst balancing the need to make progress against the desire to enjoy. By the time we leave we have a pretty good route plan for the morrow, which will be supervised by Chloe from the rear! Off to bed then, tomorrow will be a long days riding it seems.

An early six thirty start sees us waving goodbye to Colin and heading northwest through the urban sprawl that is Bournemouth. The weather has improved marginally, in that it's only grey and miserable rather than wet, but this happy state of affairs is short lived. We are no more than about 20 miles into the day before things set in like yesterday – a miserable mist and drizzle comes down to claim the horizon and a chill in the air adds it's own particular edge. Luckily, in Colin's warm bathroom, our clothes have largely dried out overnight, but it is fairly clear that this happy state of affairs will not last long. The route that we marked out the previous evening begins to puzzle me before long, as it seems to meander rather more than is strictly necessary as far as I can see. Stopping on the outskirts of Poole, I question Chloe as to her choice.

"We've *got* to go that way Dad, just look at the places we can see!" None the wiser, I ask her to clarify, and pretty soon we're both chuckling like teenagers behind the bike sheds at lunch break, as I follow her finger to 'Puddletown', 'Piddle Hinton' and 'Piddle Trenthide'. All of which reside on the banks of the river 'Piddle' itself. I find Chloe's logic difficult to argue with, and the wide-eyed awe she displays as she recites the names leaves me no choice. Clearly this is a facet of the English heritage that just has to be explored for real. We proceed along the agreed route, and I am buoyed by the sniggering behind me as each of the names go past, in the flesh. Even the weather has lost it's ability to make me miserable as we bowl along, and it seems like no time at all that we thread into the little town of Martock, home of the Treasurer's House our first Landmark of the day. It had been easy to decipher the clue in advance, 'Home of the Money Man' and the place itself was easy to find. We get our photograph and study the map once more, me suspiciously, Chloe with enthusiasm, but it seems that good sense has prevailed for the next stage and she has chosen the A303 and A30 to convey us westwards from here towards Exeter, where we'll turn south to the next Landmark at Torquay.

We take stock and check the time – it's eight fifteen, and after an hour and three quarters we have covered some 50 miles, which isn't too bad considering the conditions and the detour for the Landmark. Daisy's going beautifully, and I ponder once again how, in contrast to her passengers, she likes these wet damp conditions, in which she seems to keep relatively cool and unflustered. The mist and drizzle has not set in as badly as yesterday though, and when all's said and done we're having a good time. We thread our way back out of Martock, and onto the A303. This is a good road, officially. It snakes it's way west towards Ilminster, where a lazy turn to the south west will deliver us to Honiton just inside the Devonshire border. Honiton of course, is the home of Tri-Supply, where all parts Triumph from the 40's to the 80's can be had in exchange for any number of beer tokens. Nestling in the countryside is the authentic farmhouse and converted barn known simply as 'Meriden', and if you don't have an interest in things Triumph that's fine, for Oliver Barnes, the proprietor, runs a fine bike-friendly B&B as well. We aren't stopping there today, more's the pity, as we still have a goodly number of miles and a bunch of Landmarks to get under our belts before sunset. We press on towards Exeter.

Our next Landmark, according to our precision mapping (ahem), is situated down on the coast, in Torquay. We have already identified it as the Babbacombe model village. To get there, we have to circumnavigate Exeter, and this involves another motorway stretch before we can take a coastal route due south. Daisy is running so well that I take the opportunity to catch up a bit in the time stakes by winding on the throttle. The burble becomes a throaty growl as I watch the needle tick up.. 65, 70, 75. Just as it pushes to 80, the ancient mechanism has clearly had enough and suddenly I am watching with wonder as the thing starts jumping around wildly between 10 and 110. It is impossible to tell what our maintained speed is, but Daisy's exhaust note tells me she's stretching her legs in a most satisfactory fashion, and the vibration through the bars adds to the thrill. I glance over my shoulder as the M5 rejoins the A38, and yell a "You OK?" to Chloe. The answer is lost in the wind, but the grin says it all - we are definitely having fun now. I completely fail to spot the speed camera. Two weeks later that the Devonshire constabulary will send me the nice little demand for funds, probably to help finance more of the damn things, but I can't help wondering what the officer who vets the catch of the day will think as he gazes upon the sight of a 1948 motor bicycle, loaded to the gunnels and two up, shattering his dual carriageway speed limit. Ooops!

Oblivious to this soon to be presented opportunity to become poorer, we see Newton Abbot appear on the signs, and we peel off onto the A380 with an associated wind down on the hurtle-juice. Once below 70 again, the speedo needle stops it's wild gyration and settles at a steady 65. Newton Abbot passes by and we're soon threading our way into Torquay and hopelessly lost. My large-scale map is useless here, so we resort to stopping and asking directions - always a mistake in my experience, as there is nothing like local knowledge to send you miles in the wrong direction. Torquay is no exception to this unwritten rule of the Universe, and it's a full 30 minutes before we find the model village. Time for a rest, a map check and a little drying out, we head for the cafeteria clutching the map and settle down in a corner seat with mugs of tea and pastries. We're damp, but not overly so, and as we spread out the map to review our next stage Chloe remarks that it's only 10:15, with nearly half of the day's planned mileage done, so Daisy has done very well to get this far by now, hasn't she? I explain to her that although this is certainly true, we've only actually covered about a hundred miles so far, on mainly clear straight roads. The afternoon route that picks its way along the coast is going to be much slower going. We look at what's in store for us, continuing on south from our current location, we have a Landmark right down near Start Point to get next, which we think is a military memorial. From there we turn west once again along the coast towards Plymouth where we bear north and inland again to a rendezvous with some standing stones on the Bodmin Moor before a final long leg down through St Austell and on to the Lizard down there in Cornwall.

As we chat away, I tell Chloe about standing stones, and the mystery that surrounds such things, and we also touch on 'The Beast of Bodmin' and the stories claiming the existence of a large Panther type creature that apparently roams the Moors. Her eyes are wide with wonder as she traces her finger across the map to the area in question, and after a quick study she's eager to get at it once more.

Refreshed and rested, we continue on our way south. According to my map there are only a very few roads down to this part of Devonshire, and the road that we are on should lead us straight to a coastal stretch with our Landmark half way along it. What I hadn't noticed from the map was the large sea inlet at the mouth of the river Dart, and particularly the absence of any roads crossing it. I was certainly unaware that this is a feature of the Devonshire coastal region, and now realised that one has the choice of a long detour inland, or one waits for the little ferries that ply a leisurely trade across the inlets. Like most travellers heading west, I had always used the main routes further inland, so that this particular regional feature had been lost on me. Landmarking certainly broadens the knowledge somewhat, but it was clear there and then that it also has the ability to play havoc with any planned schedule.

The roads are getting much smaller and twistier, and if there are many more obstacles such as the ferries, it is clear that we will lose an awful lot of time – time we don't have. The ferry certainly isn't going to hurry up on our account, and we watch as it slowly comes towards us, a little platform pulled along on chains running across the seabed evidently. As we wait, I earnestly begin to review the route options, whilst explaining to Chloe that we might have misjudged things somewhat and would do well to get inland again as soon as possible after the next Landmark, in order to pick up better roads and less obstacles. Chloe doesn't agree. She is, she informs me, thoroughly enjoying herself, and don't I think this is wonderful, quaint and pretty? Isn't this exactly why we came and, not to put too fine a point on things, the whole point of doing the Landmark challenge? I countered by explaining that we have many miles to get through this weekend, still have five Landmarks to find, the weather is awful, and we have to be home by Monday evening. I show her the map, show her how pitifully few miles we'd managed since Torquay, tap my watch to focus her on the time – which is steadily ticking by, point at the ferry, and finally suggest she see things my way.

I never win arguments with She Who Must Be Obeyed at home, and shouldn't have expected much more success with the junior version. I retreat, somewhat shocked, under the withering accusation that I sound like 'an Old Fart' while Chloe turns her attention back to the map, humming happily to herself as she deliberately traces a route that stays firmly near the coast. Right, so be it then, I thought as I push Daisy onto the now waiting ferry. We will run out of time, and not get all the Landmarks, the challenge will be lost, because I certainly won't find time to come all the way back. But I have to concede that Chloe has a point and that this *is* what it is all about. I surrender, and join her at the map, still mentally chewing my blanket but resigned to just take it all as it comes. As the ferry docks and we head off, I am still smarting from the simple put down that Chloe had flipped my way. Old fart indeed! But all such thoughts are soon distant as we disembark ten minutes later and thread our way through the outskirts of Dartmouth looking for our route south and back to the coast.

Map trouble arises yet again, and somehow we miss the A379 leading to our next Landmark and end up on a myriad of roads which seem to cut across country, and are small and twisty. There are almost no signs on any of the junctions and the few that there are certainly don't show up on our novelty map. As we attempt to follow the compass, an impossible task with the 'S' bended road we're on, the grey sky descends and envelopes us in a thick, wet, miserable blanket. We're soaked again within minutes and with the overhanging trees dumping what seems to be buckets full of water on us at every opportunity it truly is a becoming a depressing experience. I fret once again on the fact that we've still got a lot of miles to cover today, and that all our gear is now thoroughly soaked through, as are we. In desperation we pull up at some godforsaken crossroads, in the middle of nowhere, confirm that we're lost and try to make sense of the map whilst sheltering under some trees.

I look at Chloe, bedraggled, wet and miserable. She has that bright shiny sheen that is the hallmark of severe wetness, and has an almost comedy look about her in the oversized waterproof trousers that she is wearing. As I watch little rivers of water run off her helmet, dripping from the edges I realize that this is hopeless. "Want to go home?" I say, feeling justified in my own cowardice because it's for the good of a young 'un. I have clearly underestimated the resilience of youth however, and am somewhat surprised as she squares her shoulders, gives me one of those looks that led to the old fart put-down earlier, and responds "Don't be silly Dad! We've only just started and we haven't camped yet!" she demands a look at the map and I feel strangely belittled as she busily traces her finger around on the by now damp paper. Only just started? That's what she had just said. I feel like I've been on the road for a week, and am so damp that I can't help but shiver as I stand there.

Chloe finds a bit on the map that might be where we are, she tells me. I can't quite work out how she has come to this conclusion, but all resistance has now deserted me and the only thing I can do is continue to strike out south at every opportunity and hope that before too long we find the coast road. It's a full hour later that we finally find the thing, the only road in the area it seems which actually appears on my map. The compass has been an absolute saviour and it would also appear that luck is beginning to favour us at last as within five minutes we're pulling up at the next Landmark, which is indeed a military memorial complete with Sherman tank - but more to the point has a big inviting, warm-looking pub opposite. As I take the photograph, the rain begins to ease off, giving way to a grey mist that cloaks everything and leaves visibility not much better than a hundred meters in any direction. But that can wait, the pub has my entire attention and I note that the time is now just after one o'clock therefore it would seem absolutely sensible to go and investigate the menu. Chloe agrees with this wholeheartedly and the two of us traipse across the road without further ado.

There's something about a good traditional rural pub that lifts the spirits, especially in this sort of weather, and restores one's sense of well-being. This one is no exception, with it's ancient, but cosy bar fronting a small dining area and a large fireplace. The fireplace is stacked with logs, and is roaring a welcome to all that enter. I order a pint of Sussex Ale and Coke for Chloe, before heading to the nearest table to that fire. We now begin the ritual that will be familiar to so many motorcyclists, peeling off the sodden jacket, working the waterproof trousers down over equally sopping shoes, now full of water, hanging gloves and scarf as close to the fire as possible. The landlord notes the activity and invites us to place my shoes, Chloe's boots, gloves and scarves on the warm hearth, whilst suggesting that we arrange some chairs in such a way that we can hang jackets near the heat as well. By the time we've finished the place looks like a hikers hostel, and I dread to think what the other patrons who steadily came into the place must have thought. Through the window we could see Daisy, poor thing, condensation gathering on tank and engine, making her take on that steamed-up-mirror look. But it's very cosy in here and with an excellent menu on offer we're anticipating a good feed and a good drying out before venturing out once more.

It's indescribable what a good pub lunch and a drop of local Ale can do for the inner spirit. By the time we had eaten an excellent meal, most of our stuff by the roaring log fire has managed to dry, with the notable exception of my gloves and shoes. As we get ready to head off once again, I mentally shrivelled at the thought of those moist articles that would feel warm at first, but inevitably turn cool and clammy within minutes. I chide myself for not having acquired any boots yet, but there's nothing to be done about it at the moment, so on the shoes go and out to Daisy we wander. As she fires up and I settle into that big sprung seat, I remark to Chloe that at least it's only misty now, not raining and we're both warm after the better part of an hour and a half in the pub. That lasts about 15 minutes as we pick our way carefully Westwards. The grey stuff descends to the point where visibility is almost zero, and as if to mock my comment that it's not so wet it makes its point depressingly, clingingly, and definitely wet after all. It's also getting noticeably cold to boot. Feeling the bonhomie evaporate we press on, round endless twisty bendy roads and soon I'm on autopilot, huddled in that pose familiar to all open-faced-helmet-no-fairing-and-it's-winter riders, until suddenly I am jolted back to reality in the worst possible way. Round a blind bend the road simply stops at a river!

This is another ferry crossing, the same little open, roll-on-get-wet-whilst-crossing-roll-off type we had come across at Dartmouth, only this one is even smaller and is, as I said, hidden round a downhill blind bend. It turns out that there are signs and stuff, warning the unwary but in the mist and drizzle I didn't see 'em. What the little chap selling the tickets must have thought I just can't imagine, as Daisy plus two screaming riders catapulted from the mist and then kangaroo'd, wobbled and finally slid to a halt about six inches from the edge. I manage to get my heart going again, eventually, by which time Chloe has climbed off the now stalled Daisy, removed her helmet and sat down by the river, flushed with the moment of excitement. The ticket seller is asking if she is all right, whilst throwing me the odd disgusted look. Clearly in his view, I am a speed-mad yobbo who should be banned from the roads without delay. There is no point trying to explain, so I stay put.

After an uncomfortable wait, during which I studiously ignore the disapproving looks from the ticket man, the ferry finally edges up to the bank and I duly push Daisy on. Over we go, after parting with a whole £1.00, and press on ever west, past Plymouth and then north towards Bodmin moor, wherein nestle the Hurlers, an ancient stone circle. Again the map excels in its utter uselessness and we almost immediately get lost. This is a truly desolate experience, with the mist and the rising moorlands making me feel very, very, insignificant and lonely, although Chloe seems unaffected by such thoughts due to the fact that we've crossed a cattle grid and are now trundling around on unfenced roads, where the sheep are free to wander as they see fit. She taps on my shoulder before long and says that we should stop – she wants to feed grass to them. I watch her wandering up the road trying to attract a belligerent looking ewe, whilst trying to work out roughly where we are. I can see nothing on any horizon, other than the grey veil, but I'm fairly sure that we have been heading steadily northwest and as such roughly in the right direction.

All we need is to find a signpost to the single village that shows on our map, and we'll at least know that salvation is close. Eventually, after persuading Chloe that the ewe is not going to play ball, we stumble across the village itself, St Cleer. I have no idea how, but I am confident that it can't be too hard to find our spot now as it's only a short distance due northeast, according to the map. Would that it were that simple! We follow a likely looking road, only to find ourselves in a farmyard after half a mile. Back we go, and select the next route out but this turns in a big arc and deposits us back in the village. Third time lucky and with no small measure of relief, there they are on a particularly desolate stretch of high moorland where we stop, get the photo and with no hesitation head back towards civilization. At Liskeard, we take a break and assess our situation: we're way behind schedule now, the time approaching five o'clock and I'm more convinced than ever that we'll not get all our Landmarks on this foray if I'm to get Chloe back to school on time. But there's nothing for it at the moment but to press on.

We find our way onto the A390 heading west again towards St Austell. We need to get past that town without any further delays, and things really start to look up as magically the mist begins to lighten, and with the hint that sunshine is trying to break through our spirits are very much buoyed. In fact, I begin to feel confident that we'll at least be able to camp within striking distance of the planned schedule, and the road is such a joy to ride that we open Daisy up once more to stretch her legs after all the little twisty roads of the past two hours. The weather continues to lift and brighten, the moist air at last becoming dry breeze and as the sun finally breaks through we pull into a little petrol station with a nice café out back, fill Daisy up, then have cream tea and crumpets to celebrate this most satisfactory turn of events. While Chloe finishes off, I wander outside to check on Daisy and make sure everything is as it should be, using my little adjustable spanner to check on the main mounts and the obvious nuts, bolts and fastenings that I can reach. Everything is shipshape except her large ornamental horn, situated just below and behind the big sprung seat.

This is flapping about on it's mounting, and is quite fiddly to tighten, but a few minutes sees it done. Daisy has fared well it would appear, and as I check her oil level I am very pleased that she is showing no signs of any oil-leaks other than the spot underneath where the engine breather is situated. I enthusiastically point out these things as Chloe emerges, but the look she gives me suggests that she thinks I'm gibbering. She does however give Daisy's pillion pad a pat, and agrees that she's a 'good girl'.

Once underway again, we skirt through St Austell and head on towards Truro. The traffic seems to be inordinately heavy, so we filter through as best we can, negotiating the half a dozen gridlocked roundabouts around the south side after which we meet the longest traffic jam I have ever seen in my entire life. Oh, the bliss of being on two wheels, but I am appalled at the utter congestion and assume, quite wrongly as it turns out, that there has been an accident further out. But the real reason for the jam becomes apparent as we leave the town behind – an endless line of caravans, stretching as far as the eye can see, is strung out along the not-that-wide road. We bowl along past these, expecting at each bend to find the front marker and a clear road ahead, but alas it's not to be and it takes us nearly an hour, dodging in and out of the oncoming lane, to cover the 15 or so miles to Truro. Bloody caravans, turning this whole area into a choked up misery and it's not even summer yet!

Finally we're through it, past Truro and riding into a glorious sunset on the last stretch down to the Lizard towards the last Landmark of the day, Goonhilly Earth Station, and hopefully an easy to find campsite. As darkness begins to close in I begin to fret about the campsite, remembering the dismal failure to find one on the foray into Suffolk. But this is the West Country and we are therefore delighted to find numerous campsite signs close by. The Earth Station, a great cluster of huge satellite dishes and domes, looking for all the world like a field of fantastic giant mushrooms, is at least easy to find. We could see the things for miles, and on arriving there we just sit for a while and soak up the peaceful surroundings, letting the day's weariness ebb away before I get out the cameras for the all-important photo. I congratulate Chloe on a fine day's achievements – we are back on schedule, have survived some pretty awful conditions, picked off four valuable Landmarks and now can relax for the evening at the nearest campsite we can find. As the sun sinks lower on the horizon and the insects begin to emerge, whining, buzzing and whirring all around, we turn and thread our way back along the tiny roads towards one of the numerous camping signs we had seen just a short while ago. Finding a camp site really is easy but I have to pause just inside the gates, in order to remove about a million bugs, moths and six legged beasties from my helmet, beard, neck and jacket before we get booked in and trundle off to find a flat spot and get set up for the night.

For Chloe this is the first real camping she's ever done and as such it's a big occasion. This modern tent is nothing like the wood and canvas contraptions that I remember from my youth, and despite two outings, I still struggle to make sense of it. In the meantime Chloe sets about doing the honours with the brand new cooking equipment that she's been carrying in the back-pack. My inexperience in preparation becomes blatantly obvious once again at this point, as Chloe empties the contents out on the grass. The bag of coffee powder has split open, and is now just a loose mess in the bottom of the pack: worse the sugar has joined the party in exactly the same way. These two had mixed with the equally mangled bag of rice. Chloe manages to salvage at least enough for a cup each, and enough uncontaminated rice for dinner, which she sets about preparing. She does a grand job too, and an hour later, stuffed with improvised chili (sweet, and with a hint of coffee) we head for the facilities block to get cleaned up.

Freshly showered, we go exploring to find the on-site bar, which is a delightful little affair, decked out like a hunting lodge but with open views to the west where the sun is making up for it's absence most of the day by putting on a spectacularly fiery sunset. Excellent beer is on offer, which I make a point of sampling several times as Chloe matched me with fruit juice, and we spend a happy evening poring over the map, with her doing the route finding with her finger again. I worry about the seemingly enormous distance to cover next day, heading first up to the north coast of Cornwall, further up and across into Somerset and eventually all the way back home. So it's off to bed early, ready for a long, long day on the morrow, and this exercise is only mildly hampered by my failure to bring along a light of any description.

Dawn. And glory be, it's a bright dawn. The sun is just poking above the low horizon, casting the eastern sky with a fiery glow, and giving the fields and distant trees, in their early misty shroud, a surreal feel. The sight makes me pause and time stands still for a magical moment - the relief is enormous after yesterday's endurance test. We break camp at a quarter to six after failing to have breakfast or tea due to a non-functioning stove. This is stupidity on my own part, I neglected to turn the thing off properly the previous evening and it had leaked the vital gas away during the night. The lack of sustenance is almost the end of the world to Chloe who does love her breakfast, and I have to promise her a Little Chef job or some-such once we are under way. We push Daisy up the driveway, to avoid waking the entire campsite, but once in the lane she fires first kick and we hit the road with spirits high.

We only have two Landmarks to get on this final day of the foray, but we'll have to cover over 400 miles as well if we're to see our own beds tonight. As we thread our way north towards Truro I begin to fret again at the seemingly impossible task. The distance itself, barring misfortune, isn't really an issue, but of course it's not that simple at all. We'll get lost, that's almost certain, we have to detour from the main routes to find the Landmarks themselves which invariably takes a lot more time than one imagines and to cap it all, we mustn't forget Daisy, who is doing fine certainly, but is not sensibly rideable all day long without plenty of rests, both for her to cool down and for us to relieve our cramps. And what about all those caravans? If yesterday was any measure of what we could look forward to today, then we're in trouble before we start. I chide myself for such negative thinking and focus instead on the plus points that are surely in our favour - the weather for one thing, has changed dramatically, and as such the miles will trundle past infinitely faster than yesterday and there are only two Landmarks to find with long riding sections in between, again unlike yesterday, so it should be possible to avoid things like ferries that ate up the time.

I am so intensely wrapped up in these thoughts that we're upon Truro and heading out the other side before we know it, looking for the left turn that will take us north again to join the A30. We are delighted to find that there are no caravans, or indeed any other traffic, which means that we can give Daisy her head once more through the gently sweeping curves that can be seen snaking off to the horizon. The early sun is burning off the wispy mist from the fields, and a glorious panorama of undisturbed countryside surrounds us which on occasion is so eye-catching that we simply have to stop briefly to savour the peacefulness of the scene. We watch a kestrel hovering with deadly silence, almost within touching distance, until it drops like a stone on some unwary, and I suspect suddenly late rodent. Chloe takes to 'mooo-ing' or 'baaa-ing' at the animals as we pass, causing me a few chuckles, and we progress steadily through the morning.

Continuing north, Camelford comes and goes, leaving a long stretch of winding, uncluttered road where Daisy can once again stretch her legs. In due course Stratton and Kilkhampton fall behind us as we head on towards the coast at Clovelly, on the border between Cornwall and North Devon. Here we bear east once more, skirting

Bideford and on to Barnstable where we plan to stop for an early lunch. And what a surprise this town is to both of us. For some reason, the name had conjured up in my mind's eye visions of some grey industrial town, disinteresting to visit and probably depressing, but nothing could be further from the truth. In fact we are enchanted as we slowly trundle around the picture postcard town centre, before stopping to indulge in Cornish Pasties (even though this is Devon) followed by a big home made ice-cream each, made with real Devon cream. Wonderful, but time is trickling past and I need to check Daisy over before we head off again, just to make sure nothing is coming adrift.

That horn is loose again, and she has developed a slight leak around the dynamo, where it interfaces with the timing chest, but it's not too bad and I don't have the right spanner or hexagon key to do anything about it anyway. A quick clean with some Kleenex will have to do, but I tell myself to keep an eye on that in case it is an early sign of worse to come. Chloe is studying the map again as I do my rounds of nuts and bolts, because from here we need to head towards the coast where our first Landmark of the day should be found in the little town of Lynton. We have not been able to decipher the clue to this one in advance, and therefore have no idea what awaits. I discuss the possible meaning of 'Raising the profile of copper and zinc' with Chloe as we prepare for the off once more, but neither of us has any inspirational ideas.

It's just after twelve o'clock as we leave Barnstable, taking the A39 and continuing to enjoy the almost perfect conditions. The early promise of that fantastic sunrise was not an empty one, and it's a glorious summer day, with the temperature rising for the occasion to give us a thoroughly pleasant experience on a thoroughly pleasant road. The hilly landscape that we are now traversing could have been made especially for classic motorcycling, with it's meandering roller coaster road winding it's way between the profusion of greens and colours that one only sees in the English countryside. And a surprise awaits us as we approach Lynton, when the road snakes over the last hill and begins a descent which takes our breath away with it's sheer, raw beauty.

To one side of us is a rock escarpment rising steeply from the very road and on the other is thick, wild, river bank woodland, following the course of the West Lyn River. Our road sweeps steeply downwards twisting and turning as it follows the contours, with Daisy's deep burbling exhaust note reverberating amidst the rocks and the trees as she lopes on the over-run in third. In the end I simply have to pull over and stop in order to just soak up the magical surroundings. I start to wonder how the people that live in such an area perceive their own surroundings. Does it simply become the norm, no more than just the everyday background to their lives? Do they travel to places like Kent and find themselves moved by its beauty, on the grounds that it is so different to this, their own environment? It's an interesting point, and one that I mentally file away for a time when I'll have the chance to discuss it with a local from some equally breathtaking region, hopefully on one of the many camping occasions the we have planned.

Just gazing around, astounded by the peacefulness of the place these thoughts keep me distracted for a full ten minutes, before my mind once again registers on the need to get underway. I call to Chloe, who has wandered across the road and is prodding around in the woods and we reluctantly get mounted up for the last half-mile down to Lynton. The town is a perfect compliment to that approach road, with its 'Olde Worlde' collection of stone-built buildings nestling between the stark coastal headlands either side. We trundle through the centre, but can see nothing that matches our clue, so we turn round and head back, this time taking a different route around.

Several such circuits fail to present us with anything obvious, but the surroundings are so impossibly pretty that neither of us is moved to care too much. Eventually, after possibly the fourth circuit of the place, we stop outside the splendid Town Hall, where a tourist information point is advertised. Perhaps, I explain to Chloe, we can get some inspiration as to the elusive clue here. Before we can go inside however, a rotund gentleman who has scurried busily from the building, urgently addressing us as he approaches, accosts us. He seems to be asking what we're doing and I suddenly realize I have parked Daisy in a spot 'reserved for the Mayor'. The gentleman accosting us turns out to be that very honorary himself judging by the gold chain, and I brace myself for the inevitable.

Just how wrong that impression turns out to be becomes clear as he reaches us, puffing slightly from his exertion. He is indeed the Mayor, introducing himself as such, but far from being upset that a pair of motorcycle ruffians have nicked his parking space with their nasty noisy machine, he is actually enthusing about Daisy! He congratulates us on the choice transport, is delighted to see such a machine in his town, and, pointing to the camping gear, wants to know how far we've come, how far we're going, professes astonishment and admiration for Chloe when he hears the answer before asking what has bought us to Lynton. Explanations follow, and in fact we find ourselves explaining the whole story of the Landmark Challenge in detail. On discovering that we are also raising charitable funds, he forbids me to move whilst he hustles into his town hall again to reappear five minutes later, waving a fiver – from the town funds – for 'my cause'! Then he turns his attention to Chloe, and I watch her almost visibly swelling with pride as he announces that she is an example to all doing such a thing requiring, he was sure, tremendous strength and effort at such an age.

The man's sheer enthusiasm is infectious to say the least and I find myself brimming with pride as well. We eventually manage to get the subject onto our immediate problem, that of the elusive clue. It takes him a few seconds to answer it, with a hearty "Of course! It's the Brass Rubbing Centre. Oh, I say how clever!" Is it? Ah... yes that fits. Copper and Zinc makes brass, rubbing would indeed 'raise the profile' so to speak. Could he give us directions to it then? He can, did and in short order we are saying our goodbyes to this wonderful character and are under way again, full of fresh enthusiasm for the task. We get the all-important photograph and reluctantly leave Lynton and it's colourful Mayor behind, riding once again up that wonderful approach road before turning east for the next leg.

Exmoor awaits us. We're both looking forward to this because it's National Park land, and that means unfenced roads and undisturbed wild countryside again. As we cross the cattle grid that marks the boundary, it's almost like turning a page onto a different scene as the lush green moor land comes right down to the road, trailing along in a wonderfully unkempt manner that will never see a curb-stone or be forced to follow a straight edge. We notice as we proceed along the higgledy-piggledy road that signposts have given way to white stones, two feet tall, and which have directions and miles engraved in them. So we're not disappointed and it's truly a marvellous ride in the continuing ideal weather. We stop on a high crest, taking Daisy two or three feet off the road onto the springy green carpet that stretches in a bumpy panorama as far as the eye can see.

Sheep interrupt their industrious cropping of the lush grass to stare quizzically at us. A hawk stops it's flight and hovers nearby, giving us an unrivalled view of it's precision use of the wind currents as it's wing-tip feathers stroke the breeze and it fixes the ground beneath with powerful optics in search of lunch. I mention to Chloe that this is what we should have enjoyed yesterday when searching for the Hurlers down on Bodmin moor, and that our current surroundings would be equally bleak should the mist and cloud descend once more. But we agree that there's no room for regret that we didn't get to sample it – we've got it now.

As I lie back on the grass and think about the day so far, I am gratified that it just gets better and better, but inevitably it's time to get underway once again and it seems only too soon that the unfenced roads give way to the hall-marks of civilization as we cross the little cattle grid at the far side of the moor. A quick map and time check reveals that we have some 50 miles to our next, and final Landmark and it's pushing towards two o'clock. I begin to mentally calculate the total distance still to cover to get home and plot that against various average speeds in my head. I didn't like the answers and suggest to Chloe reluctantly that once we have picked off the last photograph, we will have to settle for the main routes home and ride as long as possible before resting.

As usual, she is far more optimistic about things, confident as usual that Dad is merely worrying unnecessarily. After I show her the distance and invite her to do some maths involving dividing the 250 miles to home by, say, an average speed of even 40mph (which causes further debate, until Chloe understands that each stop, junction, traffic light etc reduces the average), she realises that we really are up against it. I am more concerned about riding after dark I explain, since Daisy's electrical abilities are definitely far from ideal and highly questionable in the reliability stakes. It is with a sense of urgency then that we set off once again, determined to push harder than we have all weekend. I fret about Daisy's ability to take the punishment I have planned, but there's nothing else for it really and the throttle hand winds on the juice accordingly. We're heading for a hunting lodge, owned and used by King John in the 1200's, which nestles close to Cheddar, and that hop alone will take a good forty five minutes if we're lucky. Daisy eases up to 75 on the straights, of which there aren't too many, and the miles steadily roll away beneath her wheels.

Arriving at Cheddar at around ten to three, having somehow missed the hunting lodge, we stop for a while to ease the bones, and it seems appropriate to enjoy a pint of cider (Coke for Chloe) before doubling back to find the thing and get our picture. As usual the pathetic map we have makes it hard to pinpoint exactly where the lodge is, and with a myriad of little roads in this area I begin to think we'll never find it. Round and round we go, to no avail, and the precious minutes tick relentlessly past in the afternoon sun. To add to my worries, Daisy is overheating as we stop-start-stop and in the end I am forced to stop by a little farm shop in order to let her cool down but at least this gives me a chance to ask inside about the lodge. It's easy, I'm told, as it's actually in the middle of the little town of Axbridge, not two miles up the road. Can't miss it – it's right in the town square, I am assured.

The information, against all previous experience of 'local' knowledge, turns out to be absolutely right, as we pull up ten minutes later in front of the very large and ancient lodge smack in the middle of the very small town. Whilst doing my research back at home, this little snippet had failed to register, and I had wasted a lot of time looking for my own idea of a hunting lodge, which in the proper order of things should surely be in the woods? I had therefore dismissed any route that led into a town or village! I made a mental note to check such details for the next lot of Landmarks, and certainly wouldn't get caught out again.

That's it then, and as I take the photograph I enthusiastically congratulate Chloe and Daisy. The last Landmark of this foray is safely in the can, (or cans to be more accurate, because in a very uncharacteristic fit of logical thinking back in the period of minimal planning, it had occurred to me that having a set of backup photographs in case of disaster would be an incredibly sensible precaution. I therefore had two disposable cameras in the tank bag). We check the time again and I wish we hadn't, all that mucking about has really cost us, it's now nearly five o'clock and with just over two hundred miles still to do this is no joke. We do the maths again – if we really push things and take minimal stops, we can maintain an average speed of 50 mph, probably. It's not likely however, as we're both feeling the miles now, and we're certainly not going by the motorways, so we'll have towns to slow us up not to mention the twisty roads, punctuated with regular roundabouts or junctions themselves. Call it six hours then, which will get us home at eleven if we can keep up the pace. Of course, all this assumes that Daisy's lights can keep going!

Despite the pressure to crunch miles, it is not possible to be in the area and not ride through the Cheddar Gorge. Chloe is dead keen to see it, having listened to my inadequate description, and I promise that we'll head back through Cheddar and up through the Gorge itself. This is actually an experience I have never before sampled on a motorcycle and therefore I too am dead keen. We take our time threading up through this spectacular monument to violent geography. I still find it hard to describe the gorge with it's impossibly sheer rock faces bordering the road that snakes through numerous 'S' bends as it climbs steeply up to the top into the Mendip Hills. Breathtaking – and we both agree it is a marvellous thing to do with an old classic motorcycle!

And so, inevitably, we turn towards Bath and the long haul home. Picking up the A4 heading east, we set a harsh pace for Daisy and pretty soon, with Chippenham and Marlborough behind us we take a ten-minute stop at Hungerford. I try to explain to Chloe the terrible events that took place here on that fateful day in 1987, just before she was born, when a certain Michael Ryan and his gun collection took the lives of some seventeen people before taking his own. Chloe asks the million dollar question "Why?" I find myself unable to answer – he took that secret with him. We move on, continuing on the A4 past Newbury and finally we join the M4 at Reading where we take a well deserved rest at the services. We have pushed

Daisy hard and covered some 85 miles in one and half hours, including the stop at Hungerford. The horn has come loose yet again, and that oil leak round the dynamo is noticeably worse, but nothing else is amiss. I feel immensely proud of the old bike but consider that she's in for a real test now as we'll be completing our weekend with an anticlimactic and uninspiring (but for Daisy enduring) 120 miles of motorway. It's exactly a quarter to seven as we join the M4, and exactly a quarter past nine when we pull up at home that evening.

Chloe wastes no time in claiming the bathroom, once she's managed to fight off Sheba, our dog, for whom the disappearance of two of the family again has obviously been traumatic and confusing. Chris explains that she has been pining the whole weekend, lying in the garage for long periods with her nose carefully positioned at the crack in the doors, resisting any attempts to distract or cheer her up. I take my time unpacking, only mildly hampered by Sheba's demands for attention and answering a barrage of questions from Chris. Later on, as the family sit down to a very late meal, the talk is of high adventure and Chloe gives a fairly good rendition of events as they have unfolded. The Mayor of Lynton is the high point undoubtedly, and I smile as I watch her explaining that encounter, but it was also nice to hear her describing some of the sights and scenes that captivated us so thoroughly.

Chris is very taken with the idea of national park land, and insists on a detailed account from Chloe before turning to me and asking whether he will get to see similar on his next outing. I assured him that this will indeed be the case, since one of the Landmarks is in the hills of Cumbria. There was anticipation in his manner that makes me feel enormously satisfied – my plan to broaden the kids' horizons is definitely showing dividends already, and I am delighted at the prospect of continuing to do so. By the time the plates are cleared I am under pressure from both children to confirm the rest of the Landmark campaign, and I promise that we will look at the maps the next evening – right now it is very late, and a school day to boot – so off to bed with them both, I insist. Diane is clearly pleased to see the kids so keen to be involved, and as they reluctantly headed off to their rooms, I promise everyone that we will plan the rest of the challenge in the coming week, but also remind them that before continuing, we will have to check that Daisy has handled this last test without any problems.

7. Fire in the Shires!

The following morning, with everyone off to school and Diane at her morning job, I wheel Daisy out into a glorious sunny day and settle down in the drive to check her over. A brief visual inspection is encouraging, with nothing obvious to fret about, so I open up the socket set, get my box of spanners, and set about the task of checking all the fastenings and mountings. Rocker box and cylinder head bolts have all loosened off slightly, with the beginnings of an oil-leak around the rear pushrod tubes – this is fixed easily with but a few moments of tightening whilst carefully observing the torque settings of 18ft/lb. The horn has come loose again, so it is time to take it off and after checking the threads on both nut and bolt, simply re-mount using some thread-lock. The dynamo has continued leaking but it is a minute's work to slacken off the clamp, tighten the nut to pull it harder against the timing chest, and do up the clamp once again.

The engine mountings and those of the gearbox take but a slight turn on the sockets to nip them all up, but the fuel tank is a different matter. Daisy's tank is secured with four bolts to the underside, one of which is now conspicuous by its absence. They're special bolts on these older models, with a shoulder that ensures that you can't tighten them too far and thus pierce the tank itself, with the inevitable results. I have no spares and decide that Daisy can live with it until later in the year, when doubtless other such items will be joining this one on the list of things to be replaced. Next up, I check the chain tensions of both primary and secondary drives, giving each a small amount of adjustment, before turning my attention to oil. This needs changing I decide, as she's just completed the best part of a thousand miles on her fairly new engine. Once that's done I spend the rest of that relaxed morning with a bucket and soapy water, before finishing off before lunch by giving her a well deserved wax and polish.

All told, she has done rather well I consider, as I tidy away the tools and cleaning gubbins. If this is what could be expected from the old girl, then the long haul north should hold no worries for Chris and myself at all. In fact Chris is still very wary of Daisy's manners after the troublesome Norfolk experience, despite no sign of any such problems on our unplanned detour to Le Mans. It seems she will have to deliver more than one trouble free journey to convince him that she has been properly fixed. Putting the tools away then, my thoughts turn to what else needs doing before we take to the high roads of Scotland. The tent has proved adequate, albeit a bit small, but I have suffered mightily from sleeping on the hard ground with just the thickness of the sleeping bag for padding. I have also discovered just how cold mother earth can get in the wee, small hours, as the cold from the ground had sometimes left me quivering and so cold that by five in the morning I had, in desperation, attempted to light the stove inside the tent, in order to heat the place a bit. That had led to the discovery that we had no gas and at that point I had given up, got dressed and gone off to stamp around the place in an effort to get warm again.

Chloe has suffered no such ill effects, and I guess this was age creeping up on me in yet another small way. So, a bed roll of some sort is definitely required and I need to consider other small items whilst at the camping store, such as a gas cylinder for the stove, an additional one as a spare, and some proper storage containers for the likes of milk, sugar and tea bags. Maps have also proved to be a problem thus far, and I begin to wonder where to get larger scale maps of the areas we have yet to visit. We have managed with the 1:250,000 scale that I was carrying for both forays to date, but it has proved useless once off the beaten track and it is clear that life would be much easier with more detailed items, especially when considering the wilds of Wales, Scotland and Cumbria.

Later that evening, I sit down to make a list of all these necessities, and then begin looking at the choices for the next attack. It occurs to me that the school holidays are a good few weeks away yet and with Scotland and Wales both requiring more than a normal weekend to complete, and both kids determined to share the experience, I have to concede that these epics must wait. I have to look closer to home for the moment, and having already dealt with the southeast and East Anglia there aren't actually that many 'odd ones' left. My eyes turned to the little marks on the map in Surrey, Middlesex, Berkshire and Gloucestershire, wherein nestle a Landmark apiece, and would make for an interesting weekend's worth of adventure I reckon. These lie in a logical progression, heading northwest from our little corner of the land and we can call in to see my other brother, Howard, and his family on the way through Wiltshire too. I decide to make that one a surprise visit for him and also for Chris, and therefore leave it unmentioned for the moment.

As it turns out, Diane is going off to a music convention in London this weekend, taking Chloe with her. Something I have utterly failed to remember until the Friday morning, when I am reminded not to be late picking her up from work, Chloe up from school and delivering both of them promptly to the station. I duly do all this, and on his arrival home from school Chris was quick to accept my suggestion that we may as well take the opportunity to go camping again. Of course I haven't had time yet to go and purchase the items on my list, and I certainly can't face another night without some padded insulation, so with some urgency we jump on Daisy there and then, Chris with the back-pack on, and ride the seven miles to the camping shop, arriving just in time to stop the old boy there turning the sign on his door to 'closed'. After begging to be allowed in, he tells us we must be quick, and we hurry round the place grabbing all the things that I can remember on my list, which I have of course forgotten to bring.

On the counter at the end our little stash grows – half a dozen plastic pots with screw on lids, a bedroll, some extra bungees and some gas cylinders. I rack my brains but couldn't think of anything else. Chris declined the offer of a bedroll, taking the opportunity of dealing me another mental shock when, like Chloe before, he suggests that only 'old farts' needed such things. But the shopkeeper is pointedly looking at his watch, so I let this latest insult go as we shove all the purchases in Chris's back-pack, pay the man, and climb back on Daisy. Just as we are about to pull away, I remember the thing that I have been racking my brains over, the camping light! I jump back off and just catch the 'closed' sign going up for the second time. Under the disapproving stare that is now being aimed at me I babble something about the need for the light, apologise for my idiocy and the inconvenience it is causing, take the first one tersely offered, wave some more money at the by now thoroughly bemused shopkeeper and finally leave, slightly embarrassed, to return back home and get Daisy ready for an early start the next morning.

An hour later we are trying to work out the best way of fitting everything into Daisy's limited storage, and getting nowhere fast. We hadn't had the bedroll last time, the spare gas or the alarmingly large gas light. There seems to be no space for any of them no matter how many ways we try, and we are both getting frustrated with it and each other whilst achieving nothing. Salvation comes in the shape of Bill, our neighbour. He has been observing our various comical attempts to manage what he clearly saw as a simple task, and finally decides to intervene with a polite clearing of his throat to attract our attention. Bill is everything in life that I am not. He *knows stuff.* Specifically, he knows all the stuff that mere mortals such as I can never hope to grasp, and makes impossible and complicated things seem very, very simple. This is probably because most things are in fact very simple, but that I am even simpler than they are. Whatever the case, Bill likes to demonstrate his clear superiority and abilities over those of his rather useless neighbour, and proceeds to make suggestions that as usual leave me tingling with shame at their breathtaking simplicity, but more to the point, my breathtaking inability to see them without help.

The neatness of Bill's solution cannot be argued with. Lay out the bedroll, he suggests, and place the light cross-ways in the middle. Now, he continued patiently, place the gas cylinders, bottoms facing outwards, one at each end of the light. See how these make a natural pair of end stops, around which you can now roll the bed up, enclosing the light within. Secure with bungees, and you have a neat roll, containing bulky stuff, which you just put across the back of Daisy with the tent. I do. They do. It does, and I feel deeply stupid to have not been able to see this myself during the twenty minutes of buggering around. Bill had worked it out in seconds the smug git. I tell Chris how stupid he is not to have thought of the obvious answer, am rewarded with derision, and so grudgingly raid the fridge and produce some beer, handing one over to Bill as a thank you.

As we drink in the evening sun, I explain to him what we are in the process of doing. It is clear that Bill thinks I have lost some, if not most of my marbles, confirming this with a simple statement – "You're bloody mad" he says. I try explaining the joy of the open road, the thrill of the challenge, the recaptured fun of camping. Not to mention the camaraderie that is developing with the kids, I add. None of this seems to convince him, as he eyes me with what looks like a concerned smile: eventually I give up, bid him good night, making excuses about the need for an early night, long day tomorrow, up early and all that I explain. As I put Daisy away that evening I find myself wondering whether Bill has a point. Are we mad?

I don't think so.

It's a bit of a novelty this, I think, as we set out the following morning under a vast blue sky with its promise of a warm and sunny day to come. Daisy had even started first kick and here we are heading west on near empty roads. Early mist is hanging in the trees and clinging to hedgerows across the fields, glowing mystically as the sun slowly but surely catches up and burns off the moisture. There's a slight chill in the air, but with the sun at our back promising to grow stronger by the minute, this is sure to be a temporary inconvenience, nothing more.

We're planning on cutting across country all day long, following a route that will take us first to the ancient city of Canterbury, through the North Downs to Ashford, threading our way westwards from there through the Weald of Kent to Guildford before turning north to keep our first appointment at Windsor. Specifically we will be looking for Runnymede, the site at which King John put his seal to the Magna Carta in the year 1215, the great charter of English liberties. Being so close to Windsor, I also promise Chris that we'll stop to see the castle. I am amazed to discover that he has never even seen a photograph of the place. Well, there's no substitute for the real thing I declare, so visit it we shall. From there, we'll turn west once more and pick our way across to the A4 at Reading and on into Wiltshire for that surprise rendezvous with Howard. Daisy has other ideas.

We are in the middle of the Weald in rural Kent, stopped for a rest next to a charmingly rustic little bridge that spans some ancient stream that has been gurgling along next to the winding road for the last few miles. Chris is leaning on the bridge gazing down at the clear water as it makes its leisurely way along beneath him. He's done the thing with sticks, dropping them into the current and then waiting for them to emerge the other side, and now he's looking for fish. I am sitting on a little style by the road, having a crafty cigarette whilst dreamily gazing at the countryside around me and thinking that life doesn't get much better than this. I am also thinking that my cigarette is giving off rather more smoke than is normal, which is annoying as it is interfering with my lazy inspection of Daisy against that idyllic backdrop. Holding the thing up to inspect it I am suddenly, and harshly, jolted back to reality. It's not the cigarette giving off the excessive smoke but Daisy! It is coming from beneath the panel on her petrol tank, curling up around the tank-bag and before my very eyes it is getting thicker! I let out a yell as I scramble from my perch, and Chris, yanked from his daydreams yells a harsh query at me along the lines of "What the hell…?"

"Daisy's on fire!"

What follows is classic circus stuff. As I run full tilt towards her I cannon into Chris, who's running from the bridge. I yank the tank-bag off and fling it to the floor, but then all we can do is dance around Daisy utterly helpless. Chris, by now in a blind panic, yells at me to "do something", I yell back that I can't – I have no tools and no time. The panic deepens, the smoke gets thicker and in desperation I try to grab the edge of the panel and rip the thing off without undoing it's retaining bolt. Better that, than the unthinkable consequences of doing nothing. As I grapple desperately with the panel, it occurs to me suddenly that a fire inside a recess within a half full petrol tank is about as dodgy as it is possible to get and I yell at Chris to get away. He must have arrived at the same thought as he doesn't need telling twice!

My fingers fail to grip the edge of the panel as I heave, but as they slip off they catch the lead light, standing proud from the panel, ripping it from it's housing. Smoke boils angrily up through the hole, and self preservation finally cuts in - I abandon the hopeless struggle and flee, taking large, urgent steps in the opposite direction to join Chris down the road. We stand and watch helplessly as time seems to be suspended. Miraculously though, as we continue to watch, Daisy's tank fails to erupt into a fireball and slowly, agonisingly slowly, the smoke begins to clear. I stand trembling as the adrenalin drains away, but after some ten minutes I cautiously approach once more, ready to flee at so much as 'tic' from Daisy. No smoke. I edge closer, peering gimlet-like at that hole, and suddenly notice that the wires coming from the now dangling lead light are a melted mess, but a mess that at least is no longer burning.

I continue staring at the panel, still trembling from the adrenalin rush, desperately daring to hope that the danger was over. It was, I decided, but I still wasn't going to approach the thing until it had properly cooled down. "It's OK," I yell as I turn to Chris "It's stopped!" I nearly burst out laughing though, as I took in a scene so familiar to our last journey together – that of Chris standing forty feet away, fingers firmly in ears, a look of abject fear and deep unhappiness on his face. I walk over to him, and slide down the stone wall by the road, to sit and calm down. "Well bugger that," I offer. After another five minutes or so, we head back over to Daisy, and set about inspecting the damage. I gingerly try the light switch, which is also mounted in the panel, and we are rewarded with lights without any smoke or flames. This is good. Feeling much happier, I fish around in the lead-light mounting hole, pulling the eight feet of coiled wire that allows the thing to wander, out into the sunshine. It's a sorry state indeed, with a substantial length of it melted, but it's impossible to identify what started things off. I explain to Chris that we have had a short circuit, probably due to a section of this lead rubbing against a sharp edge or something, and that to be safe we'll need to disconnect the lead, cut it back and tape the ends up.

As I do the necessary, I get to thinking that I had not reacted particularly logically to this incident. Daisy has a good old fashioned battery mounting, with the power source in its authentic Exide box, mounted on the left hand side and within easy reach. In hindsight it's plainly obvious that the thing to have done was simply to grab the leads and yank them off, disconnecting the battery, rather than attacking the panel in the tank as I had. As I think about it, I also curse myself for not equipping Daisy with a fuse, which would have prevented the problem outright. I make a mental note to do just that when we got home at the end of the weekend. On the plus side, the crisis is over with no real harm done and we can continue with our journey as planned after all, if I can persuade Chris to get back on! He does so, warily, but is quite insistent that I give all manner of assurances that there is no possibility of a repeat performance. I show him what has gone wrong, explain why it could not do it again (whilst mentally thinking 'at least not in the same place'!), but have to smile as he inspects things minutely with a look of unconvinced doubt on his face.

We've lost nearly an hour, I reckon, but I am so relieved to still posses a functioning motorcycle that this is a small worry indeed. In fact I feel insanely happy now that the drama is over – it must be a side effect of all that adrenalin. As we pull away up the lane, I remind Chris that we have plenty of time today, and that I reckon we've earned ourselves a slap up lunch at some country pub. He agrees readily and as we're somewhere in the Weald of Kent still, approaching the Sussex border, finding such an establishment won't be hard. Twenty minutes later, we are seated outside a handsomely Olde Worlde pub. It's a quarter to twelve on the clock, we've ordered, and are both looking forward to tucking into a good old traditional ploughman's whilst laughing together as we re-live that horrible few minutes of panic. I rib Chris about the finger-in-ears approach he seems to adopt whenever anything happens to Daisy, but he gets awfully serious as he breathlessly tells me that he really did think she was going to explode. I had to agree that I had also expected the worse, which was why I too had run away. The jolly Landlord interrupts our musings at this point, as he brings out the lunchtime fare, and, noticing Daisy, spontaneously exclaims his delight to see 'such a beauty' on his forecourt. All thoughts of the tension we had shared is well and truly banished as he turns to us and says, with certainty in his voice "And I bet she doesn't give you *any* problems!" We look at each other, Chris and I, and both of us burst out laughing. We are then duty bound to recount the story for the poor man while we eat, lest he thinks we're being rude. Five minutes later, as we finish the food the stout chap reappears with a pint of Sussex Ale and a coke, "On the house" he insists!

It's not long before we regretfully leave the hilly green panorama of the Weald behind us and thread our way through the urban sprawls of East Grinstead and Crawley. We could probably cut across country on some smaller minor roads, but the last minute decision to do this foray meant that I had not got round to looking for sensible navigation aids. We are still armed only with that large scale map, which would almost certainly get us hopelessly lost on anything other than at least rural A roads. The inevitable stop-start filtering doesn't take long to upset Daisy on this rather warm day, relying as she does on the fairly primitive pre-monobloc carburettor with it's remote float and recalcitrant mixing chamber. I find myself having to constantly blip her throttle at each bottleneck, lest she sputters into silence and make us play the waiting game while she cools. We're trapped for nearly forty minutes in the choked up traffic but eventually we break through into countryside heading west and I'm able to let Daisy stretch her legs and breath once again as we sweep past Horsham on the A264.

This is much more like it. The route we have selected between Crawley and Guildford is breathtaking. We deliberately take a detour further west than necessary if direct transit were the aim, in order to approach Guildford from the southwest. The reason is simple, this route, cresting the Devil's Punch Bowl and the Hog's Back, is an absolute pleasure to ride. The sheer variety of landscape keeps one constantly refreshed as it alternates between dense broad-leafed woodland, common ground and heathland. There's the odd lake in there as well, but more to the point we pick up the beginning of the North Downs ridge blessed with it's ancient routes which have maintained their rustic winding charms to this day in spite of now being 'A' roads. The early summer sunshine brings forth an explosion of life all around; birds, bugs and a profusion of colourful plants make for a very soul boosting meander.

Moving north, we cross the M3 and it's not long before we see the little circling dots of airliners that mark the stacking airspace over Heathrow. As we get closer, I start to count the things, which are circling over a wide area before reaching the bottom of the stack and taking their slot to land, joining the long line from the

West. It's amazing to think that all day long, every day, literally one aircraft every 30 seconds joins the final approach and heads in to burn rubber on that busy tarmac. That's a lot of planes, travellers, cargo and commerce. Eventually we pass directly under the flight path and stop to watch, mesmerised, as an impossibly large 'plane, which seems to just hang in the air against all logic, passes over. Amazing, if bloody noisy!

It's half-past two when we pull into Runnymede. I didn't really know what to expect from a Landmark so steeped in historical importance, and at first it was a bit of a disappointment. Basically it's a park now, on the bank of the river Thames, populated with a number of memorials, including the Magna Carta site memorial itself. As we take a rest, and just wander around the place, I explain to Chris how the Magna Carter played such a vital role in shaping the social history of Britain. We read the plaque on the memorial and it's a strange feeling to be standing on the same spot some 800 years after the events described took place. Daisy, not to be outdone, has attracted the attentions of an entire coach-load of ex-forces OAP's, obviously out for a regimental reunion or some such event. They're crowded all round her, posing with her as their colleagues take photographs or just discussing what must be their own memories of owning or riding such machines in the past. It's clear that if we approach now, we'll never get away, and so we stay hidden in the trees until they eventually return to their coach and head off. Daisy is proudly displaying several spots of oil underneath her, and with a frown I bend down to investigate the source. It's the dynamo again and I find myself irritated by this having suffered with it in the West Country, and thinking that I'd fixed it good and proper during the week. Obviously not, as it's now taunting me, to which I add my own frustration that yet again I have come with insufficient tools to do anything about it. Will I ever learn, I ask myself?

Deciding that there's nothing to be done for the dynamo, other than to mop up the dribbles with Kleenex, we get underway again and as promised, I thread Daisy along the very busy road into Windsor. It really is the grandest of places, especially the entrance to the castle estate, known as the 'Long Walk'. A vast tree-lined avenue, along which the general public are not allowed, leads up to the Castle raised high at the end in all it's regal splendour. The scale of the thing is truly remarkable and it must have seemed an insurmountable challenge to any would-be attacker back when it was first constructed by William the Conqueror to guard the Western approaches to the capital, some 900 years ago. Of course, it's been extended and strengthened over the many years since, but all the same one can't help but be caught up with sheer ancient mystery of the place. We trundle around the town, which is impressively in keeping with the castle, before eventually threading our way out towards the M4, on which we have agreed to travel as far as Reading and the A4 junction.

As we progress through the afternoon, Chris recognises Hungerford as the town that we had discussed over dinner last weekend, questioning me to confirm that this is the place. We stop for a couple of minutes and I wonder what he's thinking as he stands with a vacant look and just gazes around him, I don't want to get back into a maudlin mood though, and so we're back on the road in pretty short order.

The architecture, as you move west from London changes steadily, becoming predominantly that of Cotswold stone. It is a charming effect, to see entire villages formed from the stuff and somehow the look is both traditional and highly characteristic. Alderton is such a place, nestling on the very Southern edge of the Cotswolds and as we pull up outside the residence of the Wiltshire branch of the Ham family, I am struck how wonderfully peaceful it is. Indeed, I'm a little worried that Daisy's arrival has disturbed the peace somewhat and can imagine the stares of disapproval, unseen, boring into us from behind various net curtains. On the other hand, brother Howard runs a Harley, so they must be used to it. Without further ado, we knock on the door, eager to see the surprise from this part of our family that we only ever see once or twice a year. No answer. This is of course the problem with surprise visits. Chris is disappointed as he had been eagerly looking forward to seeing his two cousins again, but I suggest to him that all may not be lost as I have Howard's mobile number and they may just be out shopping or some such. The village is blessed with a charming little pond at one end, and we wander down to this to sit and rest while I make the call. Chris is dangling his feet at the edge, and this attracts the attention of the local pond bully – a very large, very stroppy, black swan. It's not about to put up with any nonsense from us humans either, and I can't help but laugh as Chris emits a "Whoooa" and rapidly scrambles backwards under a swift and violent attack on his boots. The swan is here for the duration it seems, and glaring at us with it's piggy red eyes it starts a little backwards and forwards patrol, radiating attitude all the while and seems to be daring us to try it on again. We decide to keep our distance.

I make the call, and find that Howard and family are at a village community event a few miles away, and after explaining that Chris and I have dropped in whilst on the way past, so to speak, he is delighted and suggests that we head over to join in the fun. Well, why not? Directions are duly handed out, and we leave the swan to rule his kingdom and head back to Daisy.

The directions prove to be accurate, and we easily find the little village of Sherston, where we have agreed to meet. What we find there is a delightful scene. The entire village is closed to traffic and a full-on street party is under way! As Chris and I park Daisy at the edge of the cordoned-off main street and begin to wander amongst all the fun, I am overwhelmed with a feeling of irrational nostalgia for the old country way of life. Nothing like this happens in urban areas such as Ramsgate, where we live. Even if it did, the setting of a rural village in the heart of the English countryside takes some beating. The street is full with noisy, happy people, milling about in the sun. There are traditional craft stalls, toffee apples can be bought for 50p, home made bakery is displayed at several stands, with all the traditional fare on offer, ice-cream stalls promise the buyer a proper home-made treat. There are two pubs in the street, and both have joined in with long trestle tables outside with a line of barrels on each offering draft beer straight from the tap. The garden fete atmosphere is finished off with a number of country games under way. Horse shoe throwing, guess the weight of the pig, open the box and shove ha'penny are all popular attractions. Wonderful.

I call Howard once again, to find out where in this heaving throng he and his brood are, and follow his directions round to the back of one of the pubs. Here we find a boules tournament under way, apparently an inter-village competition just for kids. Howard's two are competing in this, it seems, and the proud parents are seated alongside one of the 'pistes' to watch. We exchange hearty greetings but get a traditional welcome from Trish, Howard's French wife, by way of the cheek-to-cheek kiss that is the norm for that nation. Chris visibly shrivels as the same is aimed his way, and we all laugh at the horror on his face. Clearly this is not a cool thing for teenage boys to be seen doing! Howard is quick to go for beer, returning to offer me a frothing jug of some local real-ale, and I settle down with them to catch up and just enjoy the experience while Chris wanders off to look around.

The remainder of the warm, sunny afternoon lazily passes by, but relaxing though the whole experience is, we inevitably come to the point where we must part company once again. Howard and his family are due at an evening barbecue, and Chris and I need to continue our quest, so we all wander up through the street to where Daisy has patiently waited, cooling from her earlier exertions. She has also decorated the road with more oil-spots, larger than the last collection and extremely irritating to my eye. Howard takes the opportunity to rib me over my choice of steed, commenting that no such problems bother him with the Harley. Why don't I get one? He asks, smirking – it would also get me around much faster, he adds. I point out that I prefer to travel in style, adding that the rural surroundings he has chosen to live in must be the real reason he chooses an agricultural machine to ride. I am forced to concede however, that I am getting a little perturbed about the dynamo and that in fact I'm pretty certain that it's going to get progressively worse.

With a good few hundred miles still to do this weekend I consider that something needs to be done. Howard suggests that we repair to his house once more, where I can make use of his tools to effect a running repair. It's but a ten-minute ride, and after opening up the garage they leave Chris and I to it as they go inside to get ready for their evening. I find the necessary spanner and Allen key, loosen off the mounts and pull the dynamo out from it's housing to inspect the cork gasket that serves (or not, in Daisy's case) to keep the black stuff on the inside. It's a mess, and where the dynamo has obviously been allowed to vibrate, it's been somewhat chewed up. I hold it up for Chris to see, and it's obvious that this sorry thing is not going to seal anything again. I can't just bolt the dynamo back in place without a seal – it would spout oil by the bucket-load, but neither do I have anything that will remotely do the job. Chris surprises me by suggesting firmly that we can't even consider giving up. We've come too far, he still hasn't camped yet since we started this campaign (the Rabbit and Le Mans being too organised to count in his opinion), and anyway, there must be a way to fix it. This is a very different attitude to that which he displayed in Norfolk!

Howard reappears just as we are having this discussion, peers at the mangled gasket and suggests that we attempt to seal it with Hermatite liquid gasket, a tube of which he happens to have in the shed. This isn't as obvious as it sounds – the cork dynamo seal is very thick and I'm not sure whether a thinner seal would prevent the drive pinion of the dynamo from rubbing on the inside of the casing. I try the dynamo in place without any seal, and gently turn over the engine. I am rewarded with a graunching noise that confirms my fears. We scratch our heads, and consider what can be done, but the only thing I can think to try is a very thick layer of the stuff, let it go off, and try not to do up the mounting too tight. Of course, whilst doing all that I'll pray that it will then keep the seal good. It's pressure that will confound such a bodge, I tell Howard – ask any Triumph owner about crankcase pressure and bad push rod tube seals – bloody nightmare on a good day, and could cause this attempt to fail equally dismally. It's the best plan available however, and so we carefully squeeze a fat donut of the sticky red goo all around the mounting boss and leave it to go off in the sun. I'm only marginally dismayed that the tube in question looks as though it was used to seal Noah's Ark. Chris has wandered off by now to catch a few extra minutes with his cousins, Sammy and Alex. Howard and I have a cup of tea, while he returns to ribbing me over Daisy.

As I gently do up the nut, and watch the red gunge squeeze out all round the dynamo, I am utterly convinced that this will not work. But as I wipe all round the joint with Kleenex, removing the unsightly excess, the end result at least looks like a solid seal. I prime Daisy, start her up and we both peer critically at the join. At least there are no horrible noises emanating from the timing chest and after running for a few minutes at revs, there is no sign of any problem with the seal. We decide to declare it a good bodge and without further ado, Chris and I say our goodbyes once again, mount up, and head off into the Wiltshire countryside. At Howard's insistence, I have taken the remaining gasket goo and the old cork seal, spanner and Allen key, just in case and they now reside in the tank bag.

After a few miles, I stop to inspect the dynamo, still paranoid that it will not hold, but all seems to be in order and I begin to relax a bit. Chris reminds me that it's nearly half past six now, and isn't it time to make some decisions about camping? He's not forgotten the experience we had in Suffolk, where we ran out of light and were very lucky to find that pub, and he wants to be sure of his long awaited chance to do the tent thing this time. I can't argue with his logic, and after looking at where we need to get to tomorrow we decide to press on as far as Cirencester and find a campsite there. I assure Chris that this is a very popular tourist area, and as such there should be a plethora of campsites around every other bend. I hope to hell this is indeed the case, but his look of cynicism isn't encouraging. To put him at ease, I calculate the distance to the place on the map, and he is somewhat reassured once he realises that it is only fifteen miles or so away and that we will cruise at 50mph easily on these not too twisty and apparently empty roads. We'll be there by seven for certain, I think, as we set off once more into the early evening sunshine. We make good time indeed, stopping once more, very briefly, to check on the dynamo which seems to have capitulated and is no longer displaying incontinent tendencies.

Into Cirencester we trundle, at ten to seven, and it doesn't take long at all to get through the place and out of the other side, heading towards Gloucester and hopefully a handy campsite. Against all the odds, we stumble across the much-wanted camping sign almost immediately and turn into the place without a second thought. Chris perks up considerably as we sign in at the little hut by the entrance, handing over six pounds for the privilege and receiving strict instructions on where we can camp. This seems a bit unnecessary, as there is a large field with, as far as we can see, no other campers, and plenty of space all round. The attendant however, is quite insistent that we camp *there*, pointing rigidly to a spot by the hedge that marks the boundary. He also instructs us gravely that we must be particularly vigilant when setting up, making sure that we stay within the pegs that mark our slot, and do not stray beyond them into the empty hundred yards or so of space either side. Clearly, here is a chap who takes his responsibilities very seriously indeed, and having no wish to detract from his moment of authority, we readily agree that we will indeed be careful. Once outside, Chris is agog at what he's just witnessed. "What's wrong with *him*?" he asks, glancing back at the hut. I answer with a shrug and a grin and find myself recounting an old Billy Connolly sketch, in which he rants about car-park attendants who's sole purpose in life is to be irritating. The description fits our campsite attendant perfectly and we have a quiet chuckle at the thought that, as Mr Connolly suggests, he probably has a limp! No matter, we're here and in plenty of time to enjoy the evening sun whilst sorting ourselves out for the evening. But a timely growl from my stomach reminds me that I haven't eaten since that early lunch and it's high time I did something about it - "Come on" I enthuse, "lets get set up and then we'll go and find dinner!"

Twenty minutes later I am cursing. Why do we only have one sleeping bag? It's almost unbelievable that we managed to leave one behind, especially after all the efforts to fit everything in after buying the extra gear. I am at a loss to understand and spend five minutes stomping around checking and double checking. Chris, in typical teenage fashion, dismisses the discovery as unimportant. He doesn't need one, he assures me, and this statement just serves to irritate me because it's nonsense. We spend a while bickering about it uselessly as he's adamant that I'm just making a fuss over nothing and I'm equally adamant that he knows not of what he speaks – and tell him so. I realise that the debate is pointless, I'm still hungry, time is ticking past and I therefore abruptly terminate the argument in favour of sorting out dinner. The problem of freezing to death in the small hours can wait. We have two choices, I tell Chris that we can go and find a supermarket, and buy the ingredients to cook ourselves a meal, or we can search out a pub and buy a meal there. I leave the choice to him and he quickly elects to find a pub. He goes back up in my estimation, marginally.

We secure the tent, shoving everything except valuables inside, and mount up the now unburdened Daisy. Before I can start her however, our friend the car-park attendant comes urgently out of his hut and heads our way, an arm in the air bearing an accusing finger. We are admonished that it's not acceptable to start 'that noisy thing' inside the confines of the campsite and must push it outside first. I look around the empty field but with my temper already frayed from the missing sleeping bag and subsequent argument I'm in no mood for this pillock. I point out that there's nobody here to be disturbed, and that in the unlikely event that there are any later on, or when we leave in the morning, we would certainly observe the request. Right now however, I'm hungry, and tired, and have no intention of pushing anything anywhere! With that I glare at him, give Daisy a hefty kick, and she answers immediately with her throaty bark. I nearly fall off laughing as Mr. Jobsworth, possibly realising that he's on thin ice, turns abruptly and stumps away and I notice that he indeed possesses a limp! That simple observation completely restores my good humour – the world is working properly after all.

Rural Wiltshire in the early summer is a wondrous place and as we head out looking for a place to eat, we happen upon a long straight road between dry stone walls that simply invites me to wind Daisy's throttle on and relish the echo of her deep exhaust note from either side. The evening air is warm and fragrant, the surroundings idyllic and it's not long before we find a perfect compliment to the experience in the shape of a very large country Inn, seemingly in the middle of nowhere. Round the back is a large beer garden with plenty of tables, and we are able to park next to this area, choose a table and get to the serious business of studying the menu and sampling the ale. Chris goes for a chilli, and I go for the steak in Stilton sauce. Daisy is attracting a fair gathering of admirers too and Chris sidles over to the small group to bask in the glory of being the pillion on the appreciated machine. He's soon enthusiastically discussing the Landmark with several of the crowd and I leave him to it happily. It appears from the gestures during the conversation that much admiration is being offered for the lad that has clearly travelled so far on that little pad – quite the celebrity so it seems.

The drinks and meal arrive in short order, and after finally attracting his attention with a series of arm-waving and pointing gestures, Chris reluctantly leaves his fan club to go their own merry way and joins me to eat, flushed with satisfaction and somewhat puffed up with pride. He enthuses to me that he had been asked many questions about Daisy, and had been able to answer them all, including showing off the ingenuity of her sprung hub suspension, which, he continued with enthusiasm, had flummoxed a couple of the younger enquirers. "Why" he asked, round a mouthful of Chilli, "does she attract so much attention? It's just like that guy at the other pub who gave us those drinks!" he adds. He seems to like the idea of fame, however small the dose, and I let him ramble on while we finish our meal and drinks. After a while, my attention focuses on the rapidly dying sunlight, which is busy fading into a glorious misty sunset. I remind Chris that we can't trust Daisy's lights and as it's beginning to get a bit murky, with our route back consisting of the little back roads with no lighting, we'd better get a move on. I go inside to settle our tab, and manage to buy a couple of bottles of ale for the tent – Chris will be allowed to try his first taste of parentally approved beer this very evening, but I'll save that for a surprise later.

If we had enjoyed the evening thus far, the return to the campsite is an experience beyond all expectations. As we ride directly West, heading into a deep red sunset glowing above and within a hazy horizon that merges land into sky in a misty, shimmering blur, we are utterly captivated when a large shape emerges from the mirage. For a fleeting moment, on that eerie, silent road the thought of UFO's flits through my mind, but slowly the shape takes on form and becomes recognizable as a giant hot-air balloon emerging lazily from the distance. We stop to watch it approach, but we're in for a treat as another, then another emerge in the surreal surroundings. Pretty soon, it's clear that there is a whole bunch of the things, and the Western sky seems impossibly full of them drifting along no more than a hundred and fifty feet or so up. It is the most amazing sight with that glorious hazy backdrop, made all the more surreal by the complete lack of any noise either from them, us or our surroundings. I find myself wondering what it must be like from their perspective and realise that I am envious of them.

We sit there for a full fifteen minutes watching the spectacle, and I realise with a jolt that I am now having to strain my eyes into the dusk to see. I reluctantly tell Chris that it's high time for us get a move on again and I am forced to turn on Daisy's lights, for all the illumination they offer, as we set off once again down that long straight road, with the line of balloons stretching from horizon to horizon to our right. It is the perfect ending to the day and even the attendant has shut up shop and gone by the time we pull into the campsite – which now has two more tents. We sit outside our own tent and break out the beer, Chris taking his with a surprised "Thanks Dad!" and proceeding to affect a false bravado as he tries his first sip. "S'allright" he assures me, but his face is a mask of uncertainty. As the last light fades, we can still see the occasional flare of the balloons, as their occupants adjust the fill. Presumably they must land soon, I think, or they are brave fellows indeed to risk it in the dark!

Chris dismisses any attempts to give him the single sleeping bag when we turn in, and buries himself beneath our spare clothes, jeans and jackets. There is no point arguing with him further and so I retire to doze off in relative comfort.

I wake at around midnight to find a shivering Chris fidgeting and vainly trying to cover himself more effectively. He is bravely trying to survive the unpleasant cold without making a fuss by the sound of things, but after waking up a bit I realise that I cannot just leave him to suffer. I turn to face him in the dark. "I expect you're freezing then?" I say, with perhaps a hint of smugness. The pitiful moan that comes in response is enough to confirm this, but there is no mileage in saying 'I told you so'. I need instead to work out what to do, but first off I give Chris the sleeping bag, which, on this occasion, meets with no argument. He wastes no time getting into it while I attempt to find, then ignite, our newly acquired gas lamp and I am mightily put out on getting the thing lit, to discover that Chris is now sound asleep. "Bloody charming, thanks dad and good night" I mutter to myself as already I begin feeling the night chill. I sit there and wonder what to do next.

I put on my jeans, three pairs of socks and all three shirts, before curling up under the rest of our clothes and jackets. It's apparent pretty quickly that I am going to get extremely cold, and no amount of fidgeting and arranging is going to make things any better. After half an hour, I sit up shivering, and hug myself whilst I desperately try to think what else I can do. Chris is snoring deeply, just to add to my misery. I re-ignite the gas light and then find the little stove and light that too, hoping that these two will at least heat up the inside of the tent sufficiently to stave off hypothermia. They do in fact achieve this with startling speed, rather too efficiently and within ten minutes I am sweating profusely in my three shirts. That's fine, I am no longer on the endangered list. What to do now though? I can't go to sleep with these two things burning and if I turn them off it will be no time at all before the cold is back. I curse my stupidity for the fiftieth time before settling on the best of several bad options – I'll let the heat build up for another ten minutes, and then take my chances once more under the pile. I doze off in the muggy atmosphere but wake with a jolt within an hour, freezing once more. No trace of the earlier heat remains and so once again the entire exercise has to be repeated with lamp and stove. The night dragged past as I am forced to carry out the tedious ritual every hour or so, until eventually the deep dark began to give way to the first hints of daylight, almost imperceptibly at first. I can also hear the first stirrings of the great outdoors as a blackbird tries out a few halting notes and something snuffles around in the hedge behind our tent. Chris snores on. I would make one more attempt at sleep I decide, but the next awakening would be it – time for a cup of tea and an early start to the day's adventure.

I poke my head from the tent at six o'clock the following morning, tired, desperately cold and very miserable. The warm sunny day has given way to a cold damp night, and I am starkly reminded just how cold it can still get in late July. I look around at the early morning, and my spirits are lifted on two counts – Daisy hasn't spontaneously combusted during the night, and the Eastern sky holds the promise of another fine sunny day as a blazing sun began to edge up over the horizon. Despite the nightmare of the last eight hours, I find myself thoroughly heartened by the spectacle of the mist-shrouded fields and woods, bathed in the golden glow of dawn. A heavy dew had fallen in the night, but this now gives the whole scene a magical sparkle. I wake Chris, who's never been good at mornings, and try in vain to get him up so that he can witness this sight. I abandon the attempt and decide to leave him be for another thirty minutes, and instead settle for getting a mug of tea on the go and breakfast things sorted out. I congratulate myself that this time I had remembered to bring everything required for a good breakfast and by the time Chris surfaces through the opening, I have scrambled eggs, bacon and beans well underway. We sit together as we eat, watching the day grow brighter and after a second mug of tea it's time to clear up, pack away the tent and load Daisy up for the day. I decide that before doing any of that, we'll just fire the old girl up and make sure all is well. She answers my first kick with her customary deep growl, and as she sits warming up, the heavy dew on her engine, pipes and silencers turns to steam and drifts off into the crisp air.

Chris appears to be in suspended animation. He is dawdling around as we pack up, listlessly 'helping' in slow motion. I end up doing the lion's share of everything and my attempts to chivvy him along meet with a bad tempered, tetchy response, which of course makes me equally tetchy. We bicker and grumble at each other until Daisy is ready to go, and I reflect that it's an ironically fitting end to what has, after all, been a truly crappy night. But the open road awaits, and in an effort to lighten our mood I spread the novelty map out whilst enthusing about the weather. We look at the map and discuss suitable routes. Or rather, I suggest suitable routes while Chris grunts in monosyllables by way of response, each of which could be taken as a 'yes' or a 'no'. I suspect they actually mean 'don't care' but I'm not going to get wound up, I decide, and instead put on a false jollity as I declare us ready to roll. Chris completes the morning's performance by getting his helmet strap tangled, then stuck, culminating in a bad tempered display of exaggerated gestures and general weight throwing as he stomps around trying to sort it. I sit on Daisy, watching, feeling increasingly exasperated at this sudden teenage strop, but eventually he straightens things out and comes across to take up his seat, pausing only to flick me a belligerent stare as he does so. The look seems to challenge me with an unsaid "Yeah what?"

Finally we're away. At this time of the morning there's little traffic to worry about and we put Cirencester behind us in no time at all before turning northwest towards Gloucester. We're heading for a stately home, 'Helen's' near a village called Much Marcle which I consider to be a wonderful name. The good thing about today's riding is that it's all in an area that I have never previously visited, therefore the joy of discovery is certain. Looking at the map, it would also appear that we will spend most of the morning in good open countryside, and as we put Gloucester behind and head west to Ross-on-Wye that promise is delivered in spades. The 'A' roads that we find ourselves on are not the big dual-carriageway types that bore the pants off me. No, these are wonderful twisting, turning, sweeping roads alternately bordered by open pasture punctuated with banked and wooded cuttings as they follow a roller-coaster geology, the sum total of which makes for an exhilarating and enjoyable ride. With the sun delivering all it's early promise I consider that motorcycling just doesn't get any better than this, but that train of thought is prematurely derailed because just then the noise starts.

Strange noises are nothing new to anyone that regularly rides an old machine like Daisy, and as is often the case this one starts quite suddenly. It's not of a type or indeed volume that immediately concerns me, but any sudden appearance of noise on an aged motorcycle can be the harbinger of doom so I find myself slowing down and cocking my head from side to side in an effort to pinpoint it's source. Of course, as soon as I do this it stops and as soon as I shrug and wind Daisy's throttle on again, there it is, just on the periphery of hearing, almost inaudible, but definitely there. I continue along at a slower pace than the 60mph we had been cruising at and begin analysing this sudden irritation. It's not really a mechanical or metallic noise, more like a sort of rumble or rub, that comes and goes, always just evasive enough to leave me frustrated as I try to identify it. No amount of hard listening and head-tilting helps, and so we carry on, me fighting the beginnings of a slight paranoia. We carry on as far as Ross, where I take the chance to pull up by a little shop where we take a breather and I can look Daisy over for anything obvious. At least Chris seems to have brightened up, and is quite perky as he cons money out of me for 'something small' from the shop. I take the chance, as I rummage around in my pockets, to ask him about that noise.

"What noise?" says he.

Ah. I explain further "There's a strange noise, sort of rubbing or something, can't you hear it when we're riding?" He gives me a look that suggests I'm going senile and as he takes the now proffered coins and turns away, he says

"There's no noise dad. You're imagining things!"

I have to admit as we get ready to set off again, that I have been unable to find anything amiss. I spent about ten minutes trying to find something loose, checked that nothing could be rubbing against a tyre. Nothing suggests itself as the source. I start the engine and listen hard from all angles for any hint of the noise – nothing. I spin the back wheel and critically examine it. No noise. 'Fine', I think, but as we pull away, I can't shake the niggling feeling that trouble is ahead. The roads continue to offer a thoroughly good ride as we sweep northeast, and it's not long before we find our Landmark, Helen's stately home. It's closed, and a sign at the entrance invites all would be visitors not to enter, thank you very much. Fine, I think, as I can't see Chris being particularly enthusiastic about such a place and I'd rather be riding on a day like this anyway. We take our photographs of Daisy in front of the friendly sign, which at least has 'Helen's' at the top, and then sit with the map and start to talk about the rest of the day. I explain to Chris that we have only one other Landmark to visit, and it's on the way home, so with most of the day still awaiting us we can take our time.

Taking our time, I suggest, means riding south through the forest of Dean. And we're soon glad that we did, as this is a very special experience indeed. On a bike, it's just indescribably good, so I won't try to describe the mixed foliage, broad leaf woodland that we pick our way through. Suffice to say it is deeply satisfying and, I'm sure, good for the soul. But the real pleasure comes after the forest, as the A466 from Monmouth, where we have ended up, follows the meandering river Wye along Offa's Dyke Path. The scenery and geography that we encounter on this road is simply fantastic, in a closed-in sort of way. The road is hemmed in by the river, with it's wooded banks, on one side, and rock escarpment or further woods on the other. There are no sweeping views or open plains, but it's breathtakingly beautiful to ride, for all that. Go there, do it for yourself - you can thank me later. Half way down, there is also a large pub, right on the Welsh border, proudly proclaiming it's Welsh-ness, but more importantly right now it serves food and beer. We stop and sample both, sitting outside admiring the view across the river, as Daisy 'tinc – tinc's' as she cools off. Marvellous.

We follow the Wye as it feeds down into the wide estuary of the river Severn, close to Chepstow. From there, heading east, we cross the river via the famous bridge which is pretty spectacular in itself, as it spans the great flat estuary shallows, but all the more so when undertaken on a classic motorcycle. The feeling of open exposure to the elements, even in this ideal weather, is quite pronounced. As we climb the Welsh side to the apex of the bridge, my nerves are jangled once again by the return of the irritating noise that had so plagued me earlier. It's a jarring note which upsets my otherwise euphoric state of mind and I curse out loud. But not for long – as we coast down the English side of the bridge, I lean over to shout at Chris that he must, surely, be able to hear it this time, only to discover that it's HIM making what I have thought of as the 'rubbing' sound. He's humming some sort of tune in a funny sort of way, and it's arriving in my ears, distorted by wind, as that elusive noise! "Bloody hell – you Sod!" I yell into the wind. Chris stops his humming to lean over my shoulder to shout "What?" but I'm laughing now, partially through relief that Daisy isn't in the early stages of disintegration, but mainly because of the absurdity of what had begun to be a real worry. I decide that it'll keep and yell "Nothing!" as I turn my attention back to the road.

We continue on our way in peace, blissfully lacking that noise!

Onto the M4 then, past Bristol, we turn off to Bath, where we'll pick up the A4 heading east once more. I'm getting to know this road rather well now. We're making for our next and final Landmark before the last leg home and as we enter the fascinating City in its fantastic Georgian splendour I marvel, as I always do, at the grandeur from another age. Compare this to any 21st Century architecture and there is just no contest – the modern stuff loses hands down. Where did we go wrong, and why? I stop to show Chris Royal Crescent, which, let's face it I tell him, is bloody impressive. Isn't it? He agrees and wants to know why it's only old buildings that look this way and are built this way. Good question, which causes me to lament the loss of magnificence in our apparently advanced lifestyle. Progress, I tell Chris, has its price – that price is the sacrifice of grandness on the altar of profit. Shame.

It's just after two o'clock I note, as we leave Bath behind, heading for Chippenham then Marlborough. There we'll be turning south into the Berkshire countryside to begin hunting down, if our clue solving is correct, a steam museum near the town of Grafton. The last time I had traversed this route Eastwards, Chloe and I were against the clock, but this time we are in no rush and I let Daisy lope along at a leisurely 55mph. Chris must be happy on the back there, because the 'noise' is back. I tilt my head surreptitiously and sure enough he's away with the fairies humming some racy tune that I can't pinpoint. "Having fun?" a yell over my shoulder, yanking him out of whatever inner universe he had been inhabiting "Yep!" comes the enthusiastic reply. Marvellous. At Marlborough we find the A346 heading south towards Burbage but I pull over at the first available point in order to study the map. This, I tell Chris, could be a bit tricky. The red circle that marks the spot we need is in a blank bit with no apparent roads shown. This is not a total surprise, and I'm starting to get the hang of winging it with compass now, so I discuss tactics with Chris that go along the lines of "If we can get to Grafton, *here*, and take any left turn heading north, the Steam thingy is only about two miles" Chris looks distinctly dubious. He is, after all, a veteran of the same sort of vague navigational notions from the earlier Suffolk adventure, and had swapped intelligence with his sister about Dad's apparent lack of directional abilities after her West Country foray. "Why don't you get a better map?" is his considered response. "Well, it's a bit late for that" I point out, but I have to admit that it really would have been a sensible move.

We manage not to bicker about the lack of a good map, and get underway again with my compass plan being the only one available. Finding Burbage only five miles on, we turn left and begin looking for signs to Grafton. When it appears, I am dismayed to discover that it's pointing the wrong way, assuming I had read the map properly and we are in fact on the road I think we are. We stop, and I get the map out again. Chris is looking at me with *that* look again. Clearly he thinks his father is a dolt of the first order. I'm beginning to agree with his sentiment as I stare at the useless thing. I don't understand how Grafton can be that way. The map clearly shows the place, but not, if this is the road I'm sure we're on, where this sign says it is. Bugger. I then realise that if this sign is correct, then we're already the two miles or so north of the place anyway, so where's the bloody Steam place? There have been none of those little brown signs that one expects directing the would-be visitor to such places. Neither have we passed any crossroads or turnings, along which the thing may be hiding. I turn to Chris and explain my thoughts "What do you reckon?" says I. "Get a proper map" comes the sullen reply. "Bloody smartarse - come on, get involved, tell me what you reckon we should do!" I reply with barely concealed exasperation. He shrugs. I look hard at him, and he decides to stroll over and take a cursory look at the map. Incomprehension shows on his face, so I tap my finger on the map and explain the quandary again. "It's obvious, it must be down that road," he announces after a minutes contemplation, pointing to the road which the sign suggests goes to Grafton.

I hadn't thought of that, and I wasn't convinced, but just one minute later we do indeed come across the much sought after little brown sign, I decide my first comment earlier was in fact right after all – he is a smartarse! I tell him so in good humour, and he mumbles something about me being a bit of an old duffer. He's definitely been talking to his sister! We follow a tiny road for about half a mile, over a stunning little picture-postcard bridge and there at the end is not only our Landmark, but another Triumph rider as well. A fellow Landmarker, I enthuse to Chris, we must introduce ourselves as we get our photographs, I insist, and we ride over to him and park Daisy up next to his much more modern machine. In fact, his is one of the new Hinckley Triumphs, from the current factory that is going from strength to strength in a slow but steady climb back to prominence, and it makes for an interesting contrast seeing the two side by side. Obviously the owner is thinking along the same lines as he introduces himself as Simon, and quips "You've brought granny out to see her granddaughter then?" There is actually some truth to that, we both agree, because it was the Speed Twin, unveiled in 1938 that is largely reckoned to be the design that set Triumph on the course to greatness and changed the face of motorcycle design for several decades after.

It transpires that Simon is not a Landmark hunter after all, but is just out for a ride. He is a member of the Owner's Club however, and has heard of the Challenge but doesn't really know much about it. Chris, seeing another chance to display his knowledge and indeed bask in the glory of participation, is eager to explain the details and recount the story so far. I realise as I listen that he truly is proud of his involvement in the challenge, and also of his sister as he explains her own adventures thus far to the now amused Simon. We spend a good twenty minutes there, basking in the afternoon sun in the wonderfully peaceful surroundings, but it's time to get going again on the final leg home. I look at the map again, but Simon produces a much better one and offers to share his local knowledge regarding the best route towards home. He is amazed when I tell him where home is. We'll need to go back to Burbage, then take the main road south from there, joining the A342 to Andover after about six miles. From there it's on to Basingstoke where we'll pick up the A30, which is the Daisy-friendly alternative to the M3. We discover that the museum is now closing, and can't go in, so I tell Chris that we may as well get going and at this point Simon offers to take us as far as the junction with the A342, where he will be heading in the opposite direction. Rather than getting lost in all these little roads, we readily agree. He asks what speed should he keep down to, but I assure him that Daisy will cruise happily at 60 mph or even above. He doesn't look convinced! He mounts up and presses his finger on the little button that whirrs his engine into life, then sits with a big grin as he watches my own starting routine with Daisy. Petrol on, choke lever under seat a quarter turn, ignition advance/retard lever on handlebars to full retard, lean under tank and press the tickler button on top of the ancient carb float, ease over compression and give the kick-start a mighty heave. Daisy responds immediately and now I knock the choke back to full off, advance/retard lever to three quarters advance, and I grin back at Simon and give the thumbs up as he shakes his head in amused disbelief.

Fifteen minutes later, we wave goodbye to our guide and continue at a steady pace in the glorious early evening sunshine. I estimate that we'll get home at around eight o'clock if we take the twisties rather than the motorway, and this we do, eventually picking up the same route through Guildford and the Weald of Kent that we had used on the way out yesterday. We stop at the same pub that we had lunched at, but this time the landlady of the establishment is in charge, so there is no free beer. We stop again at the little bridge, the scene of near disaster so recently, and Chris recounts the story with me, asking, "what would really have happened if Daisy had stayed on fire?" What indeed, I wonder, but in answering I suggested that it never pays in life to wonder or worry about what might have been, just accept, and in this case be very grateful, for what *is*.

8. Northern Landmarks and Punctured in Durham

You can't take a fifty-something year old motorcycle, ride two up loaded to the gunnels, and simply ride it all round the place with no maintenance and absolutely no preparation. It's obvious to anyone that this is asking for trouble, and if you actually manage to make it without problems, you will almost certainly find a host of them on checking over the machine back at home. Things will have come loose, fallen off, started leaking or simply broken. I have been assured by many that this is the case, almost written in the scriptures, so it is. These thoughts haunted me as I opened up the garage on the Monday, to give Daisy a full check-over. I was feeling mildly guilty at my lack of proper attention to Daisy's mechanical well-being in the last few weeks, having hardly looked at a nut, other than the necessary dynamo fix in Wiltshire since putting in the new engine. But Daisy is clearly made of stern stuff I discover, as with mounting respect for her I find nothing amiss. There is a school of thought that says any regularly used machine will 'settle down' during it's first few thousand miles from a rebuild, at which point nothing comes loose any more and only things like the chains and tyres need any real attention. It would appear that Daisy has attained this much sought after state of being – there really is nothing to do to her except a slight adjustment to primary and final drive chains. Even that troublesome dynamo is still on as firmly as it can be, and the really impressive bit is that she doesn't seem to have leaked any oil, anywhere. I am absolutely delighted with this, and my determination that the Landmark trophy will be ours is now underpinned with a growing confidence that Daisy really will simply breeze through it all.

That evening, brimming with enthusiasm once again, I start to think about the next adventure, to find, record and cross off the numerous Landmarks in Scotland, Cumbria and the north of England. There are a lot of pushpins in the map, and they are well and truly scattered, but after a while we had the beginnings of a plan. We had to have a plan this time, or chaos would result, so an evening of umming and aahhing saw one thrashed out, at least in theory. If all went well our plan would see us complete a large anticlockwise sweep, starting from our jump off point in Cambridge. The problem was one of logistics, and although we could in theory work our way up-country from south to north, this would involve a huge amount of to-ing and fro-ing from east to west and back again, and would actually require a large number of additional miles for each decisive move north. No, far better, we decided, to find a steady route north, from which we would only divert for Landmarks to the east, leaving any to the west for our return leg Southwards, unless they were very close.

Of course, now that we have the long southwest, Wiltshire and French trips under our belt, we can use that experience to sensibly predict how far each day will take us. I explain to Chris the effect of having to leave a given route to divert in search of Landmarks, but he tersely reminds me that he was on the back in Suffolk, and could well remember that particular fun. We have also learnt that regular breaks made the whole experience far more enjoyable. Where Chloe and I had stopped regularly to absorb the delights of Cornwall and Devon, we had remained comfortable throughout the day, but on that last day, pushing for longer in order to get home, Daisy's antiquated seating and rider positioning had made themselves felt in spades. I talk this through with Chris and we settle on a limit of three hundred miles a day and having decided that we are able to put some timings on a rough schedule, starting with a seven o'clock start each day (as in wheels turning on the tarmac – preferably with Daisy packed with all of the various items that we're meant to have with us) and ending no later than seven in the evening, by which time we would, we declare, be choosing a spot for our tent. It seems dead easy when approached like that, and with increasing enthusiasm we settle down to drawing up a plan for each day, starting with Day One, a nominal Saturday morning, and plotting the whole thing from there. We are aided immeasurably in that exercise by the use of some computerised route planning software on the family PC, another trick that I have failed to utilise up till now. This approach, for the first time, gives us the luxury of having some idea of just how well/badly we are progressing once out there on the road - a comfort I had not had with Chloe in the southwest, and the lack of which had led me to fretting far more than perhaps I should have done!

After a couple of evenings, involving much map scrutiny, head scratching, debate and argument we have agreed that the start point shall be the lay-by in Cambridge that we had used earlier, and the route from there will be the A14 initially. With no intention of suffering a long and boring motorway stint on the M1, we will instead be picking up the A1 for the main trek north. The plan is to pick off four Landmarks on the way up to Newcastle, where our first overnight stop will be made. From there, we will pick up the A697, and then make for the Scottish border, onwards to Coldstream, Edinburgh, Perth and then a long haul through the Grampian mountains to our second overnight stop at Elgin with, if all has gone well, a further three Landmarks in the bag. Day three will take us round past Inverness, across the Moray Firth and up into the Highlands for roughly forty miles before turning back on ourselves and heading south again, along Loch Ness, Loch Oich, through Fort William and finally on to Stirling where we'll stop. Two more Landmarks will have been visited along the way, in theory. On day four, we continue southwest, back into England, through Northumberland and into Cumbria before jinking southeast once again, then down through the industrial Northern sprawl that is Preston, Bolton and Manchester. In theory, we will have knocked off another five Landmarks by the time we camp, somewhere in the region of Runcorn or Chester. Finally, we will meander through the Midlands heading for home, picking off a further four Landmarks on the way, making a grand total of nineteen in the week, which when added to the twenty already in the bag takes us a quantum leap towards completing the entire challenge. Simple, we both rashly agree.

Having constructed the grand plan, I am able to print off strip-maps and route directions from the computer and am astounded that it runs to thirty-six pages. This seems ridiculous to me, but once I start to read the thing it becomes apparent that the actual directions are very detailed and I realise that I won't really need most of those. The strip maps that accompany each page of drivel will, by contrast, be extremely useful. They contain more detail than our now dog-eared map of Britain and It's certain that the two used together will offer a far better navigation aid than we have been used to so far. Chris has remembered national parks, and wants to look at the big map with me again insisting that I point out the areas that will be unfenced roads and cattle grids. He seems to be fascinated by the thought of such an arrangement and as we look he begins to grill his sister once again about her own experiences on Bodmin and Exmoor. I smile as I listen and reflect on the fact that to Chris and Chloe open National Park land is indeed a novelty, they have only ever seen the countryside 'at arm's length' really, what with it's fences and 'Private, Keep Out' signs everywhere you go.

I remembered an episode when they were both much younger, when we had taken a picnic and wandered off into the wilds of Kent to find some real countryside. We had found an idyllic little copse, surrounded by green fields and woodland and had stopped the car on the verge for our picnic. We could see nothing that even hinted at civilisation and all was peaceful as we happily sat watching the kids exploring the hedgerows and woodland. Suddenly, seemingly from nowhere, a well-to-do Lady of the green-welly set appeared and in short order proceeded to lay into us verbally. Her language was shocking, as she lambasted us for daring to stop and enjoy ourselves in 'her' countryside. She accused us of 'being out of our element' and scolded us for bringing our 'shitty suburban brats' (they were the actual words she used) to a place where they were neither 'suited nor welcome'. Our tormentor was clearly going to make a point of seeing us 'orf', and harsh words followed as I invited the inbred throwback to do something interesting, and possibly amusing with her head, but our relaxed afternoon had been utterly spoilt and we never took the kids to the countryside again in the same carefree way. To this day, I have no idea what sparked such an aggressive and unnecessary tirade, especially as we had been very careful to make no mess, and had seen no signs or anything else to suggest we shouldn't be there. We were doing nobody any harm, as far as I could see.

I recount the story to Chris and Chloe as they sit there poring over the map and Chris admits to a vague recollection of the dreadful harridan before exclaiming suddenly in an alarmed voice "There won't be people like that in the National Park will there?" I could only hope not.

Finally, the big day arrives. School's out for the summer and we have six weeks in which to do the remainder of the challenge. There is nothing left to plan, buy or fix and I declare us ready for the big trek north. Chris is almost bursting with anticipation and with no reason for delay we set off very early on the first weekend of the holidays. We want to get to our base camp and be ready to hit the road by seven o'clock, which means a five am start from home, but at least the traffic is very light as a result. We make good time and after arriving at the lay-by, getting changed into riding gear, extracting Daisy from the interior of the long suffering Espace, we soon find ourselves exiting Cambridge on schedule as planned. And it's one of those days for which motorcycles were invented, warm even at this early hour, with the promise of a long balmy day reflected in the golden shimmer dancing in the misty fields. Daisy is positively purring along beneath us as we settle down to a steady fifty-five mph heading towards Peterborough and the A1. Our first Landmark is not much of a detour from our main route, and lies some seventy miles North.

I congratulate myself for making the effort to actually do some planning this time round, happy in the knowledge that we can take a leisurely ride in order to stay on schedule and get there by nine am. That's what my computer directions tell me, I recall, and it seems like child's play to me as the sun strengthens, burning off the early mist, and we leave the A14, turning north onto the A1 to begin the long haul. After putting the initial motorway section behind us, we're soon passing Peterborough and before long we pull in, stopping for tea and a ciggie. I tell Chris that I have travelled this road many, many times in the course of my working life, and it must have more little tea stalls than any other in Britain, I reckon. They seem to be in every other lay-by, sometimes a caravan, sometimes a shack, the occasional porta-cabin but all offering a good cup of tea and trucker-sized bacon rolls. This one is a caravan, with awning, and we present ourselves at the chin-high counter in order to acquire some traditional traveller's fare. As we wait, the smell of sizzling bacon drifts over to mingle with the earthy smell of early morning mist, and we sit quite happily just enjoying the experience. It's not long before a pair of king sized baps, stuffed with bacon, and two Styrofoam cups of tea are exchanged for five quid – which I think is extremely reasonable.

As we eat, I show Chris the map and remark on the fact that we're going to spend nearly the whole day on this one road, give or take the odd diversion for the Landmarks. Not quite route 66, but an impressively long road by Britain's standards, stretching as it does from London all the way up into Scotland. He wants to know if there's any National Parks on the way. The idea really has caught his imagination, and he looks disappointed when I tell him that it'll be a good few days before we see any of that. Our immediate focus returns to today's plan and our big map showing the Landmarks. We calculate that we have covered some thirty-five miles already this morning, and have approximately the same distance again to the first official stop of the day. It's just after eight now, which means that we'll easily stay within our planned schedule, and with that, we get togged up and we're back on the road again in short order. Daisy really is running faultlessly, seeming to shrug off her heavy load with no fuss at all, settling to a relaxed fifty-five once again.

It seems like no time at all until we leave the A1, just before Grantham, and head east into the lush green lanes of the Lincolnshire/Leicestershire borderlands. Proper English countryside is this, with it's gentle rolling landscape, criss-crossed by ever smaller roads with their high grassy banks. The springtime explosion of growth has given way to the wild colours of summer and flowers, butterflies and numerous buzzing things proliferate all around us. I slow Daisy to a sedate meander, allowing us to take our time in savouring this veritable Garden of Eden and I also realise that for once, we're not lost. Our target is extremely well signposted, and we have no trouble following the little brown heritage signs as we thread along numerous little lanes to arrive at the Landmark, Belvoir Castle almost bang on time and very relaxed. As we park Daisy up in a suitable place for photographs I reckon that this is not so much a castle but rather more like a stately home. Certainly it's got turrets and crenellations, but it's lacking that essential raw brute feel of your proper castle.

After taking our photographs, we wander around outside and I find several information plaques that inform us that the original structure was believed to have been built in the eleventh century by one Robert de Todeni, who's main claim to fame was that he had served as William the Conqueror's Standard Bearer during the Battle of Hastings. The story board took us through a potted history of the place since those early origins, telling a tale of medieval upheaval, treachery, treason and war. I find it fascinating stuff indeed and enthuse to Chris that this is just one local story plucked from centuries of upheaval that is English history. He gives me the 'old fart' look, but then gets interested himself as I read out the bit about one particular family who lost their ownership of the place when, in 1464, Lord Thomas Ros, the then Lord of the Manor was executed for his support of the Lancastrians during the Wars of the Roses. I find that I am experiencing the same eerie feeling that I had felt at Runnymede and wonder aloud if, with all turbulent events it has seen, the place is haunted. This thought captures Chris's full and undivided attention and as we wander back down to Daisy I find myself deeply debating the existence, or not, of ghosts, ghoulies and things that go bump in the night. He's particularly taken with my line of reasoning that suggests that ghosts are quite possibly restless spirits, yanked from life before they were good and ready, or with unfinished business that must be cleared up before eternal peace can be achieved. I explain, by way of example, that having your head lopped off for liking the wrong colour rose could, by some, be construed as a good enough reason to stick around and scare the pants off of the living.

What I can promise, I assure Chris, is that we will be visiting a number of places that have equally deep and tumultuous history attached, equally good candidates for a good haunting. I smile inwardly as I can't help noticing that he keeps flicking a worried look back up towards the castle as we walk and in a moment of wickedness I suggest to him that if he really wants to investigate the possible existence of ghosts, then I am sure we can arrange to camp at one of them and keep a vigil. His interest, it seems, does not extend to actually staking out a dodgy old ruin, and he dismisses the suggestion rather quickly with one of those looks and a firm "er...*no* Dad!" Back at Daisy, who is gleaming in the early sun, we have attracted another set of admirers. An old boy and his equally ancient wife are remembering their own younger days, which apparently featured a Triumph 'just like this one'. It's amazing how many folk had one, or at least think they had one, and we spend a little time chatting to the current veteran, Chris taking the lead with his by now familiar and enthusiastic diatribe into the merits of all things Daisy. While they're twittering away I pull the wad of strip maps from the tank bag, shuffle the used ones to the bottom, and study our next leg which takes us back to the A1, where we'll head north again for about eighty five miles before another detour to pick off Landmark number two of the four we're hoping to get in the bag today. With Daisy able to cruise happily at sixty to seventy mph I reckon this will take a couple of hours, including the detour, if the old backside holds out and we don't have to stop for a stretch too often.

The old boy is showing no signs of leaving, lost as he is in a dreamy haze of nostalgia that is being fuelled by Chris's enthusiasm. I start to make obvious getting ready to go motions coupled with exaggerated inspection of the watch, and eventually Chris gets the message and begins to prepare himself. The old boy stays until Daisy is prepped and kicked into life, and as she fires he turns to his wife and exclaims "Cor, 'ark at that! If only we could turn back the clock, eh Lil?" I am amazed to see what looks like a tear in her eye, as she puts her arm through his and squeezes, and I feel it's time to go before they both start. With a wave to the old couple, and a big smile, off we go again. We can't follow the brown signs this time, and I can't remember the twisty route we took to get here, but the A1 is due east and we are once again thankful for the little novelty compass as we pick our way across a myriad of little crossroads and meander amongst the fabulous greenery. It's not too long before we find it, and turning north I wind on the throttle once more, listening to the exhaust note deepen as we climb through the gears until Daisy is thrumming along happily at a steady sixty-five.

Now that we have put the far southern section of this road behind us, it begins to dawn on me that the A1 is actually quite a pleasant ride. Our schedule, which was oh so important on setting out, seems to be less so now as we simply settle down to enjoying what, after all, we came to do - ride. The café's, tea huts and caravans continue to populate the numerous lay-by's, which gives us plenty of opportunity to take a rest and be tempted again with their bacon sarnies and large mugs of tea. We steadily knock off the miles, ever northwards until suddenly, and without warning the (M) part of the route imposes itself on us as the road turns into three lane motorway once again. We stick to the near lane, as all the traffic speeds up around us but after a while, with everything going so well, I decide to get this over with and back onto the smaller sections by letting Daisy stretch her legs a bit. Seventy five, eighty and eighty five duly tick up on her ancient speedometer, at which point the thing decides that that's quite enough of that thank you and the needle starts to bounce wildly between twenty and ninety, not to mention all over the place in between. It becomes impossible to read, but I am revelling in the sheer joy of the first real test of the rebuilt engine, which is making no fuss at the demands suddenly placed upon it. In a particularly brave five minutes we actually overtake a number of slower cars.

Daisy's making a most satisfactory howl, but the vibration is awesome and it seems appropriate, after a while, to ease back somewhat and give the old girl a breather, not least because my fingers and feet are tingling with the first signs of the dread numbness that one can expect from such frivolous abandon on an old machine like this. The speedometer agrees, evidently, it's needle settling down to a gentle wavering once I get back down to about seventy. The vibration is much less harsh at this more sedate speed, and I fight off a slight pang of guilt for treating the old girl so hard and silently promise that we'll sit at this speed and no more. It seems to be Daisy's 'smooth spot', I consider, and she feels totally at ease, unstressed and has a wonderful exhaust burble that cannot fail to please. I realise that as I think all this I'm grinning like an idiot, a situation I suspect is well known to many classic riders. After a while, the motorway duly becomes dual carriageway and lay-bys again and we settle down once more to an enjoyable ride. Everything is right in the world, life is marvellous, there is not a hint of anything other than sheer enjoyment stretching ahead. Even the traffic, what there is of it, seems to be behaving in a fairly sedate and non-threatening manner. I can't help but grin even more as a familiar noise intrudes on these thoughts, but it no longer causes me to worry, and I chuckle that it merely means that the young man on the back is happy and away with the fairies again.

I am yanked from this reverie by a sudden cessation of the noise and an urgent tapping on my shoulder. Chris is attempting to yell something, which I can't hear in the wind-rush but he's agitated enough to suggest that all may not be well at the back, but as I drop off the throttle and look round I can't ascertain what's wrong immediately. Judging by the gestures though, I'd better pull over onto the shoulder. All becomes clear as we coast to a halt - Chris has noticed that we're about to lose our tent and baggage, which is hanging off the side of the bike at a wild angle. I had considered getting a proper rack and panniers for Daisy, before setting out on these adventures, but somehow I had not got round to it. The panniers we have are soft throw over types, which whilst eminently suitable for use on a broad dual seat as fitted to the vast majority of motorcycles, are faring rather less well on the rigid mudguard of our mount. The whole lot has slipped to one side and is barely hanging on at all. We take it all off, reposition the panniers and tighten up all the straps. Back goes the tent, bedroll and bits, with bungee straps re-applied as best we can. It all looks pretty solid again and declaring it sound, we take the opportunity to check our route sheets. We've made excellent progress, and I enthuse to Chris that we should arrive at our next jumping off point soon, to look for what I believe to be an air museum of some sort. By my calculations we've put over a hundred and forty miles behind us since starting out, and it's not much past eleven, which means we're easily on schedule for our day one target of being in Newcastle by evening, even with the detour we're about to take. I should have realised that it was all going too well.

Leaving the A1 and heading east for fifteen miles or so, the expected air museum is uncovered with consummate ease and we get the all-important photos without any drama. We decide to take a rest before setting off again. Relieved at the rapidity with which this particular Landmark had surrendered we break out some crisps and a Mars bar each whilst contemplating our next leg, which circumnavigates the historic town of York to the north before heading east yet again almost as far as the coast. I have not identified the next site from the clue, which refers to Adam and Eve putting up a tent in the garden or something. Neither of us can think of anything remotely useful or likely, and we agree that we'll just have to wing it and hope that something obvious shows up once we get there. It really doesn't seem to matter, we've made such good progress this morning, the sun is shining and no problems seem imminent. Twenty minutes later we discover Eden camp, and obviously this is where 'Adam and Eve set up their tent'. A large sign assures me that this is, in fact, the country's most popular theme attraction and I find it strange that I've never heard of it. Chris is all for exploring the place, as he would be I suppose, but our schedule won't allow for that and anyway, I have by now discovered somewhere infinitely more worthy of a visit, some fifteen miles to the northwest, and therefore worth a little detour, if my map is to be believed. 'Scagglethorpe' it says, and I can only marvel at such a splendid name for a village. We simply must go there, I enthuse, but the withering glare of incomprehension somewhat douses my spirits. Clearly the old man is having one of his moments, the look says, and is not to be encouraged. I look again at the map, and have to admit that it's quite a detour really, and I'm slightly saddened that I am alone in my delight at the quirky place-name. Oh well.

Back to York then, or at least round it once more on our double-back trek west to rejoin the A1 yet again. The weather is playing ball, getting warmer as we progress through the day and Daisy's still behaving remarkably well, so all's well with the world. But the going starts to get tougher now, as we begin a series of long climbs ever northwards, leaving the Yorkshire moors behind us and enjoying the sheer freedom of a relaxed ride in increasingly interesting country. I marvel at the enormous power stations looming on the horizon, built to feed the ferocious appetite of an industrial explosion in years past, and I wonder what it is that they now feed, given that the huge manufacturing and steel industries have largely given way to a lesser breed of lighter activities. But my thoughts are interrupted as I notice, seemingly for the first time, that a tingling vibration has crept up on me and the beginnings of a pins-and-needles sensation is setting in. I lift my hand and the sensation is markedly increased and I take the first opportunity to pull in to yet another lay-by.

Happily, the duty tea hut is in residence, and Chris is happy to trundle off to do the honours after I explain that we've got some loose nuts and bolts somewhere that need some attention. This is easier said than done. The spanners, a woefully inadequate collection though they may be, are buried in one of the panniers, which in turn are supporting the camping gear. It all has to come off, and the contents removed to get to the bottom where the sad little bag of rusty implements has hidden. There is one mighty adjustable as well, and I spread the motley collection on the ground and start the process of checking the forward engine mounts. They seem solid, so I move onto the underside and rear mountings, but they too are solid. This is curious, I tell Chris, who has returned with some steaming cups. I fully expected to find some loose nuts, to explain away the vibration, and the absence of anything even hinting at slackness is worrying, for if that's not the cause then what is? And will it prove to become a drama later? I move onto the gearbox mountings hoping that the culprits will show themselves here, but they are also solid. Stranger still, and I sit back on my haunches with the tea whilst my paranoia takes over, populating my mind with disintegrating clutches or crumbling bearings. Chris has a more relaxed approach; "You imagined it," he suggests. Resisting the impulse to bounce my half full coffee cup off his head, I explain about the definite vibration through the handlebars and the tingling fingers, but he remains sceptical. After checking for any obvious signs of any other traumas, and discovering that Daisy's big ornate horn is about to fall off again, I reluctantly accept that there is nothing useful I can do and we pack everything back up again, reinstate the camping gear on top, and head once more out to the open road.

As we accelerate up the slip road, taking her up through the gears, my attention is immediately focused on that vibration. It's still there, and I know that it'll fester in my mind like a cancer until I can find an explanation for it. We settle on the main carriageway and I realise that over the past few months I have come to know Daisy intimately. I know all her little foibles and characteristics. Every little noise and rattle (of which there are always a few on any old Triumph) is known to me, and I realise that the current object of my attention is actually not that bad – just not usual. But if I've learned one thing in my many earlier years of riding a variety of old bikes, it's that the appearance of a hitherto unknown rattle or vibration is almost always followed by drama of some sort. But there is nothing I can do right now, so we continued on our way, and I begin to mentally chew my blanket (an old family saying – I had a granny, bless her, who when worried about something, which was nearly always, would sit in the corner with a blanket on her lap, and busily chew the corner, even though she had no teeth!) deciding that I would have to investigate a little more once we have managed to make camp later in the afternoon. By mid afternoon we are approaching the general area that marks our first overnight stop and the road has once again become motorway. We pull up in the services at the Bishop Auckland junction to get our bearings, study the map and generally decide what we should now do.

We only have one Landmark left to get today, and according to the map the thing can't be more than twenty miles away from our current position. It's another cryptic and crafty one, but we were able to solve it in advance with the help of the online ordnance survey website. We've had no trouble with the others, today has gone exceptionally well so far and it's only half-past three so we decide to press on to get the thing discovered and photographed, and then take the first chance to camp that presents itself. I tell Chris that we should camp as early as possible so that we can investigate the source of that vibration. His response, "I still think you're imagining it - I can't feel it" doesn't help. But, buoyed by the progress on the day my confidence is high and I'm not too worried about much at all. I'll find the source this evening and fix whatever it is that's causing it, and we'll go on tomorrow to another highly successful day's adventure. I was about to discover that I was entirely wrong in this belief – and about a great many things.

It starts here, the general downturn in our fortunes, because this next Landmark is conspicuous by it's absence. We simply can't find it. It's now ten past five, and we have been riding round in circles for the last hour utterly failing to find anything remotely matching the clue 'Sounds like a pigeon loft of warm metal' it says, and right on the map reference, or at least very close, is supposed to be 'High Forge' a heritage site by all accounts. It's a very well hidden heritage site, we both agree, as we pull up for what seems like the fifth time at a road junction which we have already traversed from every conceivable direction. I'm pretty sure that we have now tried every single road within a three-mile radius, and there are only two notable things to see, other than endless cornfields. One is a particularly uninspiring industrial estate, seemingly completely out of place in the otherwise pleasant countryside and the other is a famous Landmark indeed, but not what we want – the Angel of the North stands impressively, albeit a tad rusty, on the horizon. We are both fractious by now and it seems pointless trundling around any more lanes, so we decide that the best bet is to enlist some local knowledge and accordingly set off to the nearest place to us, Stanley, a few miles to our west. We find a large pub just on the outskirts and suddenly a pint of warm real-ale seems like an incredibly good idea whilst picking the brains of the locals.

"No, can't help you, sorry" this is the third local we have talked to, after extracting a blank from the barman and his assistant. I stare into my beer and begin to wonder what to do next as nobody, it seems, has ever heard of High Forge, or a local heritage site of any description. As I study the faces, It occurs to me that in the present cloth-capped company, we must look a proper pair of Charlies, a couple of soft southerners, appearing from nowhere on this old wheezing motorcycle with a tent and not a lot else and asking obscure questions about non-existent forges. In an effort to demonstrate that we're not in fact barking mad, and salvage at least some self esteem, I explain about the Landmark challenge to our by now small audience and in desperation we show them the clue seeking any ideas as to what it

Daisy

Chris

Chloe

The infamous Sprung Hub

Daisy at Le Mans

Grandad and Chloe at the Rabbit Rally

Will it fit back on...?

Chris takes a break

At the dam in Central Wales

The Angel of the North

What it's all about - Daisy in The Lake District...

...and at the campsite in Coldstream

In deepest Wales

Early morning mist

Visiting castles

Chloe at the Silver Mine

could possibly be "No, sorry …" is the collective response. This is beyond belief and I turn to Chris, "Right, let's 'phone Ken Talbot!" I declare, which is met with the predictable response from Chris, "Who?" But I'm striding outside now, heading for the mobile 'phone and only slightly perturbed by the several locals who, not wanting to miss some good free street entertainment, are following gleefully. Ken Talbot, with a number of his stout fellow members of the Birmingham and Wolves branch of the Triumph Owner's Motorcycle Club, is the creator of our current problem. He's the organiser and official contact for those of us stupid enough to actually take up this challenge. I have his number along with all the clues stashed in Daisy's tank bag, right there with the 'phone, which is an unusually sensible precaution that I had taken in an unprecedented fit of clear thinking and good planning whilst packing for the trip. I certainly couldn't face another hour of hopeless meandering around the hills with only a rusty angel and some cows for company, not to mention a decidedly irritable Chris, so a call to Ken is clearly the thing to do. I find the number, and dial the digits, giving the now gathered audience a raised eyebrow and an expression that I hope suggests that the person on the other end of this call has got some explaining to do. I connect to whatever cleverly hidden mast services this area, and in short order I hear the brusque tones of the man himself.

"Ken… Is that Ken Talbot?" I enquire, beaming at the now rapt audience.

"Aye, who's this then?" Explanations follow, and I end by telling him "We've been all over the place now, and we've stopped at a local pub right here, and there's no sign of this forge and nobody's ever heard of it! I know it's on the maps, but has any of you actually ever seen the bloody place?" I realised I was sounding tetchy, and there is a moment of silence, then Ken offers some help

"Forge? What forge?" another pause "It's not a forge you want young man, no, it's a bit bigger than that, it's a steelworks, the Dovecote Steelworks, see?" I let this information sink in.

"What! There isn't a steelworks anywhere near here either!" I exclaim, "Just fields – are you sure this map reference is correct Ken?" If nothing else, our Ken is a patient man and isn't at all ruffled by this gibbering madman raving down the telephone at him.

"It certainly is, and it's definitely there!" he assures me in a steady confident drawl. "You can't miss it, bloody great place is a steelworks," he adds. A bloody great place indeed.

"Well it's bloody well camouflaged then!" is all I can think to say, and I can't help noticing that our audience is looking particularly happy with the exchange, as several of the cloth caps nod with barely concealed mirth. I ask another important question.

"Has anyone else doing the challenge had a problem here?" Apparently not, as Ken confirms no other callers have asked about this one. Great. Just marvellous, I think, but our Ken is a charitable soul and offers me a lifeline.

"Listen, if you can't find it, that's OK. Get a photo of something recognisable from the immediate area and we'll accept that. It's about participating, and getting folk out on their bikes lad, so we'll not punish you for summat silly like this!" I thank him, promise we'll have one more try at finding the thing, and if not we'll get a photograph of something else recognisable.

"How about the Angel of the North from across these fields?" I suggest.

"Aye, whatever, but just enjoy yourself!"

I end the call, to the evident disappointment of my new fan club, and beckon Chris over to explain the plan. We check the time and I'm irritated that we have lost nearly another hour, haven't found our last photo of the day, haven't found a campsite yet and still have that vibration to track down before I can truly relax tonight. But it's a glorious summer evening and we at least have a solution that is definitive, so I tell myself to take Ken's advice, stop fretting and just enjoy myself. We get our gear together, bid the still present audience a hearty farewell, and head back out for one more look around. It occurs to me that the industrial estate we had seen earlier, looking so out of place, may well be hiding the steelworks within it's boundaries and with no better plan I suggest to Chris that we try to find it again. That's not quite as easy as it sounds as we thread our way through the myriad of little country roads, but before long the rusty angel appears once again on our horizon and we know we're close. Riding up through a little copse and round a bend at the top I recognise from our earlier criss-crossings of this area, we sweep down the other side to break into a wonderful sun-soaked little valley, bordered by meadow each side. I realise in that instant that nothing in the world actually matters right now. The vibration, our schedule, this elusive Landmark – all fade into insignificance as we simply enjoy the experience of being lost in picture postcard surroundings, just us and our old motorbike. We sweep through the valley bottom, take a long right hander up out of the other side and broach the top of a another wooded hill, down into a sweeping bend the other side and suddenly all hell breaks loose.

Daisy just loses it completely without warning. Her rear end jerks violently, and then jinks sideways yanking Chris, with a yelled "Wooooah!" out of whatever reverie he was enjoying and causing him to grab hold of me. Shocked from my own daydreams, I find myself suddenly fighting the handlebars, which have taken on a life of their own, as we career towards the verge, narrowly missing the trees to our left. Suddenly we are plummeting down the hill, completely out of control, with Daisy bucking and sliding beneath us. She goes into an almighty and violent tank-slapper and in that moment I am certain we're going to come off. I have no time to think, react or do anything remotely sensible and all I can do is hang on as the frightening toboggan ride unfolds, ending with us careering to a sliding halt at the bottom, skewed diagonally across the road, hearts pounding and knees trembling like crazy. I think Chris actually nearly swallowed his tongue, judging by the gurgling noises coming from the back but I am in shock and just sit, motionless, for about two minutes. Neither of us moves or speaks but eventually we come round.

"What the hell...?" I began, but Chris lets loose his tension straight over me with a violent exclamation.

"Bloody hellfire! ....!" and with this he catapults from the pillion and stumbles off to the verge, discarding his gloves on the road and pulling violently at his helmet before thumping down on his backside to glare at Daisy. I dismount in a less theatrical manner, push her over to the verge, and the drag draws my attention to the fact that her rear tyre has blown, explaining the sudden descent into chaos. I drop her on the side-stand and follow Chris's example by divesting myself of gloves and helmet. I reach with trembling hand for the tobacco tin but find that I can't actually control my fingers to roll one due to the shakes. I look across at Chris, and without knowing why I say "looks like I picked the wrong day to give up smoking!" It wasn't likely to break the ice right at that moment, and indeed it didn't. Chris looks pretty shaken up.

"Are you OK?" I ask.

"No I'm bloody not!" is the terse response. Strong language indeed from a fourteen year old in front of his father, but I let it go in the circumstances.

We finally get round to inspecting Daisy. A puncture it is all right and in the sprung-hub rear tyre at that. This is absolutely the last thing we need and is as depressing as it gets with a rigid framed motorcycle of this age. The process of getting the rear wheel off is protracted, torturous and dirty, requiring at least two pairs of hands and ideally a decent tool-kit and workshop. What's clear is that there is no way I'm going to attempt a repair here in the sticks, so I decide to waste no time at all and make use of my recovery insurance, get them out to pick us up and take us to the nearest campsite. I make the call, and immediately we have problems as the controller asks the fateful question.

"Where exactly are you?" which, I have to admit is a remarkably good question.

"We're in the middle of the countryside" I say "er... about five miles south and a bit west of Newcastle" I add. It strikes me that these people must get a lot of idiots like me 'phoning them, because he sounds awfully patient as, without a pause he smoothly says.

"That's OK sir, but we'll need to give the driver a bit more, so, do you know what the last town or village was that you went through?" I explain about Stanley, and the pub.

"Great, so you're definitely between Stanley and Newcastle. OK, can you see any features or landmarks near you?" I nearly laughed at his use of 'landmark' but I suppress it and explain that on the horizon to the east of us is the Angel of the North.

"Right, OK sir this is what I'll do – I am giving your details to a local recovery company, with as much information as I can about location. I am going to suggest that they telephone you directly and hopefully you won't be too hard to find" He went on to tell me not to leave the vehicle (as if we would – where would we go?) and that we could expect the call within thirty minutes. I thank the guy, who has impressed me with his handling of our situation, and with nothing else to do I explain to Chris what the score is and we settle down to wait.

I sit and think about getting the back wheel off, and with the paltry tool-kit we have with us it's not a comforting thought at all. Then there's the tyre, which is a struggle at the best of times but is likely to be quite a challenge out here in the wilds with only Chris to help. I sink into a depressed state of mind but am brought round by a deep rumbling sound approaching from the direction we had just come and as I stand up a guy on a Harley comes over the hill and slows to a stop. Explanations follow, and it's clear from the look he gives us that our new friend thinks we're quite mad. We obviously don't look too well equipped, and having explained that we intend to fix the thing and carry on northwards, he begins questioning me about my readiness for such a problem.

"You've got a heavy duty repair kit with you?" Good grief, what does he think we are amateurs? I have a superb repair kit, there in the panniers, and I scrabble about inside, looking for it to show off our preparedness for such things. It's not there. Strange, I could have sworn it was in the left pannier, with some big tyre levers. I switch to the other side and scrabble about in that one but it's not there either.

"Must be in the tank bag." I say, beginning to wonder. It's not. I begin to feel pretty stupid and I can feel my face redden as I am forced to admit that, in fact, we don't after all have a repair kit of any sort.

"But you've got a spare inner-tube, surely?" No we haven't and I mumble this dreadful admission as I suddenly realise how foolish I must look to have come on this trip with no way to deal with a puncture. I looked at the incredulous rider, expecting derision of the highest order, but without further ado this knight of the road declares that it's not a problem – he'll go and get an inner tube from his garage, which he assures me will fit. With that, he promptly about faces and heads back off leaving me with a mixture of feelings. I'm utterly embarrassed at our ridiculous plight, but this is tempered with a feeling of pride to be a motorcyclist, as I ponder that his actions are entirely typical of the breed. It's built into us, I reckon, no matter what we ride or where we're from – or indeed how stupid the object of our assistance appears to be.

These thoughts are abruptly interrupted by my mobile, and it's the recovery company. The guy's in Stanley already, which is impressively fast, and wants to know more about our location. I explain about the pub we were at, and he knows where that is, so I describe as best I can the route we took. No problem apparently, he knows exactly where to find us, and ten minutes later we hear the truck approaching. He takes one look at Daisy and exclaims, "Well, I'll not be fixing *that*! Where are you from and where do you need to get back to?" We explain that we just need to be taken to the nearest decent campsite, and with that he proceeds to load her onto his truck. Minutes later, our other Harley-mounted saviour returns and I'm left speechless as he proceeds to hand over not just the inner tube which is indeed exactly right for Daisy, but tyre levers and a foot pump as well. He explains that he lives not far away and has had the tube hanging in his garage for ages. We watch as the recovery driver makes things secure, and settle down to chatting. Chris comes to life again and explains where we've been with Daisy on the other forays so far; I reflect that it does actually all make for a good yarn, to which this episode will only add flavour.

The recovery man finally declares us ready, and as I enquire as to how I can return the pump and levers, the guy insists that we keep them, and will accept no payment for them or the inner tube. As he straddles his ride once again and fires the engine, he pushes up his visor and offers a piece of good advice. "You really ought to get a repair kit and fix that other tube for a spare!" I nod and grin enthusiastically and we wave him off. Hurrah for Harley-riding Mark from Gateshead – you know who you are, and you are a credit to your peers.

The recovery guy had insisted that we unload all the gear, so now we must shove it all into the back of his cab, before settling into the big bench seat up front. We confirm once again that the nearest campsite is where we want to go. He threads his way back onto the A1, turns south and delivers us after a while to a campsite right on the Durham junction 10 miles or so south of Newcastle. He wishes us luck as he heads off, leaving us to check in, and all I want to do is get the tent up and find some food. It's a quarter to nine by the time we've unpacked and got ourselves sorted. As we get out spaghetti, some mince and a tin of sauce that we bought at the site shop, it's obvious that I'll not get anything much done to Daisy tonight. I'm suddenly exhausted anyway, and Chris looks pretty tired, and so by mutual agreement we decide to leave everything until morning and accept that the day's schedule will have to go to hell in a handcart. As the sun finally disappears over the western horizon, I stare at Daisy, with her flat tyre, and try to think the job through. She was made in an era when solidity and strength were the main design criteria for a working motorcycle. Quick access to such things as the rear wheel were not high on the agenda: the thing is firmly surrounded by solid bits of metal fixed firmly with a plethora of stout bolts. I wonder if there is a trick that will allow me to get that wheel out more easily, but I can't see it. I get up and go over to her, crouching down in the last of the light for a quick inspection but it's depressingly obvious that there will be no shortcuts here. It's then that I notice a little sign stuck in the grass nearby, next to the little looping road that runs round the site. It says 'No way out' and I reflect that nothing could be closer to the truth!

An early start is essential and we're up at seven. A mug of tea is a prerequisite to any serious activity and that is sorted out before I get round to dealing with Daisy. It's a warm morning with a light cloud, but there's enough sun coming through to glint off the heavy dew that has fallen, making this first ten minutes of contemplative mental preparation rather pleasant. But I can't put it off any longer, and pausing only to focus Chris on the task ahead, I stride purposefully over and make a start. Daisy's rear stand, which resides right at the back and serves to elevate the rear wheel from the ground, has sunk into the earth overnight. I need that to be firm and so we push her over to the road, where things are more solid. I explain to Chris what's to be done, and which bits are going to be painful; Disconnect chain, remove brake arm securing bolt, remove the stay retaining nuts, loosen the flange nuts that join the two mudguard halves which will allow the rear section to be lifted clear of the wheel, loosen the main wheel nuts. When all that's done, placing any removed parts safely, we can lift the mudguard clear and pull out the wheel.

Easy to do, I tell Chris, but I know from previous, bitter experience that the real trick is getting it all back together again – because that very heavy back wheel, with it's rotating central spring-box has a little locater bar, which has to fit 'just so' into a little slot in the frame, which of course is hidden and inaccessible. This must be done whilst keeping the mudguard clear, pulling the two rear frame lugs apart to accept the hub width, holding the brake arm in the right place and pushing the whole lot into position. Difficult enough in a good workshop with stout able-bodied assistance, but quite a challenge on the edge of a field in the middle of Yorkshire, with a very slim toolkit and an inexperienced fourteen year old apprentice. Fifteen minutes later, phase one is successfully accomplished, with the wheel out ready for inspection. Unfortunately, the removal of chain and brake arm has left my hands and lower arms smothered heavily with thick greasy oil. I despatch Chris off to find anything that he can by way of rags or paper towels, whilst I begin to survey the next, almost certainly challenging, task – that of removing the old inner-tube. By the time Chris returns I am surveying the remains of Mark's tyre levers, and cursing the fact that the tyre itself is still firmly in place. The levers are too small, and have simply given up the unequal struggle and bent. I only posses some smallish screwdrivers, one of which, having been brought to bear on the recalcitrant tyre-bead is now also bent. I curse again. Clearly I need bigger, stronger weaponry if we're to make any progress.

It's seven thirty on a Sunday morning and we're in a field just off the A1. The nearest town, Durham is five miles away and the on-site shop doesn't open for another hour. Chris is moping around getting bored, I have no obvious way of getting the tyre off and our schedule is looking to be in tatters. Bloody marvellous, I should have known that it had all been going too well yesterday. I suddenly realise that we haven't had breakfast yet, and there is bacon, eggs, beans and bread in the tent, bought yesterday evening at the shop. With nothing else to do until the shop opens, so I can find out where the nearest Halfords is, it seems the sensible thing to do and my stomach growls in agreement. I call over to Chris to get the stoves fired up and put on an enthusiastic face as I wander over. Yes, a good breakfast will make all the difference I enthuse. We cook up a handsome feast and a fresh brew to wash it down, but as we sit down to eat Chris is getting morose about our current predicament. He's convinced we'll be stuck here all day, and with nothing to do or see that is a boring prospect indeed and he makes the fact well known.

"Rubbish" says I, with a bravado that I didn't really believe myself, "We're close to Durham, which is a city. There's bound to be somewhere we can get big tyre levers and then we're sorted!" He fiddles with his breakfast and grunts, before an inner thought occurs to him.

"How do we get there then?" he asks, but I was already ahead of him there.

"We're going to call a taxi from that shop, and the driver will know where to go!" I declare triumphantly. Another grunt, and I admit that it's not the very best plan in the world, whilst cursing myself again for forgetting to pack the puncture kit and stout levers that I had prepared at home. We finish our breakfast in silence, then clear up the rubbish before collecting the dirty stuff and heading for the wash-block where the fairy liquid deals with it and the grease on my hands and arms. We need to take a shower before hitting the road, but I point out to Chris that there is no point doing this before we've fixed Daisy – we'll get handsomely dirty again trying to put her back together.

With the shop open, we discuss our predicament with the proprietor, who quite rightly points out that although there most certainly is a trading estate not far away where we'll get what we need, nothing would be open until ten o'clock, what with it being a Sunday. More time wasted, and I begin to think that fate is conspiring to spoil our day, but nothing to be done about it, so we do what we can, which is to call the local Durham taxi firm and book a cab for nine forty-five. It's nearly a quarter to eleven when we arrived back, thankfully with a set of three stout car-type levers and a heavy duty repair kit, and after handing over the best part of fifteen quid to the cab driver, including waiting time, both of us are keen to get straight at the job. Getting the tyre off is now easy, but getting the thing back on is less so, especially as I'm acutely aware that pinching the thing would be bad, given our circumstances. But eventually it's done and the donated pump is brought into service without delay. I tell Chris that we need to leave the thing for a while, just to be sure that it's going to stay up, and in the mean time we apply a patch to the punctured one that we've just removed. Both stay up, which is at least a minor victory, but we approach Daisy again with a degree of trepidation for what comes next will not be fun at all.

Chris holds the rear mudguard out of the way, while in his other hand I have him holding one of the levers, to insert 'twixt frame and wheel in order to pry the frame lug out past the spindle bush. This is incredibly hard to do, especially as I have to have the other one ready to do the same on the opposite side, whilst at the same time trying to marry up the extraordinarily heavy wheel to it's lugs, all whilst keeping the little locating arm straight and stopping the brake arm going out of position and getting tangled with chain guards and frame. The first two attempts are nothing short of comical and end, in each case, with the wheel jammed at some obscure angle and a goodly number of my fingers jammed with it. On the third attempt, the wheel slots into place, only for me to discover that the brake arm had become jammed in the wrong position. It all had to come out again. It is something like the fifth attempt and some twenty minutes later that the nightmare thing finally slots into place, and we sit back on the grass, tempers frayed, glaring at the thing with malevolence. But it is in and the relief is palpable - the rest should be plain sailing. I roll a cigarette, study my oily black arms and the lacerations to my fingers whilst rattling off a silent mantra of things I'd like to do to the bloke that designed this particular wheel arrangement. My watch tells me that lunch time has been and gone, so we've lost half a day so far, but I console myself that the rest is just so much meccano, and we should be on the road within the hour. Little did I know that this was just Daisy's opening salvo in what was to become a battle of wills – man against machine and may the most belligerent win!

9. *Mountains, Rain and Perilous Descents!*

Finally we finish the job, pack up the tent and after a miserable attempt to get clean in a cold shower-block with lukewarm water, we finally thread our way out of the campsite turning north once more. It's a quarter to two, and we must still get the Landmark photograph that we were forced to abort the previous evening. I've agreed with Chris that we're not about to go hunting for the cursed steelworks again but will instead find anything that's recognisable nearby. The Beamish steam museum is close enough, we agree, being on the outskirts of Stanley, and then without further ado it's Scotland here we come! I confess to Chris that I've never been there, so it's a first for both of us and I'm looking forward to it more than ever having overcome the trials of the morning.

We're soon past Newcastle and, anxious to make up for lost time, I open Daisy up as we push onwards north. The weather's holding up well with a light but warm breeze caressing us as we finally peel off the A1 onto the A697, and strike out for Coldstream and the Scottish border. I reckon It's about 70 miles and if all goes well I see no reason why we can't ride later into the evening in order to make up for lost time. After all, we have not been riding this morning and as such we are pretty fresh. Chris is happy with the plan and we make good steady headway for a while, but our luck is obviously on the turn downwards – Daisy starts to miss-fire. This is all we need, and I try the usual tricks to clear the problem like dropping a gear and winding open the throttle, but to no avail. With only a paltry thirty odd miles behind us we are forced to stop once again.

We find ourselves in a truly nasty lay-by full of rubbish, making a sharp contrast to the picturesque Northumberland landscape of gently undulating greenery and as I explain to Chris that we'll be here for a while he agrees to get the camping stove out for a brew. I begin to tinker with Daisy, but after prodding various bits I can't find anything obviously wrong. We seem to have a good spark, and with Daisy's early ignition system there is only the magneto to worry about, which appears to be fine, so all I can think to do is change the plugs and generally clean all the HT connections. By the time I've done that Chris has the tea made and as I let mine cool I start the engine. It seems to be better, with a couple of experimental revs showing no signs of the dread miss-fire, so we finish the tea, pack up the stove once more and set off again, hoping to hell that the problem is cured. Fat chance, Daisy's not happy at all and I begin to fret about what else I can do. We proceed slowly, inside the hard shoulder of the road, trying to pinpoint something, anything, that will give me inspiration. I discover that as long as I build up the revs slowly, the misfire doesn't seem to occur, whereas any attempt to accelerate normally produces an immediate faltering sputter. I am loath to stop yet again, opting instead to build up speed until we're cruising along at around sixty-five or so. This is fine as long as we hit no junctions or roundabouts that will force the whole frustrating charade to be replayed over again. Chris is leaning over my shoulder enquiring, "what exactly is the problem?" and I can tell he's getting despondent again, as well he might. We've got a long way to go, or, if we are forced to turn round we're a long way from home! But progress is being made and so we just push on until eventually, as we pull into Coldstream, Daisy forces me to deal with the problem by stopping dead and refusing to start again. There is a sign just in front of us that says 'Welcome to Scotland' and we have stopped ten feet short of it. An omen, or just a quirk of fate?

We take stock of our situation, and agree that it's not looking good. I have to confess to Chris that short of some obvious fiddling, I'm at a loss what to do next but at least we can see what appears to be a pleasant little campsite not far away, on the bank of the river Tweed. This is the obvious first move, I suggest. We'll push Daisy down to it and set up camp early and once that's done we can consider our options. What looks like a short distance turns out to be nearly a mile's walk as we have to follow the road into the town, round through the main street and down to the river via a looping back lane. I am exhausted by the time we get there and my spirits droop even further when I realize that our luck has completely gone now, as a dark threatening sky begins to creep over and a steady drizzle starts falling. By the time we get camp set up, the light has faded to nothing, the drizzle has intensified and we decide to leave Daisy until morning. I realize suddenly that Chris is holding his spirits up remarkably well, bustling around helping me with the tent and then asking if we can get to the supermarket and buy 'something special' to cook for dinner. I agree that this is a damned fine idea, after all there is nothing else we can do right now and I reckon we've certainly earned the most slap-up feed that can be concocted on a camp stove. Darkness is crowding in remarkably fast as we walk up the little lane towards the town, and stock up with the makings of Spaghetti Bolognaise, Chris's favourite food, some chocolate goodies for afters and a four-pack of Newcastle brown ale to finish off. We sit under the little porch section of our tent, listening to the steady patter of drizzle, but buoyed all the same by the feast that we have just consumed.

After dinner, with the time still only seven o'clock, I suggest a walk round the ancient town, with it's historic attachment to the Coldstream Guards, and we set off along the river bank path up towards the town. Out of the blue, Chris pipes up that if nothing else, at least we're in Scotland and the talk turns to Scottish people. Chris wants to know if their accent is 'worse' than that of Newcastle, the people of which, to our southern upbringing, spoke an almost foreign language. I decided to lead him on a bit, and described not only a very different accent to our own, but also a slightly fairy-tale picture of the violent history between England and Scotland garnished with a depiction of your average Scotsman, who, I said earnestly, tended to be towering ginger-haired brutes of men that, to this day, harboured a deep grudge against Englishmen with a particular distaste for soft southern Englishmen. This was received in contemplative silence, as we trudged up the hill, but any questioning of my tale would have to wait, for there, beckoning warmly in the dark, was a very pleasant looking little pub. "Let's go in there and have a drink" I declare, and move purposefully across the road. Chris however stays put. "Come on" I enthuse, but he's definitely looking uncomfortable and I suddenly realise that I must have overdone things on the raving Scotsman front. I cross back over and reassure the poor lad that I had been pulling his leg, mention that I can see a pool table through the window, something I know he enjoys, and with that he follows me in, albeit somewhat warily. The first thing I see as I enter is a huge Scotsman leaning on the bar, with a shock of ginger hair and a brutal looking face. Even I am taken aback slightly by this mountain of a man, but for Chris it's simply too much. Before I can even turn to say anything, he's gone, straight back out of the door like a human Exocet, leaving me standing in the doorway feeling rather self conscious. The huge man turns and studies me, as I stand in indecision by the door, and straightening up he lets loose a loud belch before turning his back on me. It's enough, and I quietly exit in pursuit of Chris. I have to walk fast to catch him as he retreats rapidly back down the path and no amount of persuasion will get him to go back up to the town, so we spent the evening in the tent with a slightly strained atmosphere and me feeling rather guilty to have overstepped the mark and genuinely worried the lad.

We're up at seven, and it's raining. A steady, unrelenting downpour, but there's nothing for it, so I struggle into all my clothes, jacket and waterproof trousers and out I go to look for the trouble that had caused us to stop the previous night. As I've already done HT leads and plugs, I reason that the problem must be with the magneto itself, and waste no time pulling off the cap. It's immediately apparent what the problem is now, as the points, which have fallen apart, drop out and disappear into the long grass. I scrabble about trying to find the bits, and discover that the little rivet that holds the contact itself onto the points arm has come off, and the little round contact has been rattling around in the cap. It is also apparent that the remaining assembly is loose and flapping about. I gather up all the bits and retreat back into the tent where Chris is just beginning to come round, and after lighting our little gaslight I set about reviewing the situation. After numerous attempts I eventually manage to affect a repair on the contact by poking the bent rivet top back through it's proper hole in the points arm and peening the edges back over. The result isn't at all convincing, but the thing is back where it should be and I hasten back outside to replace the assembly in its rightful position, reset the points gap and tighten everything back up. So, petrol on, flood the carburettor, and with one hefty kick I am delighted to hear the engine roar into life. I grab my helmet, and telling Chris that I'll be two minutes, I'm off for a test ride around the town. There is no sign of the misfire and I return back to camp with an absurd feeling of triumph and achievement. But reality soon asserts itself as I begin to prepare breakfast – the repair is at best a bit of a desperate bodge and realistically I have to wonder how long is it going to last? If it gives out again, which could be just a few miles into the day, will I be able to fix it again, or will it be broken irretrievably? Do I even fancy being in that position, out in the sticks in what looks to be increasingly appalling weather?

As bacon and eggs sizzle away and I turn my attention to the kettle, Chris finally crawls out from his cocoon, and immediately grills me for details. I answer his questions regarding the cause of Daisy's woes and the fix I have applied - then we discuss what to do. Our schedule, which took a big hit yesterday, is now even more over-optimistic than before, and I explain to Chris that there is no guarantee how long the fix will last. Should we carry on or do we strike for home? "Well", I say, "isn't that why God gave us Carole Nash recovery?" Chris agrees, having lost none of the enthusiasm he displayed when setting up camp the previous evening, so onwards and upwards we declare – bulldog spirit and all that. We break camp and with the time just nudging nine-thirty set off towards Edinburgh. Out on the road, I'm relieved that the miss-fire is definitely gone, at least for the moment, and the journey looks like it will be uneventful, if a trifle miserable, in the constant drizzle. Our next Landmark is due south of Edinburgh and from there we have to go into the city itself for another one before we can cross the Firth of Forth and venture further into Scotland. Chris remarks, as we stop for a breather, that he thought there were supposed to be a lot of mountains in Scotland, but now we're here he's very disappointed. I explain to him that we're only in the relatively low southern region, and that we won't see much in the way of mountains for a while yet. But see them we shall, I promise, and tell him that he should keep an eye to the north as we approach Edinburgh and cross the Firth. "How long will that be?" he wants to know, and there's a clearly suppressed excitement about the lad. I realise that I am also seriously looking forward to my first experience of the Highlands, and there is no denying that I share Chris' eagerness to get there, but before that we have two Landmarks to knock off.

We arrive at the rough spot on my strip-maps, but we have no idea once again what we're looking for. 'Where little Bob set the press rolling' says the clue, but as we scan the area we can see nothing that suggests itself. Up and down we go, nothing. We have passed some small side roads however, and it seems hopeful that one of them will yield up what we need, so we systematically begin to quarter the area in what is becoming a familiar routine. Half an hour later we are still none the wiser, but I'm determined that this time we're not going to lose too much time and decide, once again, to place the call to Ken for some inspiration. Ken is at work apparently, but his charming wife is obviously well used to Landmark calls and very quickly identifies the clue and tells us what it is we're looking for. "It's the Robert Small print works," she informs us. This doesn't help much, as we've seen nothing of the sort as we did the circuits, but at least we now know and can seek some of that 'local' knowledge. We thank our informant, and head to the nearest petrol station to seek enlightenment. "Never heard of it" is the rather disappointing answer we get, and several other locals profess to the same complete ignorance of any such place. Eventually, having now lost nearly an hour yet again, I decide to get a photograph of the village sign just up the road, as proof of us being here, and move on. At least the next one should be fairly easy, I tell Chris, for it's the Royal Yacht Britannia, and that can't be hard to find surely? It wasn't, although the process of threading Daisy through the nightmare traffic of the City leaves me feeling pretty fraught and strained – and we have to get out of the place again yet. Finally, by mid afternoon, we're through Edinburgh, and striking out towards Perth on the M90.

As we approach Perth, the dark shape of the looming Grampian mountains fills the horizon to the north and west, the higher ridges and peaks shrouded in grey foreboding cloud and Chris, his excitement growing, is constantly tapping me on the shoulder to point out particular peaks or features. Perth passes behind us, and we branch onto the A9 and head straight into the mountain range proper. The long climb begins; noticeable particularly as Daisy's exhaust note deepens with the uphill work and it seems that with every metre we rise the weather is getting correspondingly worse. I begin to regret, yet again, my failure to purchase proper heavy-duty bad weather clothing. Both our jackets, being straight forward leather, are soaked through and seem to now weigh several tons. Our gloves and boots have capitulated completely, and the flimsy waterproof trousers we have are simply not up to the unequal battle with the highland weather, with seemingly every seam and join now liberally funnelling water to the most inconvenient of places. As we struggle ever higher, the sky darkens further until I am forced to turn on Daisy's paltry lights and just when I think things can get no worse, the heavens open, Scottish Highlands style and we are battered by some of the heaviest rain I have ever seen to the accompaniment of violent blustery gusts from every direction. There has been a marked drop in temperature too, and we are soon desperate for a campsite, but it seems an eternity before we find the blessed sign that promises respite and follow it. Pulling up at the entrance lodge, we both all but fall from Daisy and I turn to look at Chris, who I am sure must have absolutely had enough of this adventure. Our eyes lock, and I am amazed as an ironic half smile breaks out on his face, as he makes a theatrically exacerbated gesture, flinging his arms wide and surveying his own disastrous appearance whilst uttering a sharp exclamation; "Bloody hell!"

Having booked in, leaving something akin to lake Wichita spreading around us in the little reception, we are directed along a path down to a river bank to what in better weather would have been an ideal site. The rushing river Tay tumbles and roars along not ten feet from the spot we are given and we set about unloading the sodden mass that is supposed to be our tent and belongings. There is nothing more miserable than trying to put up a wet tent in torrential rain and this particular occasion is, without doubt, the most depressing experience of the whole challenge so far, with not just all our gear soaked through, but all our spare clothes too. We huddle in the badly erected tent and try to take stock; the clothes we are in are sodden, all our spare clothes are sodden and our bedding is equally unusable. What we need right now then, is a mug of tea, but this just leads to another depressing discovery – "Where's the bed roll?" I ask Chris. "What? – I dunno" comes the answer. I look around, and then crawl outside into the downpour to look for it, but the roll, which contains our gas cylinders, is nowhere to be found.

"Just bloody marvellous" is all I can think to say. So, with no tea or food that can be cooked (the little shop on site closed just as we had arrived) we decide to venture out to the local town in search of a warm dry place to eat. The local pub is three miles away but provides us with a steaming hot steak & kidney pud which restores us somewhat, and whilst we eat we hatch a plan to get a lot of change and spend the rest of the evening in the launderette trying to get warm and dry whilst in theory watching our clothes and bedding spin round and round in the big dryers. At least this idea works out exactly as planned, and we hog all three dryers feeding bedding into one, all our clothes into another and jackets and boots into the third. We then change out of our damp set and shove them in for a session, but sitting there feeding coins into the machines, I reflect that I have never felt lower in my life. Neither of us says very much, but we share the opinion that neither of us wants another day like today and one thing we both agree on is that if the weather hasn't improved by morning, we will stay put and stay dry.

I wake at six thirty, to find that the river has swollen overnight and is now generating a quite unbelievable roar as it tumbles and crashes over the rocks close by. But it's immediately apparent that the weather is much improved and I poke my head out to see broken cloud scudding across the sky in the fresh cool breeze. The site shop won't open for another hour and a half yet, and I decide that we should forego breakfast and get an early start in an effort to make up for lost time. After several attempts I manage to rouse Chris only to be rewarded with a very grumpy teenager as a result, but the mention of a day's riding in the mountains soon has him up and about. We break camp amidst the glorious panorama of dark peaks shrouded with raggedy clouds, and in short order we have packed up and are off towards the peaks for what we both hope will be a fantastic day's riding up to Elgin on the Moray Firth, east of Inverness. As we resume the long climb, Daisy toiling beneath us, it's not long before an urgent tapping from Chris draws my attention to our first sighting of a snowcap in the distance. "This is what we're here for" I shout, and suddenly I am absolutely delighted that we had pressed on after all, as the stunning landscape spreads around and below us. We simply have to stop numerous times in order to marvel at the stark, dark beauty, which to us soft southerners is a completely new and wonderful experience. On one occasion, parked at the top of yet another steep rise, we are utterly captivated by the sight of a large cotton wool cloud scudding along below us, and eventually breaking across the road and spreading it's way upwards towards us like a special effect in a Hammer Horror film. I move next to Chris as he watches this display in awe "You wanted wild National Park Chris? – Well you've got it mate!" Daisy takes the morning's hard work in her stride, although at numerous times I have to drop down a gear and settle for a slow, laboured ascent up yet another long, long incline. At the top of these, I invariably stop to allow the old girl to cool down, but with so much to take in this seems to be a bonus rather than a chore. By mid morning, we have left the Grampian range behind and find ourselves threading our way between the Cairngorms on our right and the Monadhliath range to our left, so that no matter what direction we look there are distant peaks shrouded in cloud, set in a glorious panorama of raw heath. Bright yellow gorse bushes compete with the purple heathers to make for a colourful vista all around, and the air has a crisp clear quality that is never to be found in our normal daily lives. I suddenly realise that Chris, who has been asthmatic since he was two, has not produced his inhaler at all in the last two days – a situation I haven't seen for many, many months.

Eventually, Daisy can take things easy, as we finally broach the highest points of the snaking road and begin the long descent towards Inverness. The landscape becomes gentler as the white peaks are left behind us, but I wonder that Chris won't have a permanently cricked neck as he keeps a constant awestruck gaze over his shoulder. The morning's ride has made everything suddenly worthwhile, but we were about to enjoy an even better highlight of the day. Leaving the A9 at the point at which it turns northwest towards Inverness, we join the A95 northeast towards Elgin and our next Landmark. We find ourselves in a much gentler environment of pleasant rolling green hills and one of those lazy twisty roads that we all dream about. Coming over the crest of a hill, and down into the sweeping bend the other side we see a railway line coming across from the east which turns to run parallel alongside the road about a mile away. There is an old steam train chuffing across the low valley and as we get closer to the point that road and rail meet, heading the same way, we end up side by side with the engine thundering along at a good lick. I am almost immediately overwhelmed with the sheer sense of nostalgia and let out a childish whoop as we hurtle side by side up the straight. I'm not alone in my delight either, as the old buffer driving the thing (a strange profusion of whiskers, overalls and oily rags) starts hanging off his foot plate and waving at us madly in between various gestures of appreciation for this old motor bicycle that has suddenly joined him from nowhere. We grin and nod back and suddenly he's giving me the 'throttle' signal – he wants a burn up! Unfortunately before we could find a winner of such an unlikely race, the railway line peeled off to the east once more and the train and its occupant were gone as quickly as they had appeared. It was a strangely exhilarating moment though, and made for the icing on the cake in what had already been a stunningly good day.

The next Landmark, bizarrely, was a petrol station. The clue had urged us to 'fill up under the sign of the Jolly Roger' or something like that, and all became clear as we reached the Buccaneer service station just outside Elgin. Taking a rest here, we share some food and tea from the little shop, and congratulate ourselves on our progress so far today. We have covered only seventy or so miles, but much of that has been hard terrain for Daisy and it is only lunchtime anyway we agree. The remainder of the day looks positively easy by comparison; west towards Inverness for forty odd miles, north once more, taking us over the Moray Firth and along the raggedy coast line for another thirty or so, where we hope to find the Shin Falls, our final Landmark of the day. From there we plan to come back down to Inverness and begin our southward leg at Loch Ness, camping at the first place we find. Easy, we both agree, and before long we're off once more. Over the Firth of Inverness we go, and onto a delightful coastal road. Daisy is still running fine, and I have a fleeting thought that the repair, affected so long ago at Coldstream, is obviously holding. These thoughts are interrupted as we are treated to yet another sight that neither of us has ever seen before - the stark, imposing silhouettes of a number of giant North Sea Oil platforms, 'parked' in an estuary. The sight captivates us because that close the things really look pretty impressive. That surprise gives way to another delight, in the shape of a long, low, arched bridge stretching across the estuary, and I begin to wonder as we burble across, just how many surprises and pleasures one can have in a day?

Eventually cutting inland once more, we follow a superb road up to Shin Falls, where we stop for a very late lunch. This place is apparently famous for it's spectacular salmon run, and we follow the signs to a wooden walkway that winds down to the face of the steep rapids where the fish power their way up to their spawning grounds upstream. Standing feet away from the roaring torrent, it seems unbelievable that anything could swim against it, but we fail to see any salmon leaping the falls. We stay for ten minutes or so before heading back to Daisy, but half way up Chris has a shock when a wizened old Scottish lady, looking tougher than my leather boots and possessing a sharp piercing voice, grabs his arm in a vice like grip, fixes him with an intense stare from gimlet eyes and demands "Jeearseeum?" He stutters and tries to back away whilst giving me a desperate glance beseeching me to help him out of this sudden, startling confrontation, but his captor is not to be ignored.

"Th' *fush*!" she elaborates "Jeearseeum?"

For a second, Chris looks like he may dive in blind panic over the walkway safety rail, but the tough old harridan has him in a grip of steel, and before the situation gets out of hand I step forward to help him out of this hilarious situation.

"Fish, Chris – the lady is asking 'did you see them'!" Seeing a sudden way out, he responds to her saying "Oh! No….no, we didn't see any fish" and with that she snorts at him but mercifully releases her hold to hurry on down the path. I am trying not to burst out laughing as Chris shakes his head, tries to straighten his jacket, whilst his cheeks flush a deep red. He sets off up the path at a vigorous and exaggerated gait, and I follow at a more sedate pace, chuckling. At the top, Chris is slouched by Daisy staring intensely at his boots in a deep scowl, but on seeing my face, still barely controlling a smirk, he stomps off exclaiming "Shut up Dad! Just go away!"

I decide it's best to let him cool off, and tell him I'm going to find the gents. I am not prepared for the next surprise in this day of the things, but here it was. I went into the gents in a hazy sunshine, to come out less than five minutes later to an absolute downpour. The sky had suddenly turned dark, almost from nowhere, and we were back to the awful weather of yesterday. "Bugger", is my immediate thought. I had been looking forward to the late afternoon ride back down to Inverness, and on to Loch Ness but with the weather deteriorating so suddenly, with a rapidity that's truly startling, I am deeply depressed at the thought of another miserable soaking like yesterday evening. Chris is sheltering by the shop doorway, and I run through the maelstrom to join him.

"Where did this lot come from?" I ask.

"It just came – and I'm not going out in it!" is the reply. I tend to agree, and so we wander into the dining area for another pot of coffee in the hope that things will settle. Half an hour later the rain has eased to a steady drizzle but it's clear that this is it for the day and so we reluctantly come to the decision to press on back down to Inverness and stop at the first campsite we can find. Neither of us is impressed with the idea after the experience of the previous evening but things couldn't be as bad as that could they? We set off shortly after, heading south for the first time in four days, hoping to get a reasonable distance and find a haven before getting too wet. We were about to discover Lady luck had other ideas.

Rural roadworks can be a pain, but this lot seemed to be more painful than any I had ever encountered. We are on a high, twisty road heading back to the east coast above Inverness, and have been hopping between a series of stretches that have been dug up for a hundred yards or so each. This is the third set of red lights in ten minutes, and I vaguely consider that we must have been lucky earlier, coming the other way to have hit green lights all the way. We wait, I have my chin tucked down to keep the drizzle out, and as I stare vacantly at the rear lights of the car just in front of us there is a 'thunk' noise and Daisy, without warning, lurches forward into the back of the thing. Caught utterly unprepared for this, I lose balance and feel Daisy falling, made worse by Chris on the back struggling to regain his own composure. Over we go, in slow motion, to end up in a straggly heap behind the car. The owner is out in a flash, exclaiming something that I can't quite decipher, but rather than demand what the hell we think we're playing at he helps me bring Daisy upright again. Chris has scrambled over too, having been ejected sideways. "What the hell happened" he demands, but the cause of the mishap is obvious from the floppy lever on Daisy's left handlebar – the clutch cable has snapped! I quickly point this out to the car driver, in an effort to show that I am not an inconsiderate maniac, and he seems to understand that this was an unavoidable incident. We both inspect his car, but there is no damage either to it or to Daisy, and after agreeing that there is nothing we need by way of help, he's on his way. Chris looks despondent, but I cheerily assure him that far from being a problem, this is in fact cause to celebrate clever forward thinking. There is a spare clutch cable taped to the broken one! Fitting it only took a few minutes, and we're soon ready to go once more, but as we pull away Chris leans over my shoulder and gives me a slight chill with the comment "What do we do if *this* one breaks as well?" Good question.

By the time we get back to Inverness, and find the top of the long road that runs the length of Loch Ness, the rain has become persistently heavier and we're soaked through again. We struggle on as far as Drumnadrochit, with no sign of a campsite, but in truth I have already decided that camping in torrential rain a second night is not an option. Having said that, I am not at all clear what we will do instead but I pull Daisy up to the curb in order to try and take stock of our situation. It's grim that much is clear as yet again I curse the very inadequate provisions I had made for bad weather. We climb off stiffly onto the front forecourt of some kind of Loch Ness Monster visitor centre, and survey the rain swept street looking for inspiration, but there is nothing to see in the gathering gloom other than the little pockets of light under each lamppost where a dim shiny glow highlights the myriad of constant pock-marks created by the relentless raindrops. My spirits droop further, and I suddenly feel really sorry for Chris, who has sauntered off into the doorway of the building to seek shelter. To him, this is meant to be a great adventure, something that he's looked forward to over the previous weeks and days and although we've certainly had some fine experiences, he has had to pay a pretty steep price in terms of endurance, and it's not been quite the idyllic escape that we had planned. I reflect that all in all he's handled it pretty well and I resolve to try and make the best of things, starting with the need to try and lift our spirits. I join him in the doorway and with a confidence that I don't really believe myself I say, "Right, bugger this. We're going to find a hotel. We'll get a room with a bathroom, and it must have a warm bar, and we'll sit in there and get a bloody great feed, and then we'll sleep in warm comfortable beds! – What do you reckon?" He looks at me, and I nearly laugh out loud as I watch a little river of water running down his nose, dripping off the end.

"Where?" he says morosely "There aren't any here."

We had to get lucky. We deserved it, and we couldn't get luckier than finding 'Fiddler's Bar'. As we stood in that miserable doorway, I had caught a snatch of laughter from round the corner and immediately set out to investigate. And there, like an oasis of dryness in a cold, wet desert, was possibly the most welcoming sight I have ever seen. It was an Irish bar. More to the point It was a warm dry Irish bar. Even more importantly it said B&B on a little sign, and it said 'vacancies' underneath. I urgently call to Chris, pointing out this stunning find and suggest that without wasting any more time we push Daisy round there and book ourselves in pronto. They have one room left, but it's a twin with en-suite facilities says the man. I assure him that I don't care if it's the proverbial stable out the back, because right now anything that isn't a tent, isn't wet, isn't cold and, most important of all, posses a bar and serves food is simply bloody wonderful. It turns out to be even better than that: the place even has a lock-up garage for Daisy, just across the road. We unpack everything and ferry it all into the little room at the back of the bar, and before long the place looks like a back street in Chinatown with clothes draped from or over every possible surface. Chris takes the first use of the shower while I go down to put Daisy to bed and then once I've freshened up as well we head down to the little bar enthusiastically, with Chris burbling that I had promised him a big feed, and he intended to abuse the offer mightily. We had the full works of starter, main course, dessert, washed down with Guinness for me and bitter-shandy for Chris. Compared to the last few days and against the backdrop of rain drumming on the windows, this, we agree, is absolute heaven. Although tired from the day's exertions, we are in no hurry to turn in, being quite happy just relaxing there chatting away about the day's events, the highlights, the low points and I realise that I haven't sat and just talked to Chris like this for a long time. It felt great to do so and I was happy to stay there as long as he did, or until the bar closed. Eventually it did, and we spend the last fifteen minutes before turning in just standing on the fire-escape to our room sampling the crisp clear air and chuckling over the funnier parts of the day, like the frightening woman that had captured Chris at Shin Falls. I went to bed feeling strangely contented.

The sight outside our window was well worth waking up for. We had arrived in darkness the previous evening in a shroud of mist and rain, which had entirely concealed the dramatic skyline around Drumnadrochit. But this morning it was there to see in all it's splendour. The rain had given way once more to broken cloud, threatening in parts but with plenty of bright, clear patches and it looked fine for the morning run down the length of Loch Ness and Loch Oich to Fort William. Breakfast is traditional Irish fare and after that we collect all our gear, which, after hanging all round our room for the night has dried quite well. The jackets are still fairly damp, but hopefully the morning ride will see to that. I push Daisy from her shelter and remark to Chris that she is looking strangely clean. This Scottish rain must be better than our stuff because after a day's wet riding she normally looks like she came last in ploughing competition on account of getting stuck in the mud. Chris pipes up with a query – hadn't I noticed yesterday how *soft* the rain was in Scotland? He was right now I came to think about it. We're soon underway and heading down the long and pleasant road that runs alongside Loch Ness, we stop briefly at the famous Urquhart Castle, with it's eerie tower that features in so many photographs of this most mysterious of Scotland's Lochs, and it looks in the flesh exactly as I recall – dark, lonely and foreboding. The weather's holding up for the main part with only occasional drizzle, but it's infinitely more bearable than yesterday as we eventually leave the home of Nessie behind and head on down to Loch Oich, our next Landmark and another piece of gruesome history.

This is the well of seven heads, and history tells us that in the proper tradition of brutal treachery and murderous intent that passed for political correctness in the 1600s, two brothers of the MacDonald clan, daring to lay claim to the Chieftainship of Keppoch, were stabbed to death by some seven of their own clansmen, whom, we must presume, had other ideas about who should be running the show. This little coup went unchallenged for a couple of years, but then for some reason it was declared to have been not quite cricket by the Privy Council in Edinburgh, who issued a 'Fire and Sword' death warrant against the perpetrators. Unfortunately for the seven they found themselves amongst the kind of people that weren't about to pass up the chance to exact a legally swift and brutal revenge, and they were promptly hunted down and executed via that well tested method of lopping off their heads. Of course, it was considered only right and proper to display the macabre exhibits afterwards, but being a bit messy the story goes that the heads were washed in this well before taking up their new role as decoration in nearby Invergarry castle. Eventually they were moved to make a fine display on Gallows Hill in Edinburgh, presumably because someone thought the place needed brightening up. A Gruesome story, and it's amusing to see the look of horror on Chris's face as I read off the details from the little plaque by the well. For all that, it's a strangely peaceful place and we decide to knock up a quick brew before continuing our way south once more.

Our next Landmark on this tour will see us back in England once more, but the afternoon's ride to get there will take in yet more famous, or at least well known places that are probably familiar to most people. Fort William, Glen Coe, Loch Lomond and Glasgow are all on route and I can't wait to get at it. I show Chris the map, and decide to build up the anticipation and give him something to look forward to; "You know what's at Fort William?" I ask him. "Dunno ... a fort?" is his less than inspired answer. "More mountains" says I, "bigger than any you've seen yet" I add. This gets his attention, as I knew it would judging by his enthusiastic recounting of our elevated experiences in the Grampians and Cairngorms, over dinner last night.

"Do you know what the highest mountain in Britain is?" he doesn't, so I point it out on our map, or at least I point out the place it should be on our map, if the thing was any use and had any detail worth mentioning. "Ben Nevis" I declare "and not only are we going to see it today, but in fact we have to go round it". Suddenly Chris seems in a hurry to get back on the road heading for what surely must be the best experience we'll have on this adventure. I was to be wrong about that, it would turn out, but at the moment I was every bit as eager as Chris and so we set off with renewed vigour and a heightened sense of anticipation. Unlike yesterday, the skies are much clearer and we see the Nevis range on the horizon long before we get amongst them. It seems that we are riding towards them forever, making no progress as they grow in our vision only millimetre by tiny millimetre. But it soon becomes apparent that this is merely because they are impressively large (maybe not by the standards of the Alps or Himalayas, sure, but to us they are magnificent) The last five miles into Fort William has us utterly captivated by the natural beauty of the range, off to our left, and we are thankful for our luck that in clear skies the snowy peaks make a display of grandeur that's both awesome and breathtaking. I find that I've slowed Daisy to an almost pedestrian speed as we pick our way past these silent giants, because this is not an experience to be rushed. Fantastic.

We stop at Fort William for fuel and a cup of coffee, before reluctantly taking a last look back and putting it all behind us. I felt a sadness to be leaving, and sensed the same in Chris, both of us knowing that we may never be back, but as we head south once more the feeling is soon lost in the contrasting splendour of the ride through Glen Coe and across Rannoch Moor. In a very different way, it is still nothing short of breathtaking with its fantastic views, wonderful roads and it's just an all round uplifting experience. In the middle of nowhere, we find a Scotsman in his traditional national finery, playing bagpipes in a lay-by overlooking a deep valley. It's a charming sight and although the guy is obviously a tourist attraction, we declare him a Landmark anyway, asking him to sit on Daisy for a photo and he seems pleased to oblige before we're off again on the long run down to Loch Lomond. And what an experience this is too. The loch seems to be impossibly large, and the road hugs the western shore all the way down, passing through deep wooded sections on the way. There are little lay-bys right on the waters edge every so often, and pulling into one of these I am amazed to discover that after eleven miles riding along the shoreline we are still only half way along it's length. It's incredibly peaceful, and I suddenly realise that all thoughts of our original schedule have gone during the morning. It simply doesn't seem to matter any more, even though I have arrangements back at home that I should keep. With Chris on holiday from school, I find myself thinking so what if we're two days late? I can always rearrange things rather than rush this experience, and certainly the thought of returning to any kind of routine after the freedom of the open road seems a poor reward to be hurrying towards. I determine there and then to take things easier where the surroundings demand it, and stuff the schedule. This decision lifts my spirits even further as we mount up and set off once again towards Glasgow, after all, this is what it's all about, what I set out to achieve when I changed gear in life – freedom and spontaneity.

Approaching Glasgow, we are dealt another flash surprise that seems to sum up the Scottish weather. From almost nowhere, a dark foreboding sky closes in with a rapidity that's startling and as we enter the city the heavens open once more. This time, with my new relaxed approach to time, we pull over quickly and dive for shelter in a bus stop. If I thought the rain was heavy as we dived for shelter, then what follows is nothing short of biblical. The noise from the rain drumming on the shelter roof is so loud that conversation is rendered all but impossible and we simply stand and watch the incredible sight of a two foot deep fog of spray created by the huge raindrops hammering into the ground. It looks surreal, an impression that is strengthened as something akin to a river rises before our very eyes and flows past us, engulfing two thirds of the road and lapping up over the curb to submerge the pavement right in front of our feet. Traffic slows to a virtual standstill as we watch and unbelievably the thundering on the roof increases yet again, beyond anything imaginable. By now, the bottom four inches or so of Daisy's wheels are engulfed by the torrent of water flowing past us, and I realize that once again the tent and all our clothes will be hopelessly wet. I wonder idly whether Daisy will actually start again after such a dowsing, but there is absolutely nothing to be done right now but watch, which is what we do for nearly half an hour when, almost as suddenly as it had arrived the downpour slowed and promptly stops as if someone had turned off a tap. I suddenly realised how dark the day had become as the sun breaks through again and illuminates a spectacular rainbow that reaches right across the sky. The clouds disappear almost magically, and we watch as the torrent flowing past us slowly recedes to leave a curiously fresh smell in the air and the inevitable sound of dripping water all around us. "Bloody hell that was really bad," exclaims Chris and that just about sums it up I reckon.

"Well, it's gone" I reply, as I head purposefully out of the shelter "and after that little lot, we'd better see if she'll start!"

Old British motorcycles are not known for their waterproof electrical systems and it seems impossible that the magneto on Daisy can possibly function after such a drenching. I position the kick-start and take a big heave knowing with almost total certainty that nothing is going to happen. In fact, so convinced am I that the deluge will have got into everything, and so certain am I about the futility of the gesture, that the deep bark that meets my effort startles me and makes me jump. Amazed, I give her a couple of blips and as she responds crisply I grin at Chris and make my feelings known "Wahey!" I enthuse "Way to go Daisy!" I add, as Chris views me with a fishy eye and shakes his head, but I don't care, and leaving her ticking over, steam broiling off her exhausts and cylinders, I retrieve my helmet and gloves and chivvy Chris along. "C'mon, let's make a dash before the next lot gets us!" This at least he seems to understand, and within minutes we are off once more marvelling at the fact that other than the shiny roads, all signs of the dreadful weather have completely gone, with even the rainbow disappearing almost as quickly as it had popped into existence. As we follow the main ring road through the City, I am taken with the feeling of space and openness of the place, which doesn't fit with the mental image I had developed for some reason, and the earthy smell produced by the rain makes the experience rather pleasant.

As we leave the more industrialised southern limits I have to make a choice of routes into Lanarkshire, where our second Landmark of the day, which I believe to be a beam engine, is waiting. The M74 is the most direct route, taking us to straight down to within a few miles, whereas the A73 meanders off to the east before turning back to cross the motorway at the same point that we would turn off to reach our next stop. Having already come to the liberating conclusion that the touring experience was more important than any schedule, we take the 'A' road and settle down to a sedate progress through the green expanse of the Southern Uplands, with not a care in the world. But pretty soon I am discovering that this wasn't quite such a good idea as we struggle with the results of the recent cloudburst. Some sections of the road, where natural dips occur, are still underwater and even the clear sections often have a slick covering of mud that is running from the hedgerows and banks. Progress slows to a virtual crawl in places, and I find that it's mentally hard work keeping Daisy's upright and her wheels firmly in line as we negotiate treacherous stretch after treacherous stretch. On more than one occasion we have a heart stopping moment as the rear wheel twitches away from us and it takes an inordinately long time to reach the motorway junction that signifies that we are only ten miles or so from our next target. To our north another dark band of weather is building, and it's hard to decide which direction it's heading. We keep a constant eye on it, having no intention of being caught out in the open in another flash flood, but it seems to be moving east to west in a direct parallel to our own course.

A steady climb takes us to the little cluster of cottages that is Wanlockhead which, at fifteen hundred odd feet above sea level has the distinction of being

Scotland's highest village. This was a centre for lead and gold mining back as far as Roman times and finally came to a stop sometime in the nineteen fifties, but the history is preserved for posterity in the form of a delightful living museum encompassing the majority of the village, allowing visitors to walk the entire place and finish up marvelling at the well preserved beam-engine dating back to the eighteenth century. It's an enlightening experience, capped off by the wide vista of rolling hills all around and a crisp fresh quality to the air that takes some beating. So peaceful is the place that Chris and I spend over an hour wandering around, absorbing the strange contrast of this little oasis of industrial concentration with nothing around it for miles. Eventually we make our way back to Daisy, and look at our maps to work out what comes next, and my spirits are buoyed even further as I explain to Chris that we are now heading for Cumbria and the lake district, which is not only one of my all time favourite areas for sheer natural beauty, but also contains some of that National Park he's been so looking forward to. We take stock of our progress so far today, and it's a surprise to find out that we have already covered some two hundred plus miles since leaving Fiddler's bar this morning. Our next Landmark is hidden amidst the Coniston hills, and we're not sure what it actually is yet, but we will have to ride nearly a hundred miles to get there. As it's already gone five o'clock, and after agreeing that we shall shun the motorway, in preference for the meandering 'A' roads, it seems unlikely that we'll reach it today but so great is the anticipation we both feel, that we agree to make the effort and ride until the light goes somewhere around nine.

We are able to pick up a meandering road that winds its way south from our current location all the way to Dumfries. With the late afternoon sun illuminating the patchwork of fields that span either side of us it makes for a wonderful ride and Daisy revels in the relaxed canter, her exhaust note bouncing from the stone walls that enclose the roads. We slowly descend from the heights of Wanlockhead into the lower lands that run to the coast of the Irish Sea, and in what seems like no time at all Dumfries falls behind and we turn slightly east to round the inlet that dissects the land between Scotland to the north and England to the south. Next stop Carlisle and a much needed petrol stop and we find a pleasant little café where we decide to get a meal before our final leg of the day into the Lake District proper amidst the wilds of Cumbria. As Chris finishes his meal, I take the chance to do some quick checking of nuts and bolts and finding nothing particularly amiss, top up Daisy's oil tank, noting that she has consumed half of what I had fed her the previous day. This is nothing particularly unusual and certainly nothing to fret over, other than the cost of the stuff, but I can't find the preferred 20W50 multigrade in the station's shop, and have to settle for a thinner 15W40 instead. As I pour the fresh stuff in, I catch myself hoping that Daisy doesn't take it as an invitation to leak it out of any weak joints. Chris emerges just as I'm doing up the cap, ready for the off once more it seems but then I think about what's ahead and signal to Chris that we should go back into the shop. "We need to get something for supper, and stuff for breakfast, so we'll get it here in case we arrive at camping too late," I tell him. That done, it's back out on the road and underway once more, straight into the sun which is slowly sinking ahead of us.

It's just past seven when I notice the looming peaks of the Coniston hills for the first time, away to our front and left. We had studied the map back at Carlisle and decided that the best way to our next Landmark would be to take the A595 south west, skirting the northern edge of the Lake District National Park, before turning west and then south at Cockermouth and enjoying the marvellous unfenced roads that will lead us to our spot in the hills. Chris is ahead of me, tapping urgently on my shoulder to point ahead and shouts something about mountains over my shoulder. I give him a thumbs-up and just after that we bump across the cattle-grid that denotes entry into the park. Almost immediately the banks either side of the road close in, and although this serves to narrow the road the absence of any fencing gives us the opposite feeling, one of open expanse. We slow to a sedate crawl, threading our way into the wild beauty of the low hills and almost immediately have to stop just to take in the surroundings. We have to wheel Daisy onto the lush springy turf in order to allow any other vehicles that should happen along to pass, and after ditching helmets, gloves and jackets we simply wander a little way up the nearest slope and enjoy the fantastic view. It occurs to me that this is, for us, the ingredient that was missing in Scotland. This closeness to the surroundings offers the ability to simply stop, walk twenty steps and be right in it. Most of our experience of Scotland had meant that whilst the raw natural landscape was grander and far more spectacular, we were mainly on bigger roads, with very few smaller ones obviously available to ride and on the occasions we had been able to stop like this, inevitably a wall or fence prevented us from truly feeling a part of it all. What the Lake District lacks in the scale of its splendour, it seems to make up for in sheer availability. It's the difference between say *admiring* a favourite motorcycle from afar, or actually *riding* the thing for real – both give satisfaction but they're not the same thing at all.

We waste a whole twenty minutes at this spot, sitting at the top of a rocky, turf-studded outcrop, watching a stream tumbling past just below us. Some sheep eye us vacantly from under a nearby tree, deciding evidently that we aren't edible, and therefore not worth further attention, so they wander off higher into the hills. I could sit here all evening I reckon, as the sun sinks low behind us, casting long tall shadows across the area, but we need to find a place to camp before it gets too dark. And this is the reason for my earlier eager anticipation, because I've got a surprise for Chris that I have kept quiet about. The fact is that we will be doing proper camping tonight, out on our own in the wild. There are no campsites in the national park area, but instead of skirting round it until we get to the south side, camping at a proper site and then in the morning cutting into the park to find our photograph, I intend to enter the area from the north and simply get lost right up in the heart of the place. We'll find a spot such as this one, preferably complete with a stream tumbling past, and just set up right there. It will probably be the only time we can do it like this on the whole challenge and quite possibly the only time I'll do it in my life. And having dismissed the schedule as not important any more, I do not intend to miss the chance to really do things properly. I study the strip map, and realise that we're in trouble if we expect to be able to use it to any great effect in this area. Most of the tiny roads are simply not shown at all and in particular our Landmark is shown as occupying a large white square with no roads any where near. But I'm not worried about it; I had identified this one at home, and I know that it is on little more than a track known as the Hardknott Pass, but it can't be that hard to find surely?

I show Chris the map, and suddenly want to unveil my little secret; "This it where it gets interesting" I tell him, "we can carry on down using the big roads, and there will be campsites down here" I point at the area. "But we've done enough of all that, and as the weather's marvellous and we've got food, I thought we might head straight into the national park, where we'll almost certainly get lost and just camp in the wild when the light starts to go!". His face registers a conflict; He's clearly excited at what I've just suggested, but his natural instincts are telling him that there's something wrong with the idea and he voices the obvious concern, which had also been bothering me slightly.

"We can't Dad, it's not allowed and we'll get told off," he declares. I wonder if, like me, he's remembering that dreadful woman who raided our picnic all those years ago, but I'm ready for this and I've made up my mind.

"Well, we spend all our lives being told what we can or can't do. If it's fun, you can't do it these days, but just for once we've got the chance, and we're going to do it anyway" I surprise myself as I say these things, but it's true - just for once I really am going to do what I want to do, no matter what. Chris is looking far from convinced however, and I almost regret bringing him up to be so observant of the laws of the land and society that we live in.

"Look" I say, tapping the map, "This area really is the wilds. There are loads of tiny roads criss-crossing the whole place and by the time we get down here" I show him the area just north of our target, "There will be no-one around to bother us. And we'll make sure that we are very careful to make no mess or leave any sign that we've been there – nobody can complain about that!" I can see that he's still unsure, but his underlying eagerness to actually do what I am suggesting wins the internal struggle, and with a shrug he quietly reaches for helmet and gloves and looks at me with an expression that says "Come on then". I fire Daisy up, and discarding the maps I fumble in my pocket for the little compass, which I slide into the see-through panel on the tank bag. This will be our only real means of heading in the right direction but I realise that right here, right now, it simply doesn't matter. I don't actually care where we end up tonight and with that, I select first gear and slowly bounce off the springy grass, turn left into the National Park and set out with a feeling of complete contentment. Progress is promptly halted round the very first bend however as we enter a stretch with high stone walls either side of the narrow tarmac - and a large horned obstruction standing in the middle of the road between them. We stop, for there is no way round the thing, and I have a fleeting panic that this may be the male variety, which might also take exception to us disturbing whatever deep bovine contemplation it has been occupied with. It's jaws, which had been lazily working, stop the side-to-side motion as it's ears cock forward and a keen, piercing stare is directed at us. I note the bulging udder with relief, but although the cow decides that we are not very interesting and returns to it's industrious chewing, it shows no sign of moving. We sit and stare at the beast; it continues to idly watch us. I wave my arms and toot Daisy's feeble horn causing the chewing to stop momentarily, but my failure to follow up with something more worthy of reaction soon sees the slow grinding return and a complete lack of any other movement. We appear to have a standoff, but the cow has the advantage that it has nothing else to do and nowhere it wants to go.

"What do we do?" asks Chris after several minutes.

"Bloody good question" I reply, "and one to which I have no ready answer! - I'll have to get off and try to get it moving I suppose" but as we put Daisy on the stand I am anything but confident because after all, what exactly does one need to do to get a cow to do anything at all, let alone move, if it doesn't want to. I approach the thing cautiously, speaking as I go and hoping that it will get the hint and back away. It doesn't move, but the jaws stop again and I am subjected to the keen stare once more. "Shoo" I suggest, flapping my arms and stamping my feet from only five feet away. The cow stares but moves not one inch. "Bang!" I try. "C'mon SHOO!" I add, jumping around like a mad thing but reluctant to go any closer. The cow continues to stare, whilst continuing to move not at all. I realise that I'm getting nowhere and I'm completely out of ideas. I return to Daisy and Chris, shrugging my shoulders and feeling helpless, but before either of us can speak the cow decides that it's had quite enough entertainment from this gibbering human doing the rain-dance and with a disdainful glance at us it saunters idly past and ambles slowly round the corner, pausing to deposit a steaming pile as it goes. Charming, but at least the road is clear once more and with Chris sniggering that the cow has made me look stupid, we mount up and get underway once more.

Half an hour later, I am standing at the top of a sharp rise surveying the immediate area to the side of a road that can only barely make the claim, being little more than a raggedy edged tarmac strip snaking higgledy-piggledy amidst the rolling landscape. To our left the ground rises sharply, the lower levels of much higher hills and a tumbledown array of loose boulders interspersed with the spongy, springy grass that populates every flat surface. Through the middle of this, and running off down the slope to our right, is a delightful stream, splashing and tumbling it's way from the higher peaks to the low valley that we have just ridden through. There are a few sheep standing higher up the hill, inspecting us intently as their jaws work busily from side-to-side and I can see the little road stretching away below us, looking like a carelessly thrown bootlace on a manicured lawn. We are on a wide flat ledge half way up the rolling landscape, and it seems the perfect spot to make our camp because we are able to get round to the other side of the jutting promontory formed by a large boulder, and effectively be out of view from the road. The view is simply stunning and I can think of no better place to spend the night. Chris has already climbed up to where the stream breaks over the outcrop of rock to tumble in a little waterfall down its face, and I've never seen him look happier. Simply put, it's absolutely fantastic.

As I sit some while later, watching our little stoves hissing away in the last of what has turned into a glorious sunset, I know that this evening will remain etched in my memory for ever. It's one of those things that you just know you will never, ever forget and I feel privileged to be here. We have no real idea where we are, and it matters not. All thoughts of a schedule or even the next day's ride are somehow irrelevant at this moment. Supper is nearly ready, tinned Irish stew that we had grabbed at the shop, we have two cans of Newcastle Brown Ale for afterwards, and a full compliment of breakfast ingredients. We have nothing to do this evening but watch the sunset, eat, drink and then just talk and so it goes. The darkness, when it comes, is absolute but glancing upwards we are thrilled to see the amazing panorama of the Milky Way, clearer and crisper than we have ever seen before. The general pollution down south means that we never see such a sky so we get our sleeping bags out and just lie out there in the open air, inevitably ending up telling ghost stories until, much later a deep rhythmic breathing suggests that Chris has fallen asleep.

I continue to lie there staring up at a billion pin-pricks in the sky, but as the bright point of a satellite passes across the starry vista, I'm reminded that even out here in the wilds we can't escape modern civilisation completely. The next thing I know I am waking with a start to see the first hint of a fiery dawn to the east - the beginnings of the new day. I sit up and realise that during the night a heavy dew has permeated the sleeping bag. It's soaked through and now that I have moved and disturbed it the water collects in the creases and sends icy trickles running inside in a most uncomfortable way. I try to ignore it and lie down again, but the damage is done and I can't get comfortable. I get up, find the kettle and stumble off in the chill air to fill it with some of the water at the stream, which I am guessing and hoping should be fairly pure. I decide to make sure it's well and truly boiled, just in case, and once it's on the stove I begin to sort out the stash of breakfast food we had bought at the shop in Carlisle. With that lot on the go, I wake Chris so that we can hang the sleeping bags over the rocks and hopefully get them at least partially dry in the early sun, the top of which is just making it's first tentative appearance on the horizon.

It's hard to describe in mere words what unfolds before us as we wait to eat. The low ground falling away beneath us is shrouded in a layer of early white mist, but it's one of those surreal bands that hangs about four feet above the ground and is only a few feet thick. The air is clear underneath and on top - Chris points out a tree, a few hundred yards away, with just it's trunk and it's uppermost branches in clear view and it's middle shrouded in white. This mystical ribbon is lit up by the low sun which itself is set in a fluorescent pink sky. A few thin clouds move slowly across in the distance, their edges fiercely silhouetted in fire, and all around us we are aware of the absolute calm stillness which is that most magical point at the end of the dark night - the breaking of dawn. Neither of us says much, for there is nothing to say at such a moment and then it's gone, the spell is broken and the new day has arrived. Then we notice that the odd quiet cheep or chirp that had been discernable for the last ten minutes has become a constant and loud twitter all round us as various birds awake once more.

Breakfast is ready, and is soon devoured hungrily, followed by a mug of coffee, and soon after we break camp and prepare for the days ride. Before setting off, we scour the area to ensure that no sign of our stay is left behind us as I explain to Chris that it simply wouldn't do to leave a wrapper or even a teabag behind to spoil the next visitor's enjoyment of the natural splendour of this little spot in the Cumbrian fells. Finding nothing, Daisy is fired up and allowed to warm and then we're off on that little strip of raggedy tarmac looking for the Hardknott Pass further south.

Twenty minutes later I'm thinking that this must be the challenge organisers idea of a little joke. We have found the start of the pass without much difficulty, and a little sign for the Roman Fort half way through the Coniston hill range and skirting the heights of Harter Fell. The road, if it could be called such a thing, is quite indescribable. It's even narrower and more raggedy than the ones we have been picking our way along since yesterday, but worse by far is it's route, which follows the bumps and curves of a myriad of small hillocks, outcrops and dips as it winds it's way up into the fells. At several points, we are faced with a sudden sharp change of direction, incorporating a steep rise or drop which, often coupled with an acute angle to the road makes for some hairy riding. At one particular perpendicular hairpin we have to stop and actually unload Daisy, as I cautiously take her up what appears to be a near vertical rise, seasoned with a right angle bend five feet up just to make things interesting. I would imagine that on a modern trail bike this road would be huge amounts of fun, but a 1948 clunker with hardly any suspension and pretty poor brakes makes it a dangerous experience in places. We reach the fort, and it's hard to believe that it is only two miles along the pass to this point, because I feel completely exhausted. Worse still, we have to go back along the thing to reach what, only half an hour ago, I had thought of as tiny roads but now consider to be the heights of sophisticated civilization by comparison. The fort itself is barely more than a raised floor plan of stone wall now, but for all that it's very clear to see what it used to be like. Built in around AD130 or so, it is believed to have been a very remote outpost indeed and one has to wonder why on earth they built the thing here. Presumably it served as a staging post for patrols and traders, a haven of respite on an otherwise tough and hostile route between population centres. Who knows, but the size of the thing and the number of structures within suggests that it was a fairly imposing place in its prime.

Looking along the pass from the fort, I can't help but wonder whether the Challenge organizers have ever actually been here themselves, or was this just a ready Landmark picked from the map with no realization of just how remote and tricky it is to actually get to. If they are aware, I would have to say "nice one boys – remind me to bring you here on Daisy's pillion some day!" But like anything in life, there is a benefit to be had from the effort, and there is absolutely no denying that our current spot takes some beating in terms of being a sheer uplifting experience. In most directions there is no sign whatsoever of humanity, just the rolling foothills overlapping each other as they build up to the high peaks all around us. The imposing height of Scafell Pike dominates our view, reminding me that we are actually standing on the lower slopes of the highest ground in England and it's quite simply fantastic, but after a while, inevitably, we must go and I look back along the pass with some trepidation as Chris jumps onto the back once more and we begin the return to civilisation. We take it easy, but before long that vertical right angle bend is before us and we have to stop to survey the task ahead. It's down hill this time, and once again I take the decision to unload all the gear from Daisy and walk it down, leaving Chris at the bottom to wait for me to climb back up and retrieve Daisy. I edge towards the top of the drop, and ease onto the sharp slope but we gather pace in seconds. Panic sets in just before the canted bend, as Daisy's brakes stop working with a startling rapidity, failing miserably in an uneven struggle to hold our momentum back and I suddenly understand the true horror and meaning of brake-fade. We're going too fast, and even though I have her in first gear with the clutch out, both brakes anchored on as hard as I can, we are simply gathering speed straight towards a rock face where the road does it's right angle drop. There is absolutely nothing I can do.

To this day I am fuzzy about the details of what happened next other than abandoning all attempts at braking, jamming the heels of both boots into the tarmac and physically attempting to heave Daisy round the bend. We hit the wall in a side-on slew and by rights it should have ended there, but incredibly we bounce off it and we're suddenly careering down the slope past the bend, accompanied by bits of rock and mud from the wall, and straight towards Chris, who, white faced and panicked, takes flight up the grassy bank. I narrowly miss the gear that we've stacked at the bottom and mercifully come to a halt some thirty feet further on as the road rises once more. I can smell the harsh burnt tang from the brakes and I can feel pain in both my left arm and leg. The trembles set in as I hear Chris running up the slope behind me, breathless, and the most ridiculous thought pops into my mind; "He'll need his inhaler" was my rather peculiar observation.

We stand Daisy by the road and inspect the damage. Her clutch lever has been bent where it hit the rocks and the left hand handlebar rubber has been ripped at the end and has bits of stone stuck in the tear. Similarly the footrest rubber has been torn at the end but miraculously there appears to be no other damage at all. My jacket has a large grey/brown scrape down the entire length of the left arm, and both my jeans and left boot have suffered a similar scrape to match. Neither the jacket or jeans has actually torn, but the fiery sensation up my leg tells me that the impact was quite hard. The biggest thing for me is the adrenalin flood that makes me feel almost physically sick and totally spent as I slump into a sitting position on the road and reach for the tobacco tin. I am about to voice my feelings but Chris literally takes the words from my mouth – "Bugger that!" he exclaims, and the outburst breaks the tension and suddenly I find it hard to suppress a maniacal laughter that wells up within me from sheer relief to be in one piece.

Eventually we get back to the relative civilization of small single track roads that at least have the benefit of following a more sedate geography, and we skirt around the northern edge of Lake Windermere before stopping for an early lunch. We've earned one I reckon, and we also both need to visit the gents for a call of nature that would not have been acceptable in the hills. I take the chance to inspect my leg, which is still feeling chaffed and raw, noting that indeed it has an angry looking pattern of scrapes and the beginnings of a lovely bruise on the knee. Back outside, where we find a picnic table bathed in sunshine in the beer garden, we take stock of our progress so far and begin to plan out the rest of the day. The next Landmark is seventy odd miles to the southwest at Skipton, and only twenty odd miles north of the great urbanised sprawl that stretches from Leeds, through Manchester and all the way to Liverpool. We study the strip map and it's good to see that a large part of the route takes in the Pennines - the 'roof of England' I explain to Chris. That is certainly something to enjoy, but we need to try and decide whether to take things easy and stay to the north or press on and get past the heavily urbanised areas before evening. We agree that this will be harder than it might sound, because there are two more Landmarks on the northern side of Manchester and Liverpool that require a diversion straight across country, east to west, before we can turn south and pick our way through the inevitably busy built up areas. We decide that our target will be to take our time, pick off the three and call it a day, hopefully finding suitable camping somewhere in the green belt between Preston and Liverpool. Having made that decision, it is clear that with only a hundred and fifty miles to cover and all afternoon to do it, we can take our time over lunch, set a steady but unhurried pace through the Pennines and take time to enjoy the surroundings before covering the last fifty miles which encompass the three Landmarks and then finding a campsite fairly early for once. I turn my attention to the menu, and enjoy the rare feeling that the only thing I need to worry about is whether to have the ploughman's or the steak and ale pie.

The afternoon ride is both uneventful and every bit as enjoyable as we had anticipated. Although we climb steadily into the Pennine district, the landscape is vastly different to that of Scotland and Cumbria, lacking the stark imposing peaks in favour of wide open, high spaces from which grand views are on offer in just about every direction. The hedgerows and grassy verges of Cumbria have given way to endless dry stone walls and a myriad of little byres and outbuildings made of the same stuff seem to populate the many fields, presumably serving as rudimentary food stores for the countless sheep or cows that dot the landscape all the way to the horizon. We stop numerous times, just idling the time away and marvelling at the remoteness of these high slopes, but even when we're moving we keep the speed down to around fifty and simply drink in the freedom of so much natural splendour and space. As we pick our way ever southwards I develop the distinct feeling that it would be no place to roam in winter, as even on this summer's afternoon the odd cloud passing over makes the shadowed areas look bleak and foreboding and there is a raw quality to the stiff wind that plays across the high vista. I can't help but notice that the few trees up here are bent in their eternal struggle against the constant force that would have them over if it could. But eventually the land begins to drop away and we see the first signs of civilisation once more as we drop into the chocolate box prettiness that is the Yorkshire Dales. James Herriot country I recall, and I can suddenly understand why he wrote about the place and his life here with such passion. I remember devouring every one of his books back in the seventies, and could only imagine in wonder what the places he described so well would actually be like in real life. Well, now I know, and it's no kind of disappointment.

All good things come to an end, and we eventually find ourselves at the edge of the dales and on a far more featureless road that leads to Skipton, a few miles from which the Embsay steam railway awaits our cameras. I position Daisy on the road next to the little ticket office, and short of taking a train ride into the dales there is nothing else to be done here so we take our photographs and within minutes we're off again towards the western boundary of Halifax and another unidentified clue. We have to ride about twenty miles, and it is a strange mixture of heavy suburbs interspaced with startling raw countryside, often switching from one to the other and right back again in the space of a mile or so. We make a wrong turn somewhere and get sucked into a nightmare one-way system that deposits us in the middle of Halifax itself, from which a Herculean struggle is required to escape again. We seem to go round the place about five times, and, although I swear each time that I've taken a different road, it is only a matter of time before we end up back in the centre again. I curse as we pass a familiar filling station from yet another different direction, and decide that to trundle off in some arbitrary direction yet again is hopeless because all roads seem to come right back here. I have given up on the compass, being unable to maintain a westerly route from this point and as we need petrol anyway it seems sensible to fill up and try to explain to the attendant where we want to get to and ask for advice.

I am no kind of racist, and I happily accept that we live in a multi-cultural country, but I must confess that nothing in all my years has prepared me for what now transpires. Quite simply I find that here I am a foreigner in my own homeland, and an unwanted one at that, as I try to converse with the attendant. He doesn't appear to speak English, or at least not any kind of English that I have ever heard, but worse than that I get the distinct impression that I am not at all welcome here. Any doubt about that is removed when another customer begins a heated conversation with the attendant, and both of them begin making exaggerated gestures in my general direction, leaving me with no doubt whatsoever that whatever else is being discussed, I'm not about to be invited home for tea. As the customer, a thuggish looking young man with rather more gold jewellery and face furniture than would strictly be necessary for mere decoration, continues his amazing tirade, we make eye contact and I am shocked as I recognize something that has thankfully been almost non-existent in my life - hatred. An older guy touches my arm, and in clear English he says in a matter of fact way "They want you to leave - it would be best if you did that".

What I actually want to do is punch furniture-face straight in the ear hole, but with a fourteen-year-old standing outside waiting, in what must now be declared as hostile territory, that's not an option. I hold my hands up in what I hope is a placating gesture, take the map from the counter and back away saying "Fine - don't get so excited - I'm going!". The two stop their jabber and stare at me but with no intention of allowing this to develop into any more of a drama, I head for the door with a swelling anger barely controlled within me. I stride over to Daisy, grab my helmet and swing my leg over her, but can't stop the outburst; "Bastards!" I declare, staring at the shop. "Bloody arseholes!" I add and Chris, who hasn't got a clue what has just occurred within, immediately wants to know why I am cursing. I just want to go, and I'm short with him as a result "Just get on" I tell him, and he's sensible enough to just do it. With his feet barely settled on the pegs I have let out the clutch and we are mobile. A hundred yards up the road I take a left turn and then a right, left, right, left and so on until we suddenly break out into countryside again. I stop at the first available point, kill the engine and walk over to the fence to stare across the fields, still seething about the unbelievable and deeply disturbing events just a few miles back. Chris is clearly unsure what has gone on and hangs back next to Daisy and I realise that I owe him an explanation, so I turn back and begin to recount the story. As I tell him what happened it sounds incredible even to me and Chris adds to that feeling with a string of questions that can only come from one naive to the ugly reality of modern Britain "Why do they hate us? We haven't done anything to them have we?" seemed the most poignant, and was a question to which no easy answer was available, or at least not in a lay-by on a small road in North Yorkshire.

From what I can work out, we have come out on the northern side of the built up area again and, determined not to get sucked back into that nightmare one way system, I suggest to Chris that we should continue to head north for about five miles where I hope we will hit a junction with the A6033 - the road we should have been on earlier. This will take us to the west of Halifax before turning in towards the town. Our Landmark should be on route, right on the outskirts. The clue is ambiguous to say the least, being simply 'amiable' but as we finally come in on the right road the answer is blatantly obvious as we are invited to drive carefully through 'Friendly'. As I take the photographs and zip the two disposable cameras back into their pockets in the tank bag, a sudden thought occurs to me that lifts my spirits after the unsavoury incident earlier on. I laugh out loud as I turn to Chris and tell him the good news.

"Hey, you know that petrol station back there that didn't like us?" I ask, "Well, we came out getting one over 'em because I've just realised something - I didn't pay for the tank of petrol!"

Into the late afternoon then, back out into the lush green countryside and we hope, heading for an agreeably early camp. We have accepted that we'll have to do a bit of motorway to our last Landmark of the day, skirting through the southern edge of Blackburn and on towards Preston on the M65. Somewhere between the two we'll be jinking north for just a couple of miles to find Hoghton Tower, a renaissance manor house.

The place is closed when we find it, but the photographs are taken at the entrance to the impressively long driveway and it's all we need. The good news is that we now have all evening to decide where to go for the night's camp, the bad news is that we are pretty much surrounded by urban brown-belt with Preston to the west, Blackburn to the east and Manchester, Bolton or Liverpool to the south. We have no local knowledge to assist in the decision making and without that it's hard to know what to do. I lay out the large scale map in order to look at the Landmarks we'll be chasing in the morning, but with both of them situated to the south of the sprawl, I tell Chris that it makes no difference where we go from here as long as it's not north.

"Why can't we go north - why can't we go here?" he says, pointing to an area higher up the map.

"Well, it's in the wrong direction see? We're heading down *here* tomorrow!" I tap my finger on the first Landmark.

"So? You said we didn't have to rush at anything and that we could take our time if we wanted to, so why does it matter?" I look again at the area he had indicated, and have to concede that it looks to be far less populated and far more inviting than any other direction. It's clear that the lad is right, I have been behaving as if we're back on that schedule again, always looking at the next target instead of the best experience and it's daft when only fifteen miles or so the 'wrong way' there is open country and what looks suspiciously like national park again.

"OK, you win!" I confess, "Go on then, you choose where to go, and go there we shall – within reason!" he simply taps a petulant finger on the same spot he had already highlighted.

The immediate problem is how to get out of this urban jungle. There are no obvious roads that will take us straight up to where we want to go and it seems that we'll have to do another stint of motorway, this time on the dreaded M6. My eye catches a place name that I feel is a worthy target, and Goosnargh is on the southern edge of the Beacon Fell National Park. Couldn't be better, so with no further ado we set forth in the late afternoon sun in search of another inspiring place to camp, this time early enough and in weather that is good enough to really enjoy it. The M6 has other ideas about enjoyment however, for we join it at just about the worst possible time of day, slap in the middle of the evening rush hour. We don't even manage to get off the slip road before the huge tailback begins and brake lights are all that can be seen for what looks like miles ahead. We edge out into the slow river of metal, easing into the gaps until we have worked our way over to the outside lane. As a big BMW with panniers and top box glides past us between the stationary cars we tuck in behind it and begin to filter through the nightmare of congestion that is the modern British motorway in rush hour.

I find my mind wandering as we thread our way through: we had just spent a night under the stars, had awoken this morning to the wilds of Cumbria where no car, house or even much tarmac could be seen and we had spent the whole of the morning threading our way from there up onto the heights of the Pennines and down into the Yorkshire Dales, hardly seeing any other vehicles for much of the time and revelling in the uncluttered freedom of the ride. Then came Halifax and the disturbing events there, followed by urban congestion, motorway, more stop-start frustration in the middle and now this. I know that tomorrow will bring a lot more of the same, because there is no avoiding that huge sprawl, but right here, right now I yearn to be back in the green lanes and can feel a huge almost irrational impatience as we follow the BMW at something less than twenty miles per hour past endless cars, vans and trucks. The six miles that we have to cover on this blighted road seem like sixty, but at last the sign appears that heralds our exit, and with a huge relief I filter across and finally break free up the slip road and the promise of freedom once more.

We amble into the smaller lanes getting happily lost but our camp site is absolutely ideal nestling in a quiet wooded area between rolling hills, and with a river bending round its far end where a number of tents are already in place. It's a small site and peaceful as a result, but it still sports all the facilities that we are in dire need of – a toilet/shower block, launderette and a little shop. We bump across the field to a spot by the river and enjoy to the full the feeling of coming to rest after a long day's wandering. Chris wanders down to the river and I lie back on the warm grass, arms spread wide and think lazily about how the rest of the day will go. Putting the kettle on seems to be the way to start, followed by an unhurried erection of the tent. That done, I'll discuss with Chris whether to bother with cooking tonight, or should we walk down to an inn which we saw not far along the road? We have surely earned a slap up feed and a pint or two of something this evening. Daisy must need some attention too, as I realise guiltily that I haven't paid much attention to her nuts bolts or fluids, and this I decide can be done before taking a shower, changing clothes and finally visiting shop and laundry. Chris returns to interrupt my daydreaming, readily voting for the inn option when asked and also agreeing on the rest of the plan. Tea, tent, Daisy, shower, shop, launderette and pub – in that order, and we have a couple of hours to do the first six, with all evening to enjoy the last one. A plan with no downsides, I declare, and stir myself to dig out the stove and kettle.

Fiddling with Daisy an hour later, it is pleasing to find almost nothing amiss. She has used oil again, as usual, and her gearbox and rear wheel need adjusting to take up a slight slackness in the primary and rear chains. A couple of nuts are slightly loose here and there and she is weeping some oil from the dynamo housing, but apart from that I can find no real work for the spanners. As I work my way from front to rear, I realise that the vibration which had set in and so worried me on the way up the A1, has not got any worse. At least, I haven't noticed it getting worse, which is tantamount to the same thing, and I start to wonder again what had caused it to appear in the first place which leads me to fretting for a few minutes about the meaning of it's sudden presence. No good can possibly come from that line of thinking I tell myself, and remember instead the frightful bodge that had been carried out on the ignition in Coldstream. With all thoughts of mysterious vibrations banished in favour of a far more tangible and obvious thing to fret about, I remove the end-cap from the magneto and peer inside at the points. It all looks as it should, which is most gratifying, but with an almost morbid curiosity I give the little screw that retains the points a prod. This is stupid because I immediately become deeply alarmed when the whole assembly wobbles before my eyes. Magneto points should not wobble because the little screw that I have just prodded is there to hold the entire assembly tight, in an exact relation with the cam ring which opens the points at something like the correct moment as the whole assembly spins round. I try to tighten the little screw, but it is already tight and I can't see how this very critical arrangement can possibly be working properly – or at all in fact.

If it ain't broke, don't try to fix it. This old saying has served us classic motorcyclists well, and I have just fallen foul of it. I know this is true, because having finished fiddling, I find that Daisy won't start anymore and, after expending numerous kicks and even more curses, I am left sitting on a non functioning motorcycle which had been running perfectly before I had touched it. My mood is not helped by Chris, who having watched the entire sorry episode, points this out to me rather unnecessarily. I climb off and reach for the magneto again, although I don't really know what I'm going to do. After taking out the spark plugs to ease turning the engine over I ask Chris to come and do just that with the kick-start, so that I can watch what is happening to the points. And there it is; as the points rotate and the little arm pushes against the cam, the whole assembly moves sideways from the pressure and the points are not opening at all. I don't understand how this can be, or why my simple act of prodding the thing can have suddenly caused the problem. Confused, I sit back and wonder out loud "How the bloody hell has she been running so well since Coldstream?" Chris grunts something that I suspect is immensely unhelpful, but I'm already descending into self-pity and ignore him as I continue my rant "I mean, all those miles, all that vibration and the bloody thing's solid all the way, then breaks just because I touch it? – It doesn't make any sense!" and it doesn't make sense, not at all. I reach for the screwdriver and set to work removing the contact breaker assembly and back-plate for closer inspection, but with the bits spread out in my hand I can see nothing wrong at all. I try fitting the thing on it's shaft and wobbling it and suddenly, in a blinding flash of enlightenment I can see the problem and I understand what has occurred.

The back-plate fits onto a taper, that wholly remarkable design that is meant to keep objects such as sprockets, pinions and, as in this case, contact breaker assemblies firmly anchored to their rotating shafts. It is, in theory, impossible to achieve a wobbly assembly that is pressed onto a taper but I realise that this is only true if the screw that is meant to push the thing firmly onto the taper is actually doing so. With a little experimentation it becomes abundantly clear that Daisy's vital little retaining screw is doing no such thing because incredibly it is just a fraction too long, the net effect of which is that when screwed all the way up it is reaching the end of its threaded hole just a fraction before actually pressing onto the assembly that it's supposed to be holding in place. In short, the screw can be done up tight but is doing nothing at all in the holding things together stakes. I double check my findings, and confirm without any doubt that this is the case, and now I am left to wonder how on earth the thing has managed to stay in one piece for the hundreds of miles that we have covered since stripping it apart on the Scottish border. That thought leads sets me to wondering how it has stayed together *prior* to this trip and the field repair, when we were gaily bowling around Cornwall, Norfolk, Wiltshire and the main leg up the A1 a few days ago. Surely the same problem must have existed all along? It is a mystery and I can only surmise that by sheer luck the thing must have been pressed onto it's taper just hard enough to get a grip after being put on by hand each time it had been assembled. But as I sit there I have a flash of inspiration, suddenly seeing the simple cause of our problem. It is astoundingly obvious that there is a washer missing, which, if fitted, would allow the screw to do its job by taking up that fraction of length and I curse silently. I must have dropped the thing into the long grass back there in Coldstream as I had struggled to fix it on that cold damp morning after Daisy had made her unscheduled and unexpected stop. The discovery presents an immediate problem in that the missing washer is very small, meaning that it is highly unlikely that I have any that will fit. After a quick search I am amazed to actually find a few that look like they might do the job in one of my jacket pockets. It is but a minute's work to match one to the screw, fit the assembly back together and note with satisfaction that everything is now good and tight on it's taper. I climb back onto Daisy, try a good kick, and this time I am rewarded as she responds immediately with her throaty bark. "Waheey!" I exclaim with relief, and even Chris looks suitably impressed as the engine settles down to a steady even tick-over.

We both oversleep the next morning and by the time we have breakfast underway it is nearly half-past ten. It doesn't seem to matter at all and we take our time sat by the river in the morning sunshine. The previous evening, we had managed to get a good shower and had got our laundry and shopping done and in fact, the rest of the evening had been passed very pleasantly in the local inn where, after dining on a superb home cooked meal, we had stayed for the duration of the session chatting to some of the locals. Our southern accents had been met with the inevitable questions about where we came from, what had brought us this far north and pretty soon the story of Daisy and the Landmark was being told once again by Chris. By the time the last bell had rung, we were amid a happy group whom it felt like we had known for years and I was feeling guilty because I had not been allowed to buy a single drink all evening, but the icing on the cake of northern hospitality was the landlord's insistence on a "little nightcap lad, to keep t' cold out" and I had found an impossibly large brandy in my hand "On the house!" It had been an unsteady return to our tent, at least for me, and it had seemed a good idea to brew up some coffee to assist in warding off the ill effects of so much hospitality, so we had sat ourselves down with the stove outside the tent, listening to the river gurgling along close by, while we chatted idly about the day that had begun what now seemed to be an aeon ago. It had been well past midnight when we had finally turned in but I was extremely contented as I lay there in the dark waiting for sleep to overtake me. No surprise that we had awoken late then but it felt good to have no pressing tasks to do other than eat, pack up, fire Daisy up and hit the road so we take our time over the food before turning our attention to preparing to ride.

Eventually everything is packed and loaded and we are ready to go, but right here, as we check the maps and study the route to our first target of the day, I realise that this is actually partly the reason I have taken so much time this morning - we are about to swap the idyllic surroundings of this campsite and it's wonderful surroundings for a morning of choked motorway, urban sprawl and traffic. The M6 gives us no quarter, with a seemingly endless stream of fast moving trucks in the inside lanes and much faster traffic hurtling past them and it feels like we have just threaded our way onto a free-for-all racetrack. Daisy can hold her own at seventy plus, but amidst such fast moving, and more to the point *heavy* traffic I consider it stupid and potentially suicidal to try to compete. She is after all an old motorcycle, with a far higher percentage likelihood of a mechanical failure of some sort, the consequences of which, should they occur in the middle of this rat race, are scary to say the least. With this in mind I tuck us in behind a coach travelling at fifty, keeping as close as possible to the hard shoulder and simply let the speeding world go by. Easier said than done though, because most of what speeds past us is large and carries with it a vicious wind blast that continuously buffets us which makes the going pretty hard work. As the built up areas of Wigan and St Helens sprawl either side of the snaking road even more traffic comes flying up the slip roads to our left to join the lemming-rush. It's a huge relief to be through it, after forty unpleasant miles and with a need to get our bearings we begin to look for a suitable place to peel off onto smaller, hopefully less hectic roads. The A50 presents itself, and with Knutsford on the signs, a name that rings a bell from earlier perusal of the maps, I point Daisy up the slip road.

We have a quandary now, I think, as we look at the two nearest Landmarks on the remainder of this trek. They are equidistant from our current spot, one to the east and one to the west, effectively halting any southern progress. It doesn't seem to matter which way we go first because neither of them gives a particularly better route to the next batch further south and whichever we choose we'll still have to double back to get the other one. I estimate that they're about twenty miles apart, so in truth we have to go ten miles or so one way then the full twenty back on ourselves, whilst making no progress whatsoever down south. But now that we're off the motorway and the weather is still good, we can look forward to far better motorcycling if nothing else. I check my watch and do some mental calculations – it's just gone two o'clock and whichever way we go it'll be twenty past by the time the first Landmark is reached then another forty minutes or so back again. I get to thinking that if we go east first, then double-back will actually take us fairly close to Chester, a town that I had visited a number of times in my working life but, as is often the way, not actually seen at all. I remember being told that the place was well worth a wander round, being steeped in history and still possessing a lot of it to see. The way we had done things yesterday was spot on, camping early and taking our time, so why not do that again and visit Chester today? I suggest the plan to Chris, and he seems quite happy to go along with whatever I want, agreeing that the previous evening had certainly been amongst the better ones. So the plan is good, and we set off along the A50 towards Knutsford where we'll turn east and go in search of what I believe to be the Quarry Bank Mill Museum, which is confirmed on arrival at the map-point.

It's a big place this. I have always harboured a rather dismal mental image of these huge cotton mills from my schooldays, but to see the reality of the great oblong brick building with it's row upon row of high windows and the inevitable tall chimney, so representative of the times is something else. With time on our hands it seems silly not to go in and have a look around and we park Daisy up as close as we can and head off to the entrance to the museum. An hour later, which could have easily been stretched into two or three if we had more time, we have been shocked at the incredibly harsh life-style of the late eighteenth century mill worker, including the urchins or 'pauper children' and we have marvelled at what passed for technology and raw industrial power back in those ground-breaking years of our history. There are examples of an impressive beam engine as well as a working horizontal steam engine, coupled with various galleries with all manner of widgets and gadgets based around the general theme of water and steam power. We could easily bimble around in here for hours, but we both want to follow the plan of an early camp and a visit to Chester so dragging ourselves reluctantly back outside at just after half past four, we are soon back on the route we had come in on, going west once more and in search of the next Landmark, which is a water mill east of Runcorn if my research is correct. Daisy burbles along underneath us, totally happy at the leisurely cruising speed of fifty, untroubled by vibrations, disintegrating points, sudden deflations or moisture of any kind. She is completely in her element right now, performing exactly the kind of duty that her makers had envisaged and delivering exactly that which is asked of her with such ease that I have no doubt whatsoever that if I chose to we could keep this up all day long, into the night, and all the way home. As we arrive at the mill, I am still lost in these happy thoughts, thinking that although Daisy may well take such a demand in her stride, Chris and myself could not do the same, I suspect.

With that thought I have a sudden yearning for home, to be with Diane my wife, Chloe, the dog, the luxury of a long hot bath and a real bed. I am startled by the power of the feeling which has sprung up from nowhere, after all we have only been away for six days and although we've certainly had some challenges, the past two have been a breeze really, where nothing has occurred that would stimulate an emotional pang for the homestead. I manage to shrug off the feeling, but as we thread our way back onto the road that will take us to Chester I find myself looking forward to the call I'll make this evening, as I have every evening, to check in, let everyone know we're fine, where we are and what we're up to. I suddenly wonder if Chris feels the same and half shouting over my shoulder I ask him the question, surprised by the answer that yes, getting home is quite a priority in his mind, but typically for a teenager he confesses that this is because he's missing his computer and the dog. No mention of mum or sister and certainly not the bath. The conversation falters, because we're riding a 'B' road at fifty or so and I have to keep my eyes front which makes it hard to converse, and we both settle back to our own little worlds for the remainder of the run, which ends easily when we find a campsite sign just on the eastern edge of Chester itself and make straight for it. But I have been thinking about things in the past few miles, and have come to a decision that I am sure Chris will go with although I will wait until we've set up camp and sorted out the evening meal before broaching it with him.

We've gone overboard with the food, I reckon, as we sit watching three pots bubbling away in front of us. We have potatoes boiling in one, peas and carrots in another and a mass of mince in gravy in the third. All bought at the little shop on site and smelling lovely as I realise just how hungry I've become through the afternoon. But my mind has wandered again to thoughts of home and I reckon now is as good a time as any to ask Chris what he thinks of the plan that had formed during the last miles of the afternoon, and so I float the idea while we wait.

"How do you fancy making a run for home tomorrow?" I ask "Because if we drop one of the Landmarks, which I can get with Chloe when we do Wales, then I reckon we could do it". He looks back at me owlishly, and I can see he likes the idea, but he poses a good question before answering.

"It's too far to go isn't it? How many miles is it to home from here?"

I confess I haven't actually got that far, but I was convinced it was achievable so I answered quickly "I don't know exactly, it's probably three hundred or so miles without the other Landmark, but I tell you what we'll do – finish dinner, take a ride into Chester for a wander around, find a pub where we can sit down with the maps and we'll work it out and see what we reckon." This met with agreement and we set about dishing out the food without further discussion. By now, I am determined to make the run and I knew that Chris would take little persuading.

Evening finds us ensconced in a marvellous pub right next to the Shropshire Union canal, me with a pint of Dogbolter and Chris with a coke, maps spread out in front of us. We have spent the past hour wandering around Chester's fascinating centre, with its ancient walls, castle and shopping rows from another age and now we must decide on our plan for the next morning. I explain to Chris that we were due to head southwest from here into Shropshire and to the Welsh border, which would have taken quite a time due to the nature of the roads, but I can reschedule that for later when I do the Welsh leg with Chloe, allowing us to take a more direct route, starting with what would have been the second of our three remaining targets in this trip some thirty miles to the south east. From there, we have to jink about a bit to travel a further thirty five miles east, because there is no direct route that we can identify; we'll have to head south to Stoke-on-Trent and then zigzag across to the Derbyshire Dales and the Carsington Reservoir, our final Landmark of this foray. From there we have no more distractions and can cut across the northern boundary of Nottingham for another forty miles until we hit Newark and the A1 once more and commence the long haul home. "So how many miles is it?" Chris wants to know, and I trace along the route, estimating the distance as I go until my finger rests on Ramsgate and the number in my head is three hundred and twenty, which is a lot if we allow for Landmarks and fatigue.

I tell him the news and get no reaction at first, as he sits and does some internal calculations of his own, but suddenly he comes over all positive exclaiming "That's about the same as we did the other day, you know, from Loch Ness to that fort." He barely pauses before continuing "This'll be easier because there won't be all those mountains and little tiny roads" his last statement however is startling "We could get home by lunch time!"

I am delighted to realise that he's been paying more attention than I thought to our route if he knows the mileage we covered two days ago, but I can't leave him thinking that this leg will be so much easier that we'll be home for lunch. There is absolutely no chance of us, let alone Daisy, achieving that and I tell him so. Not to be put off, he argues the point and we spend the remainder of the evening in Chester in good natured disagreement until I end up patiently explaining to him how to work out average speed, including stops and Landmark-hunting wastage. We finally settle on an agreed average of thirty-five miles per hour all things considered, although Chris is convinced it works out at forty-five, but we divide the mileage by the lower number to get a projected time on the road of something like nine and a half hours barring mishaps. We agree to get an early morning start at six o'clock or so and go for it, and I telephone Diane to tell her the good news. That done, and eager to get the night over and hit the road, we head back to the campsite and turn in. I am just dozing off when a voice pipes up from the darkness: "You're wrong about the average speed, we'll be home by lunch time!"

We wake up to the sound of drizzle hitting the tent, which is just about the last thing we want to hear. I manoeuvre myself to the door and peer out at a grey overcast sky and a very damp landscape, but there's little to be done about it so I close the flap, reach for the kettle and get the morning brew underway. It's half past five by my watch, and we have agreed to skip the breakfast routine, in favour of getting early miles under our wheels, but not until after a cup of coffee to jumpstart our metabolisms. By six o'clock we are shivering in the early chill air as we fold up the soggy tent, and shortly afterwards Daisy is warming up as I strap the thing onto her panniers. We have donned our ridiculously inadequate waterproof trousers once more, but neither of us feels much like talking as we contemplate the soggy ride ahead. But we're going home, that's the main focus of my attention, which means I can console myself that at least this time there will be a hot bath, a homecooked meal and a real bed at the other end. I turn to Chris, who is just doing up his helmet,

"Ready then?" I ask.

"We're late," he says, but then a shy grin appears as he adds "We might be late for lunch now!"

Thirty miles or so to the east, we pull up damply at our first and penultimate Landmark of the day, Little Moreton Hall, which is quite the most wondrous piece of preserved history nestling damply in the Cheshire countryside. It is truly an amazing sight even in this country of historic depth. A Tudor manor house, in all its timber glory, the classic, albeit now twisted white walled black-timbered structure bearing it's age superbly in ideal surroundings. I can't help but consider what a grand place it must have been all those hundreds of years ago, as even by modern building standards it's fairly big. Clearly a seat of power was this, and I can't help wondering what tumultuous events have passed under its very eaves as the centuries slowly passed it by. We can't take Daisy close enough for the photograph, so we have to leave her in the car park and walk the rest of the way to have a wander around, and as we do this the devil in me strikes again and I ask Chris if he can believe for one second that this place isn't haunted. He bites, as I knew he would and I find myself deep in discussion with him regarding the likely hauntees. A Cavalier, Roundhead, grey lady or a mad monk? Who knows? I suggest he looks the place up on the Internet once we get back home and I can see from his face that this is almost certainly something he'll do. In the mean time we have a challenge to complete and it's time to move on once more, on our zigzag course east and our next appointment in the Derbyshire Dales with a reservoir. The drizzle continues to hang in the air, and Daisy is covered with a film of moisture from the morning's miles, but our spirits are high as we begin the countdown to home "Only two hundred and ninety to go" I enthuse, and with that we set off once more.

Just outside Stoke-on-Trent we have to turn almost back on ourselves towards Leek in order to avoid being sucked into the town itself and certain chaos on yet another town planner's one-way nightmare. But we are forced to turn right back round and head for the place anyway when Daisy sputters to a stop and I discover that we're out of petrol. The reserve tap, I know from experience, will only give us between five and ten miles, and it's unlikely that we'll find fuel on this little road so there is no choice. We are soon swallowed by the feared traffic system and although we find fuel easily I can't find my way back to where we want to be. Round and round we go, wasting about twenty minutes, before finally exiting the place far further south than I had wanted. I had hoped to stay much further north, which would have taken us to our next target via the edge of the Dales, but it's not to be. We stop to check maps and get our bearings once more and after a few false starts we eventually manage to connect with the A50, which, with it's southeasterly direction is not ideal but at least identifiable, and means we're no longer lost. Down to Sudbury we go, turning north just before the village and heading straight for the reservoir. We have wasted a good three quarters of an hour and added probably ten miles to this leg as a result of my stupidity, and Chris is a bit fractious about it when we finally arrive at Carsington Water some two hours and forty minutes after setting out this morning. It should have taken two hours maximum, or, by Chris's more optimistic calculations an hour and forty minutes. But it's progress, still only nine o'clock in the morning, I remind him, and we have all day to complete the remaining two hundred and fifty miles without any further distractions, always assuming that Daisy doesn't throw any tantrums.

We pull into the lay-by near Cambridge at just after six-thirty that evening, tired, but elated with the knowledge that we have put a huge dent in the Landmark Challenge. Chris probably thinks that I have lost the plot completely as I kill the engine, lean forwards, give her tank a big pat and exclaim "Good girl Daisy, well done!" but we both want to get home and waste no more time in ditching our riding gear, opening up the rear door of the car and loading the bike and all our gear into the back. I divest myself of boots, changing into comfortable shoes, turn out the pockets of my jacket for the car keys and settle into the luxury of the Espace's soft driving seat. Inserting the key, I turn on the ignition and for a few seconds I gaze in confusion as nothing happens. No dash lights, no fan and no radio respond and as I turn the key further to crank the engine I am met with a dull 'click' and nothing else. I look at Chris, muttering "I don't believe this" try again, but nothing happens. I stare stupidly at the dashboard as nothing continues to happen and Chris, understanding the situation now exclaims "Oh just great!" I have to agree, and in sheer frustration that the car, of all things, could do this to us I bang the steering wheel and curse. Of all the things I had imagined could happen to us on this trip, the car letting us down certainly wasn't one of them and I feel a sense of outrage that it should be the case. We have no choice but to call recovery, wait the hour it takes them to show up and then feel foolish when, after the twenty seconds it takes the driver to give us a jump start, he points in through the back window and suggests that I turn off the rear internal light that has obviously been left on and has slowly drained the battery. I curse again at such stupidity, but end up having a bit of a laugh with the guy as we confess that we have in fact just toured a large part of Britain on the old clunker in the back only to have to call the cavalry to rescue our reasonably modern car. Even Chris can't help but see the funny side as the driver bids us farewell and leaves with a final flippant remark; "Next time mate, leave the bleedin' car at 'ome eh?"

It's nine thirty by the time we get home, but as I ask Chris to grab our jackets and helmets from the back whilst I manoeuvre Daisy out, my own voice is overpowered by a louder exclamation as Chloe explodes from the house and comes charging towards us, battling for pole position with the dog and yelling "Daaadeeee!" They arrive simultaneously, all but knocking me off my feet as Chloe flings her arms around my middle and Sheba scrabbles desperately to climb over her in an effort to lick my face. Chris eyes this whole ceremony with one of those teenage looks, but his facade is shattered when Sheba, abandoning the unequal struggle with Chloe launches herself at him instead, succeeding in planting the slobbery tongue right on the button as Chris tries in vain to fend off her attentions. With my arm around Chloe, who is holding on tight firing questions at me in rapid succession about this latest adventure, as well as demanding to know when the next one, involving her, is to take place, I open the garage door ready to put Daisy inside and I can see through to the rear garden and there is my wife, Diane, hanging out washing and it's a relief when she doesn't come charging up the path and jump on me, settling for a good hug in a more sedate fashion.

"You made it then? Amazing" she ribs me "and now I suppose you're hungry? Well it's on but you've got time for a bath first". With this she details Chloe to go upstairs and start the thing running while I bring Daisy in. I suddenly realise just how hungry I am, but more to the point it's great to be home and yes, I reckon I really could use a bath.

Dinner is a lively affair, with Chris eagerly telling our war stories to his sister as his mum and I share a conspiratorial look. He has really come out of himself since that first foray into Norfolk and it's fantastic to see him so animated, so enthusiastic. A year ago he would almost certainly have struggled with the challenges we had just come through, would have been quite stressed by it all and certainly would never have been the lively centre of conversation that I see before me now. He tells his stories in a jumble of mis-order, of the puncture, the points falling apart, the appalling weather we had endured. A look of awe and wonder settles on Chloe's face as he talks of the ride through the mountains, looking down on clouds and sleeping under the stars in Cumbria. He describes the race with the steam train and has the whole table in stitches as he tells of the 'mad old woman' at the Shin Falls, attempting to mimic that lady's Scottish accent and pronunciation. Chloe tries out the word 'fush' and then the phrase 'D'jyaseeum?' and before we know it she and Chris are conversing in their own version of pseudo Scots. Suddenly Chris changes tack completely; "When can I get a bike?" he asks. Diane gives me that look again. Dinner lasts quite a time that evening, and we are still sitting round the table an hour later. I am totally content, feeling deeply satisfied and even the ritual of clearing up afterwards, a task that I am left to do as the rest of the family retire to the living room, has the pleasant ring of home about it. I potter about doing the mundane things but before too long my mind is drifting back out there on the road, in the mountains, valleys and dales and I realise that already I am eager to go and do it all again, in Wales.

The next morning I have a long lay in, not even waking up until gone eleven and eventually coming downstairs I find that Chris still hasn't surfaced either. Breakfast is a leisurely affair as I wallow in the luxury of not having to do anything in particular, other than unpack Daisy, who had been parked and left fully loaded the previous evening. I wander out after a while and begin to un-strap and remove the various bits that make up our touring kit. She looks like an old pack-mule festooned as she is with tank bag, throw-over panniers, tent and bedrolls. All come off within a few minutes and she looks strangely bare without them, I think. I sort through the stuff, hanging the camping gear up in the garage, ferrying the laundry into the house, stowing bag and panniers away ready for next time and finally I can wheel Daisy out into the sunshine for a post campaign check-up. The first obvious thing to do is give her a good wash because she is looking very grubby, with a layer of light brown grime covering all of the forward facing surfaces, particularly those closer to the road and most of her chrome is now a dull grey colour. I notice also that where the tank bag and panniers have rested, collecting water under them, there is a smudgy pink residue smeared all over, the remnants of her previously polished wax finish which has been eroded and emulsified. She's certainly not the gleaming machine upon which we had set out a week ago. A good wash transforms her but as I scrub and polish each area and all the nooks and crannies I am building a little catalogue of things that have come loose or in some circumstances, come off altogether. A session with the spanners seems in order and while I'm at it we'll do some basic maintenance, an oil change and finally a good polish and wax would not go amiss, but first I am going to take Diane out for a late lunch.

I am surprised in the late afternoon, as I prepare to set about Daisy with the sockets. Chris has surfaced from his pit and has joined me in the garage, showing interest for the first time in Daisy as a mechanical object rather than just the source of high adventure. I do believe he's getting the bug, I smile to myself, as he asks what he can do to help and reaches for the spanners. Happy to encourage him, I talk through the list of things we have to do and decide to give him the job of changing Daisy's oil, explaining what needs to be done and pointing to the nice fresh can of lubricant waiting to go in. As we work and chat we're soon back onto the subject of a bike of his own - how long must he wait, what can he get and how much would it cost? - and I have a sudden memory of myself at his age, helping my own father with his BSA A10, a deep longing growing within me to own a machine of my own but knowing that I'd have to wait several years. I remember clearly that it seemed an impossibly long wait and that I would have given anything in the world right then to own a motorcycle of my own. I remember also the great day, shortly after my seventeenth birthday, when my father told me of a machine that was for sale for a reasonable sum, a suitable machine to learn on he suggested and a British one at that. I was in my first job at the time, earning the princely sum of thirty pounds a week and the bike would set me back some three months pay if I saved every penny after tax and my keep were deducted, but my father had thought of that and was offering a loan of the two hundred pounds asking price. Within a week I was the proud owner of a 200cc Triumph Tiger Cub and had my first accident the very next day.

I tell Chris the story as he struggles to complete the oil change. He has had no previous mechanical experience and is not a natural hands-on type at all, so he struggles with this, his first spannering job and quickly becomes frustrated. I have to calm him down as I try to help, but it's uphill work and so in an effort to explain that all new things take some mastering, I get us back onto the subject of the great moment when I sat astride that little cub for the first time all those years ago. I had no concept whatsoever of clutch, gears and a footbrake and the controls had felt alien to me as my father explained how things worked. Finally, with the engine running, first gear selected and the clutch held in, I had revved the engine far too much, let go of the clutch and we were suddenly off up the garden, completely out of control. I couldn't get my head round the controls, forgot to pull in the clutch, forgot about the brake pedal and rode in glorious disarray straight into the pear tree fifty feet up the garden. It was a complete shock and I had felt utterly stupid, but I was also drunk from my first experience of engine power mixed with adrenalin and as I picked the bike up with trembling hands there was only one thought in my mind; "Wow!" I was hooked, plain and simple, and the only thing to do was get right back on and try again, as many times as it takes, until I have mastered the basics and would dare to venture out onto the roads. The story does the trick with Chris and now we begin comparing the ease with which I had been able to take up bikes with the much harder and more restricted task presented to young riders nowadays. For me it had been insanely easy, for the law back then was far more liberal and prospective young riders could choose anything under 250cc, slap on 'L' plates, get insured with relative ease and launch themselves on an unsuspecting world with no formal training whatsoever. They could ride like that as long as they liked with no pressure to take the comparatively simple test at all. Life used to be so simple.

Chris sticks around for the duration of the afternoon's tasks, but I can't help but notice that he doesn't reach for any more spanners once the oil has been changed. But he certainly is keen to talk about bikes, biking, camping and adventure. As I work, we talk and I suggest he might consider the merits of a BSA Bantam for his first bike. He then goes quite quiet for a while and when he next pipes up, I'm amused to discover that his imagination has been working overtime as he suddenly and enthusiastically states that once he's seventeen, he'll get the bike, pass the test, and then he will ride it to Le Mans just like we had done on Daisy. A bit ambitious is that, I suggest, but he clearly has the wanderlust and dismisses my observation with the comment "It'll just take longer is all!" He goes quiet again, and I just know that he's suffering that same deep yearning that I had and just like I did he is probably thinking that his seventeenth birthday is an impossibly long way away. After a while, he wanders off into the house and I feel sorry for the lad. Still, when you wait that long for something, it's all the more satisfying when you finally get it, although I find myself wondering what the current going rate for a Bantam is, and with Christmas only a few months away, I might just have a word with the management (Diane) before the summer's out. In the mean time, I review the progress on Daisy's list. She had lost a bolt from the right hand exhaust, a nut from her front number plate, a nut from the speedometer mounting, one from her chain-guard and finally the retaining screw had gone from the dynamo cap. All of these have now been replaced, pausing only to marvel at the fact that the cap had actually stayed in place. I have checked all other mountings and found a few loose, including of course the big horn. Her oil has been changed for fresh new gloop; I have adjusted her tappets and even checked and adjusted her tyre pressures. Time for a test ride in the late afternoon sun then, and I go indoors to retrieve my jacket and report to she who commands that I won't be long. Both Chris and Chloe decline the offer of a ride, having just attached a lead to the dog in order to head for the local park.

Two immediate things impress themselves on me as I pull away and accelerate up the road. Firstly, after a week of all day riding two-up and loaded for camping, Daisy feels incredibly light and very lively, but secondly my afternoon's efforts at servicing and maintenance, far from making her all tickety-boo, appear to have done something alarming at the back end and within fifty yards I have pulled over urgently to investigate the harsh clanking noise that has sprung up from nowhere and is ringing out with every bump. I can't help noticing that she feels remarkably skittish at the back as well. I crouch down and inspect her rear section, the mudguard stays, the wheel mountings, chain guard and the chain itself but I can see nothing wrong and nothing seems to be loose or misplaced. Strange, had I imagined it? No, definitely not. I sit astride her, wobble my backside from side to side and bounce up and down a bit but to no avail. Stranger still, and definitely worrying I think, as I pull on my gloves again, select first gear and pull away once more, gently this time and with my head cocked listening for any untoward noises. There it is again, a harsh metallic clonk coupled with a definite feeling that all is not well back there, so without further ado I execute a 'U' turn and ride slowly back to the house with ears straining and my head swivelling from side to side as I try look down and backwards for a glimpse of anything doing something interesting.

Outside the house once more I park by the curb and start a manic inspection of the rear end, but there is nothing to see, the cause of the startling noise and the very disconcerting skittishness remains a complete mystery. I pull things, push bits and generally prod around. I spin the wheel, which taunts me as it glides silently and steadily on it's bearings, refusing to do anything nasty and so I grip the thing and heave from side to side but it's solid. I climb back on, bounce around and generally shake the poor bike all over the place but worrying noises continue not to happen - nothing. I consider that I must be going mad and I decide that what I should do is go indoors for a cup of tea and a bit of a fret, but half way up the drive I have a sudden thought which is startlingly, obviously the answer and would have been plain to anyone other than me in idiot mode. Something is loose in the toolbox! I do a sharp about turn and open the thing with a coin, anticipating the sight of a loose spanner or screwdriver and now I'm sure I'm going mad because the thing is empty. Back to plan 'A' then, I go indoors and I make tea, retiring to the sun lounge where I do indeed fret about phantom noises and more specifically, my total inability to identify the probably obvious source. Diane doesn't help much as she pops her head through the door and teases me "broken it then have we?" She asks unkindly.

The kids arrive back from the park to find me sat cross-legged next to Daisy and in a fractious mood. I have been up and down the road numerous times now, clanking and skitting each time but failing miserably to make any progress in identifying the cause. To help matters along, my imagination has now furnished me with various nightmare scenarios involving the inner gubbins of the dread sprung hub and I am, not to put too fine a point on things, officially worried. I am also struggling to understand the apparent suddenness of the symptoms and just to satisfy myself that I haven't imagined it I grill Chris about the final long ride yesterday.

"Had he noticed a noise, or anything like that?" He had not.

"Right" I declare, "I need your help with this!" He eyes me suspiciously, looks at Daisy and then back at me, confusion on his face as he blurts, "I don't know what's wrong! How would I know what's wrong!"

I have to quickly explain "I didn't say you did, but you can help by riding with me and seeing if you can pinpoint where the noise is coming from. I can't do that and ride at the same time, but you probably can"

He looks appalled at the suggestion, rapidly backing away and forcefully declaring "I'm not going on that if it's broken! It's dangerous!" and just in case I try to persuade him, he turns on his heel and strides off up the drive. Conversation over it seems.

"Well thanks a lot mate!" I shout after him, but he's already in the porch and not about to come back for more.

"Bloody marvellous", I rage and decide that he really can't be allowed to get away with that attitude, not after all we've just been through, and certainly not if he has aspirations to become a classic motorcyclist himself. I pursue him into the house where I make that feeling known and we're just getting into a lively argument when Chloe pipes up in the middle with "I'll go Dad" and I realise that there is no mileage in continuing to argue with Chris, even though I'm deeply disappointed with his attitude. I grab Chloe by the hand, exclaiming "Marvellous, thanks Chloe" and we head straight out to Daisy leaving Chris, hopefully, feeling a little bit ashamed at his attitude. I have second thoughts almost immediately however. Perhaps he has a point and in fact I'm being a bit gung-ho regarding the safety of what I'm proposing. What if it is something nasty? Something that is about to break imminently? Chris is right to be concerned, particularly if it's inside that hub. Am I being irrational and, when all's said and done a tad reckless? I am gripped with indecision suddenly but Chloe has no inhibitions "What do I have to do again?" she asks, doing up the strap on her helmet and pulling on gloves. I make my mind up there and then to take it very slowly and tell Chloe to hold on tight, but I simply have to find out what's making that bloody noise!

Up the road we go, slowly at first and I am amazed to note that both noise and the skittishness have vanished. We stop and I ask Chloe if she heard any noises at all. She didn't apparently so I turn us around a go back down the road, a little faster this time. No noises, and no skits. Unbelievable. "We'll go a bit further" I declare, "You keep you ears skinned and yell the minute you hear anything OK?" and with that we're off again. A ten-mile round trip later, I am thoroughly confused by Daisy's refusal to misbehave in any way. No dread clanks, no skits and in fact she feels wonderful in every way. Back at home I put her away somewhat bemused, and I begin to fret about the now mysteriously absent symptoms of doom. I had definitely not imagined it. Something had been sounding decidedly horrible, coupled with a distinctly physical change to her feel on the road, which is enough to scare any motorcyclist. With another long adventure awaiting us, for which Chloe would occupy the pillion, I can't shake the niggling worry that imminent disaster is waiting to strike. I discuss my fears that evening with Diane and both kids, and the general consensus is that we should not embark on the Welsh trip until I am able to satisfy myself that there is definitely nothing wrong. Chris has not changed his earlier stance at all, and if anything is even more adamant that he's not going back on the bike until we can be absolutely sure. I am left with no real choice but to investigate further, but that means removing the rear wheel again and investigating the scary innards of the hub. So be it, I assure everyone that I'll set about the job first thing the next day and Chris offers assistance - he's had experience of that back wheel and is happy to perform the role of chief mudguard remover once again.

Early morning finds me wheeling Daisy out for another ride around before I do battle with the hub. The noise is back with a vengeance and I suddenly realise that this is only occurring when there is no load on the back. I return and press-gang Chloe into a test ride once more and sure enough it's gone again. Off she gets, I ride twenty yards without her and there it is again. Back home I puzzle over this strange phenomenon and cannot for the life of me fathom it out. It simply must be something to do with the rudimentary suspension in the hub, so I head indoors to peruse the original manual and gaze in wonder and fear at the exploded diagram of the nightmare thing. Clearly this is no job for the faint-hearted, but then I read the description of servicing, with it's dire warnings that on no account should the thing be tampered with unless the tamperer is:

a) Properly equipped with the special Triumph jig for the job and

b) Mildly insane.

A bit of research follows by way of telephoning a couple of highly knowledgeable suppliers and the message is clear: unless I wish to end my life prematurely or risk serious injury, on no account should I attempt to dismantle the insides of a sprung-hub. I listen in awe to one fellow who tells the story of a chap that had decided to ignore such good advice, and pull his own hub apart in his shed. The resultant injuries left him in hospital for several weeks with a broken jaw and when he finally came home he was amazed to find a hole in his shed roof measuring nearly a foot across, presumably the exit point of the main spring. That was enough for me, and I had to accept that there were only three options available to me. Send the wheel off to an appropriately equipped expert, find another wheel in good order or find a rigid wheel without the hub design (Daisy's original specification in 1948 was actually a rigid wheel, with the sprung hub being an 'option' for an extra few quid). None of these options would be cheap.

Thoroughly depressed, but realising that action is the only way forward if we're to complete the challenge with Daisy, I spend the following morning making more calls and reach an agreement with one of the dealers that if I send or take the wheel to him he'll at least give me a free estimate for repairs. In the mean time, there is an auto jumble coming up this very weekend and I can go to that in the hope of finding something there, even if it is unlikely. I return to the garage to set about getting the wheel out and decide that I'll take the thing down to Hastings for the estimate straight away, but as I slot the large spanner onto the first of the big wheel nuts I stop absolutely dead in my tracks. I have just noticed something that is so ridiculously obvious that at first I think I must be mistaken. I stare at the thing in bewildered incomprehension for a minute, and yes, there is no doubt at all now - the sprung centre of the hub is upside-down! I grab hold of the rear mudguard and try to bounce the back end to check my suspicions, and it's so blatantly obvious now that I almost laugh out loud at the ridiculous reality. The whole concept of the sprung hub is to mount the wheel spindle between two mighty springs, with the whole lot locked in place within a steel spring box. The spindle is effectively offset to allow the wheel to move against the stronger spring over bumps, providing an effective two inches or so of movement. This is all fine and dandy, but relies on the spindle being at the top of the slot, and mine is clearly at the bottom, effectively preventing any wheel movement and obviously causing some kind of jarring reaction with every bump. That certainly would explain the clank, and with the wheel effectively rigid as it stands it would also explain the skittishness. Surely the designers would have thought of this and made it impossible to fit incorrectly? Apparently not.

Eager to pull the thing off and get the centre hub inverted, I summon Chris to help and in short order we have discovered that there is a design feature that is meant to prevent incorrect insertion of the wheel, but it's so obscure and vague that it's entirely easy to miss and with a bit of brute force it will go in upside down. Whilst struggling in that field near Newcastle, I had obviously failed to notice the slight offset of the locating arm and had clearly forced it incorrectly into the already worn slot without noticing my error. Now that we have it the right way round, it positively glides into position with no resistance at all and I feel utterly stupid to have not noticed the arrangement before. I grasp the mudguard once more, bounce up and down, and glory be we have suspension, of a sort, once more. Now for the real acid test, I hurry indoors to retrieve jacket, helmet and gloves before wheeling Daisy once more to the road for yet another test ride and I nearly cheer out loud as she smoothly eats up the bumps in wonderful silence. The back end is once again behaving itself and I return home with a mixture of delight and relief that the obscure problem has been overcome without either a lengthy wait or just as importantly the need for startling expenditure. I can now get right back on with planning the final stages of our campaign, which only this morning was looking to be in serious jeopardy. At dinner, I can't suppress my rediscovered happiness and monopolise the conversation, raving about the design of that hub, my own stupidity, the fears I had suffered that our Landmark challenge had hit the rocks, my subsequent delight that it hasn't and I realise as I babble away that the whole thing has become bizarrely important to me. I am more determined than ever that we shall win that trophy and after we've cleared away the plates, I spread the maps out once more, Chloe joins me eagerly and we're soon happily lost in deep contemplation of what should prove to be our final, successful foray.

10. The World Strikes Back!

The plan emerges and it seems that fate has thrown the dice on our behalf and come up with a double six. The Landmarks that remain are in fact arrayed in beautifully logical order from the Cambridge base that has become so familiar. From there we can see a clear anti-clockwise route that starts with Santa Pod, from where we'll loop to the north of Birmingham, up to Chester once more, circumnavigates Wales in a big loop to arrive eight hundred miles later at the very last target, Draycote Water, not fifty miles from the start. The large natural reservoir will be the final triumphant stop and our fiftieth Landmark, so we circle it several times in thick red marker. But an awkward moment beckons, something I had not considered at any point when I had coerced the kids into joining me on the adventure. It's simply that the great moment of completion can only be shared by one of them, Chloe as it turns out, and plainly Chris is feeling left out because I come to realise that he's been hanging around on the periphery of this final evening of planning, but hasn't joined in or said a word and is looking sullen and upset. He's been involved in more of the actual riding, and has endured some pretty tough conditions along the way, but he won't be there at the finish to share the moment. It's an incredibly emotional moment for me as I lock eyes with him for a fleeting second, the unsaid disappointment is communicated silently before he looks away quickly and exits towards his room. Chloe stares after him and says,

"What's up with Chris?" but before I can formulate an answer she's clicked.

"Oh" she adds, which just about says it all. We stare glumly at the route which we had been discussing with such enthusiasm just moments before, as I try to think how to handle the situation, but no inspiration comes so I decide to leave it be for the moment. I'll see if his mother can come up with any bright ideas, I decide, but right now it's time to call it a night.

Diane's suggestion is that I try to include Chris by way of telling him that we can't celebrate the great moment without him, and therefore he will need to be waiting near the telephone at around the right time on the great day, when he'll find that there is something special in the fridge, such as a bottle of beer, a rare treat indeed, that he can use as a toast to our success. Of course, that will require that we stay in touch so that he can track our progress and by doing that we can remind him of his own involvement and allow him to be at least loosely part of the final foray. I'll have to sell this whole idea to him carefully, but it seems to be an almost perfect answer to an otherwise unsatisfactory situation. I sleep on it and the next morning the idea is every bit as good, although I realise that at the hormone-bouncing age of fourteen, Chris will probably still see it as a less than satisfactory conclusion. These thoughts are pushed to the back of my mind by the intrusion of the telephone however and within a few short minutes everything has changed because the real world has just woken up, eyed me lazily, found me wanting and decided to intrude on my recently acquired utopian lifestyle with a sudden opportunity to be stressed, put upon and generally have no fun whatsoever. An issue has arisen within my old business, involving one of the sites for which that I had promised I would always be available when I stepped back from my Director's role - and Steve now needs me back on the case. It's urgent, will require my complete and immediate dedication and will take me eight thousand miles away from home before it's done so can I attend the offices tomorrow for a full briefing? Fate it seems, has decided to take her dice back and call 'foul' and suddenly my dream of completing the Landmark is once again under serious threat.

The next morning finds me sitting in my old office suffering an overwhelming feeling of déjà vu and cursing at the unbelievable timing of the project that has just landed unavoidably in my lap. When I had left the company, I had promised to maintain involvement and be available for any serious issues or projects involving two of the companies long standing customers, and one in particular had been so completely 'my baby' over the years that it was almost impossible for me not to be intricately involved in anything that should arise. The site that now requires me to honour this promise is in the Falkland Islands in the South Atlantic where any project timing is dictated by the seasons, not to mention the fact that preparation of equipment, supplies and logistics has to take place a full six weeks before the actual job (it takes that long to ship the stuff down there). Of course as usual everything has been left to the last minute, which taken together means that there is a blind panic going on that is now exclusively mine - it's no wonder I'm feeling put upon. I desperately take stock of my options, but it seems that whatever way I look at it there aren't any that will allow me to complete the challenge during what little remains of the summer holiday. I curse again at the unfairness of life, particularly the ironic fact that I had walked away from my career for exactly this reason - it was intruding unacceptably on my family life. How on earth could I tell Chris and Chloe that everything we had set out to achieve on the challenge was now dashed by the very pressures of business that had spawned the whole thing to start with?

The next few days whistle by as I find myself right back in the cut and thrust that is modern business, and reluctantly I am fully focused on my new project. By the end of the week I have the shape of the thing, have identified the exact requirements and know the schedule to which I must work. I have deliberately not mentioned to the kids the potential disruption this project could bring, and now that I know what's required of me I can see a glimmer of hope. There are two full weeks of the summer holiday left, and I have estimated that Chloe and I can complete the last leg comfortably in three days. Most of the next week will be taken up with specification and ordering of computers, software and peripherals for the Falklands followed by the completion of the full project plan, and finally the internal paperwork that is the bane of every office nowadays. Crucially, I will then have a whole week free whilst awaiting delivery of all the project components, after which I will be fully occupied with the preparations for the trip to the Falklands. It's clear then, that if Chloe is to join me on the last foray, it must be in that second week, just before school starts again and I'll just have to hope that Daisy doesn't decide to do anything interesting to us that prevents completion. I make a mental note to make sure we're properly equipped to deal with a puncture this time and this leads me to remember that I must also get a new set of points, rather urgently.

There are times when I can be astoundingly idiotic, I chide myself, as I realise that during the so-called complete check over and maintenance I had performed after the Scottish leg, I had utterly failed to even look at that bodge repair to the magneto. The thing must be all but falling apart by now and it would be foolish indeed to set off on another eight hundred mile trek without replacing it. It's too late now to do anything, being past five thirty on a Friday evening, so I scribble a note for myself for the next week and place it squarely in the middle of the desk. As I get up to go home, I stop and write 'urgent' in big letters at the top just in case.

A free weekend at home then, but I can't relax because I have yet to get any of our photographs developed and of course without them we have no claim to the challenge at all. For some reason I have been feeling increasingly paranoid about this. What if the cameras have been shaken about too much, or worse, got too wet and the precious film ruined? It is unthinkable, but I can't shake the growing doubt that perhaps these cheap disposable units were not the best of ideas. I have been sensible enough to carry two and record the Landmarks on both, sure, but until I am actually in possession of the final prints from at least one of them there is much to worry about. Selecting the primary three containing the vital evidence then, I head off on Daisy to the local supermarket where there is a fast print shop, hand them over to an attendant who doesn't look a day over twelve and therefore worries me even more, collect my one hour service receipt and then wander off to wait anxiously for the results. I manage to find a small cafeteria to sit in whilst I sip possibly the most foul cup of coffee I've ever experienced and I fester nervously as I convince myself that at least one of the cameras will turn out to be useless and all our efforts will have been in vain. Of course, I tell myself, the one that is most likely to have been ruined will be the Scottish leg, and with no chance whatsoever of a repeat trip this year if necessary, that would sound the death-knell of our attempt at the trophy. The hour seems to drag past at half speed, but eventually it's time and I return to the print shop with butterflies in my stomach. I nearly die on the spot when the acne'd young man gets the three packages but rather than just handing them over, he opens one, frowns, states "One of your cameras had water in it I'm afraid" and pulls out a print to show me the worst. My heart gives a flutter, but gloriously the print he's showing me is a clear photograph of Daisy in Scotland. There is a horrible pink smudge across the top left corner, which effectively ruins the thing in terms of being a happy holiday snap, but for my purposes it's absolutely fine. I take the package and riff through the rest - nearly all have at least a small pink smudge along the top somewhere, but all show what they need to and I'm massively relieved. The attendant eyes me with deep incomprehension as I look at him with a huge grin and assure him that these are just fine. Abso-bloody-lutely marvellous in fact!

Delight to deep concern in two minutes. That is what happens as I hurry from the supermarket only to find a police officer standing next to Daisy, clearly waiting for her owner and looking distinctly un-amused. I have the usual quick pang of worry as I approach, but then I assure myself that this is stupid for there is nothing, surely, that can put me on the wrong side of the law? She's MoT'd, taxed, insured and in good fettle, but then the look on this constable's face tells a different story. Oh Gawd. I approach nervously and having established without doubt that I am the guilty party the officer addresses me.

"Is this your motorcycle then Sir?" Here we go then, I am about to find out what heinous crime I have unwittingly committed and experience tells me to adopt a polite and respectful demeanour in my response

"Yes she is - Isn't she pretty?" My tormentor studies me for a few seconds before turning to Daisy with exaggerated slowness, inspecting the clearly disgraceful object in front of him.

"That's as well may be Sir, but right now I would suggest to you that it's only 'pretty' as in 'pretty dangerous!" he pauses, switches his gaze to me and adds "Do you know why it's 'pretty dangerous' Sir?" Some coppers just have a knack of getting right up my hooter, and this is one of them. I sometimes wonder if they have extra evening classes at training college on patronising sarcasm and how to deliver it. I'm not about to rise to the bait, but neither am I going to take it lying down

"Well, obviously I don't because I wouldn't be riding it if I did now would I?" is the best I can come with. I have no idea what it is that has given him cause to pull me, and I suspect that he knows it. We study each other for a moment and then, adopting the air of a headmaster addressing a particularly errant scamp of a pupil, he crouches down, indicates that I should join him, stabs a finger towards a particular place on Daisy's rear tyre and raises an eyebrow in anticipation of my response.

"Bloody hell" is what springs to mind, and in fact is what I exclaim, as I can now clearly see the two inch ragged tear in the sidewall and the strangely shredded bald patch in the tread adjacent to it. There is no denying it; no excuse for it and indeed it does look in a dangerous state. Clearly I'm nicked, as they say.

The rozzer stands up and we now go through the usual rigmarole of license, insurance, MOT the latter two of which he hands back after a cursory inspection before instructing me to stay where I am as he heads purposefully to his car with the license. He talks for a minute or so into the radio, then comes back and hands it back. He sighs, studies me for a moment, and then starts to speak.

"We seem to have little problem here don't we?" he points at the bike and raises that eyebrow again. I decide that a non-committal shrug is the best response. I can't help noticing that the 'Sir' is no longer part of his repartee, either. He's holding all the cards and he knows it, I'm just going to have to put up with his razor sharp wit while I wait for him to spell it out.

"Right, I'm going to talk for a minute and you are going to listen carefully, agreed?" we look at each other, but I'm careful to try and look neutral because this is beginning to sound promising. What comes next is almost unbearable and clearly sets out the way this interview is about to go.

"The answer I was looking for there is 'Yes officer' - do you see where I'm coming from?" at this moment I want to poke him in the eye, the one with the raised eyebrow, but I find myself mumbling "Yes officer" whilst thinking 'Git'. He relaxes, having established control of things, and launches into a little speech about road safety, the important role that a good set of tyres, for example, might play in achieving it and in conclusion he spells out what he expects me to now do.

"You take this motorcycle straight home, slowly, and before it sees the road again you will replace the tyre." He pauses and the eyebrow does it's party piece again, "Yes officer" he suggests patiently.

"Yes officer" I mimic.

"Good, and in future you will be sure to check the condition of those tyres regularly won't you? - Say 'yes officer' once more". He's had his fun and I have played my part, and with that he turns on his heel and heads for his car, leaving me steaming gently behind him. As he pulls away, he slows down and winds down his window, and I steel myself for one more intensely annoying comment. But with a genuine tone in his voice he says, "One thing Sir, I do have to agree she is *very* pretty!"

At home I dump the photographs in the dining room and head straight back out to the garage to inspect that tyre. As I stare once more at the angry welt in its surface I wonder how on earth I had missed it when we were mucking about with the wheel recently. It's undeniably knackered which is just about the last thing I need on top of the other distractions and it also means that the sodding back wheel will have to come off *again*. I am initially at a complete loss as to how this can have happened but thinking back over the events of the Challenge to date I realise that there have been a number of incidents that could have caused the damage. There was that horrible sliding skid at the edge of the river in Devon, the puncture in Newcastle of course and then the out of control descent of that scary drop on the Hardknott pass. I'll never know which one of those hairy experiences had delivered the fatal wound and it won't change anything anyway, so I focus my attention, get right down to removing the rear wheel yet again and then set to with the tyre levers for the second time in three weeks. I leave Daisy resting on her rear stand, so useful at times like this, throw the old tyre into the corner and head back indoors reminding myself that there is now an extra item to be sourced urgently before we can set out on what is trying it's hardest to be an ever more elusive last leg.

The week doesn't start well, complications and difficulties with the project distracting me to the point that by Tuesday evening I have still completely failed to source or order anything for Daisy and only realise this when I rediscover the note to myself buried under some other papers that had been given to me first thing on Monday. Someone has also pulled a flanker, for I have inexplicably found myself dealing with another project alongside the Falklands one, on the grounds that it requires kit ordering from the same suppliers that I am already dealing with as well as apparently benefiting from my experience in it's planning. From my perspective it's all going horribly wrong all of a sudden, my break from this business, working as a free agent, my new life-style, the challenge - everything. I am utterly hacked off and as I slump in my chair, staring at the note and cursing, I realise that drastic action is required if I'm to get things back on track again and prevent the inevitable black-hole type attraction that is sucking me right back into the old ways. Over my dead body, I decide, it has to stop right now. I scoop up the additional, non-Falklands paperwork that has found it's way onto my desk (and the irony that it is this stuff that had obscured my note has not escaped me) and on my way out to go home I shove it back under the door from whence it came. I will deal with the questions later, the word 'no' will be prevalent in my answers in the morning and Daisy and her needs will take priority over everything else. I feel better already.

The evening is spent finalising the route plan for the Welsh leg the following week, with Chloe and Chris joining in. I had sat Chris down before starting, in order to unveil his mum's plan for the big moment of completion, showing him the bottle of Newcastle Ale reserved for him in the 'fridge and promising that we'll be reporting in so that he can track our progress. On arrival at the final Landmark, we'll 'phone in and he can crack the bottle and share the moment with us. It wouldn't be right otherwise, I assure him and to my relief he accepts this philosophically and is soon burbling of his own involvement, reminiscing about some of the high points and low points, comparing experiences with Chloe and enthusiastically describing for her the splendour of motorcycling through mountains, a pleasure she is yet to experience, but one that is waiting for her in the Snowdonia National Park. We find it on the map and Chloe traces her finger from our start point, wanting to know how far we'll get on day one, how long it will take from our camp to Snowdonia on day two, how long we'll be in the mountain region and the time flies by as we discuss it all with enthusiasm. By bed time I am well on the way to being fully content once more, happy in the knowledge that we are getting back on track and all I've got to do is make some calls in the morning, secure Daisy's vital bits, get them, fit them and head off into yet another glorious bimble, free of pressures, deadlines, schedules and most importantly responsibilities. This is how it's going to be, there is no possibility of it being any other way and for once in my life, things really will go exactly as planned.

By lunchtime the next day I have indeed sourced and ordered Daisy's bits, said 'no' to a whole host of wheedling persuasion with regard to the additional project, dealt with the few remaining issues that had arisen with the Falklands, and completed most of the paperwork expected of me. I am determined that Friday will find me waiting at home for the deliveries, the immediate fitting of which will be my only priority of the day and that we shall be ready for our final foray starting Sunday. On the day, I prepare our computer strip maps and then top up supplies such as coffee, tea and sugar whilst waiting for the courier. Chloe has the wanderlust on her and buzzes around helping, her excitement showing as we pack the maps into their place in the see-through panel on the tank bag. She talks incessantly about the adventure to come, the mountains, Wales and the Welsh and this leads her to another thread; "Do they speak English?" she asks. I never get to answer this one because at that moment the arrival of Daisy's tyre is announced by the dog exploding into a frenzy at the front door in her normal manic postman routine. Only the tyre has arrived though, no points for her magneto - yet. At least I can get her ready to roll now and after a relatively painless fitting of the new rubber, taking care this time to get the sprung hub the right way up, she's all set and waiting to be loaded up for wild adventures in the valleys. Chloe helps with the now familiar routine and we can't help but notice that the dog has cottoned on as well, as it slinks around us looking sorry for itself, ears down and tail low. She had spent almost the entire week in the garage while Chris and I were touring Scotland, her nose pressed to the crack where the doors meet. According to the girls nothing could keep her in the house and it had even taken some considerable coaxing to get her to come for her dinner. Clearly we are about to abandon her again, and she's not at all happy about it.

Saturday evening, Chloe has happily gone off to bed before her usual time, ready for an early start, an unheard of event in any other circumstances. She has left me fretting however, because the new points for Daisy's magneto, when they finally arrived earlier in the day, didn't fit. More buffoonery on my part, it must be said, because when ordering the things I had neglected to tell the supplier that Daisy's magneto is not the Lucas item that one normally associates with Triumphs of this era, but the less common BTH. I believe that this was an option, like the sprung hub, at the time Daisy rolled out of the factory and I had overlooked the necessity to inform the guy. Strictly speaking I should do something about it, but I am lost as to what exactly. The last time I had fiddled with the things I had only managed to stop them working at all but on the other hand will they last another eight hundred miles? I decide to leave well alone and trust the great God of Triumph sparkery-things to look after us. Time for bed then, pausing only to trip over the dog, who has taken to following me around all day, absolutely everywhere, inches from my heels, lest I suddenly disappear for another week and leave her to that lonely vigil in the garage once more. I sit and take her head in my hands, rubbing her ears and talking softly to her, but I can't get the usual waggy-tailed response and I can see that she is deeply unhappy – she just knows and there's no consoling her. Perhaps when I phone in to give Chris our progress reports, I'll get him to hold the telephone to Sheba's ear so I can talk to her. That way she'll at least know we're still around, somewhere. I stop this thought dead in its tracks as I head for bed – what on earth am I thinking about? Surely that way lies madness - having meaningful conversations with a dog over the telephone!

11. Wales, Sheep and More Trouble with Landmarks

I am yanked awake by the alarm clock at six o'clock and stumble downstairs to find Chloe already up, dressed and eager for the off. I use her enthusiasm to leave as a bargaining chip to con coffee out of her, and once that has helped to kick-start my heart I agree that it's time to go. This is it then, we're on the road for the final leg and we're blessed with a glorious sunrise as we thread our way through the sleepy outskirts of Ramsgate and hit the open road towards Cambridge. We are giggling like school kids (which is fine for Chloe, she is one after all) because Chloe has coined a little saying adapted from the Star Trek series and has just announced in an attempt to mimic the voice-over that accompanies the beginning of each episode.

"Wales," she says "The Final Frontier" and continues to rattle out a version of the rest suggesting that Daisy is about to boldly go where no 'old heap' has gone before. It's silly stuff, but has us sniggering all the same as I accept the well meaning insult to Daisy and interrupt her with the odd "Oi – careful, She'll hear you!" By the time we arrive and commence unloading in our lay-by, it's become a warm, balmy day and we just can't wait to put the big roads behind us once more and start the final Landmark countdown, from the ten remaining to the last one, only thirty miles away. Before we go however, we need to make the first call to Chris, as promised, and I as I talk to him I can picture him studying the map that we've left at home for him, showing the route we'll be taking over the next three days, ticking off each target as we reach it and counting down with us to the moment when he can get that beer from the 'fridge and join us in a toast to success. Chloe is peering over my shoulder as I bend down looking at our own map tracing a finger from our current position to our first stop, the Santa Pod raceway and drag strip. Forty miles or so, a nice little first hop before the longer haul around the north side of Birmingham and so promising Chris we'll check in later, it's time to get going.

Daisy has never felt better as we cruise along in the sunshine, heading directly west on the A428. I'm not taking any risks on this, our last foray, especially with the knowledge that those bodged points are still providing the sparks and so we settle down to a leisurely fifty-five. I revel in the feeling of freedom once more as the pressures and trials of the past few weeks dissolve into insignificance. We're back doing what we want to do, success is within our grasp and everything that could be good in the world is, indeed, good. Being relatively early on a Sunday morning, there is very little traffic about to spoil the ride and it's at times like this, I ponder, that the English countryside is at it's most enjoyable. Of course, this is nothing compared to what's ahead, where we'll hopefully enjoy yet more unfenced roads meandering through the splendour of the Snowdonia National Park, but it's relaxing and enjoyable just the same. It's also true that with the long and eventful Scottish leg completed, a new-found confidence in Daisy, and my own ability to handle her few foibles has buoyed my spirits to the point that I'm viewing this last foray as virtually a formality. Nothing can, or will, stop us now. I am still pondering such thoughts as we leave the larger roads and dive into the green lanes just to the west of Northampton in search of Santa Pod. It proves to be a tricky place to find, with the poor detail of maps that we have and a surprising lack of clear signposts that I had expected to find. Indeed, when we do finally stumble across it, more by luck than any feat of navigation, I comment to Chloe that for a famous site so popular amongst petrol-heads, it's most notable feature is the fact that it is surrounded by nothing more than trees and fields. It is also shut, so after a short break and the by now familiar routine of positioning Daisy for photographs, we waste no more time.

Inexplicably, I manage to lose the road that had brought us from the A428, and after a while we are completely lost in the green lanes and almost certainly going in the wrong direction. As usual, the little villages that appear from time to time on the very few signposts cannot be found on any of our maps. I try to follow the compass instead, a tried and tested navigation method previously, knowing that as long as we maintain a vague northwesterly direction we won't go too far wrong, but even this proves impossible because the roads simply won't behave and keep heading off in anything but the direction that we want. No sooner do we find a junction that offers a route that seems to go in our required direction than we find that it's a false hope yet again and the thing invariably bends round to the east, as if to deliberately taunt us. At one point, rising through a wooded area to burst into the sunshine on what seems to be a plateau, we stop and I gaze at the horizon all around, straining to see anything in any direction that looks like civilisation. A place perhaps, where we can pinpoint our location on the maps, find bigger roads that lead somewhere meaningful, or, at the very least contain a café! But I can see no such place, and whilst it must be confessed that what I can see is undeniably peaceful and certainly pretty, I would rather be enjoying it whilst at the same time making progress towards Wales instead of Germany, via the North Sea. There's nothing for it but to keep trying really, but to negate the need to keep stopping and scrabbling around in pockets, I tape the little compass onto Daisy's steering damper knob.

Half an hour later, we finally connect with a bigger road, and even better a sign to a place that's actually on our maps. We have managed it seems, to spend the last half an hour going in circles to the southeast of our last stop, but more to the point we have achieved the princely sum of about ten miles in the wrong direction. However, this is the A6 according to the sign in front of us, which promises to at least lead us north towards Wellingborough, the only recognizable place on our maps. From there we can jink west on the A45 and with a fair wind or whatever, we'll get onto a proper Daisy road, the B573, that will shoot us between Northampton and Wellingborough. And so it goes, with almost no clownery at all, until we're once again bowling along in open country, not a care in the world. We pass under the M1 after a while, get sucked into Rugby town centre, emerge, against all the odds, heading north on the right road and begin the circumnavigation of the huge sprawl that is Coventry and Birmingham. But this is not a chore at all, the countryside and general geography around Brum is actually very satisfying as a motorcycling experience. For large stretches, where the view is obscured either by hills or trees, it is near impossible to believe that a sizeable metropolis is but a few miles away, but studying the map it is clear that we are on the very edge of the suburbs and should, by rights, be threading our way through built up areas, fighting with bus lanes, traffic lights and endless mini-roundabouts. We see none of these things at all until suddenly, almost out of the blue, Stafford hoves into view and we're drawn like the proverbial moth to a flame. It's a good place to stop and Chloe agrees. She's hungry, she informs me, and isn't it time for lunch? I have to agree – the day has flown by and it's already half past one.

I like Stafford. Always have, because it's the quintessential Olde Englishe town packed to the hilt with history. Some of the buildings, which as a rule have survived remarkably well, date from the eleven hundreds and the place possesses what's believed to be the largest standing authentic timber framed house in England, dating from the sixteenth century or so. As fine a place as any for lunch, I reckon and we set about finding a suitably patina'd pub to do the honours. The Swan hotel is just the ticket, with it's little tables outside on the pleasantly landscaped street, and we settle for a ploughman's apiece as we just relax in the sunshine, watching the world go by. The grub, and a pint of rather murky real ale, is consumed in a leisurely fashion and then it's time to press on towards North Wales where one of my all time favourite roads awaits. We check our proposed route which takes us directly west from here, through Shrewsbury, Oswestry and then turning north up towards Wrexham. But we'll cut across country at Llangollan, through the mountains, in order to join up with the north coast road, the A55, and the reason that this road is a favourite is the string of tunnels that claw through the rocky coastal headlands as it passes through Conwy on it's way to Anglesey – a good road to drive or ride but especially good on an old twin like Daisy. I estimate that it's approximately a hundred miles to the point we'll join it, and I tell Chloe that if all goes well we should get to it some time around six o'clock and can look for camping soon after. I haven't got her full attention however, because she's spotted the word 'mountains' on the map and is far more interested in what time we'll be getting to them. We'll get to the mountains at five o'clock, I declare, unaware that the dark force of Sod is gathering to practice his Law, and in fact we're in for a bit of a shock.

I had forgotten about the roads in Wales. On the face of it, they're no worse than any other rural roads, but there seems to be a break in the very fabric of the space-time continuum that causes a normal rate of progress to be absolutely impossible. If you take any given ten mile stretch of rural road, anywhere else in the United Kingdom, you can ride it's length, stop, have a picnic and probably a short snooze and maybe even wash the bike before you'll complete the same distance in Wales. Strange, but true. I have a theory that some ancient, mystical power interferes with modern instruments and causes them to misrepresent true speed. When the needle says fifty, the actual rate of progress is in fact thirty-five. Of course, the locals know about this, but aren't about to let on to us lot, preferring to save the pleasure of doing an indicated eighty on a minor public road all for themselves. Certain parts of Ireland are obviously on the same ley-line. This also explains why North Wales Constabulary have such a good track record for catching speeding drivers – their equipment tells them, as you bimble sedately along at fifty-five, that in fact you're doing seventy and being 'locals' themselves, they use this quirk of physics to great advantage. I could, of course, be entirely wrong, but as we sit in a lay-by eyeing the silhouette of the peaks, I enjoy explaining my reasoning to Chloe. "You're mad" is the rather unsatisfactory counter argument. Nevertheless, since passing

Shrewsbury, progress has been inordinately, undeniably slow, and although the view on the horizon is highly suggestive of a great ride ahead, it seems to be taking forever to get there.

Then of course, there is the peculiarly Welsh double-wammy of caravans and tractors. We are forcibly reminded of their ability to turn any given planned journey into a frustrating and stressful experience, when we come across an example of each engaged in a face-off. The particular road we are travelling should, along most of its length, allow all vehicles, of any size, to pass without much trouble. But as is the way of things, the tractor we can now see in front of us, with it's large trailer full of hay and the Volvo estate coming the other way, with it's ridiculously large caravan, have met on one of the very few stretches of road that will not. Not only can they not pass, but in trying to do so they seem to have become jammed, like corks in a bottle. Both vehicles have pushed as far into the hedgerow as they can and unsuccessfully tried to edge past each other, and the Volvo has found a ditch by the looks of things. There is no way past, so we pull up a little way down the road and watch for a minute or two before I decide that nothing is going to change in a hurry, reach out, kill Daisy's engine and tell Chloe that she can get off. As we sit by the hedgerow watching, another car towing an equally huge caravan comes round the far bend and very nearly ploughs into the Volvo. By now, both the tractor driver and the Volvo driver are engaged in a heated discussion, presumably about who should reverse, made laughable by the fact that the Volvo driver can't actually get out of his car because the tractor's huge rear wheel is preventing him from opening his door and the hedgerow is preventing him opening the passenger door. I can see his wife giving him grief in the other ear, and the whole situation shows a promising likelihood that it will become highly amusing when he breaks off the argument with the tractor driver to start one with her instead. I can't lip read too well, but the expletives exchanged are so very obvious that I don't really need to!

I consider the phenomenon of caravans and tractors. I'm sure that if a statistical analysis were to be carried out, Wales in mid-summer would be found to posses a far and disproportionately higher concentration of the things per square mile than almost any other place in Europe. With the possible exception, when it comes to caravans, of Cornwall. But this train of thought is interrupted as the main matinee gets under way down the road. The tractor driver, obviously growing weary of the verbal haranguing from Mr Volvo, has decided to act. He revs the tractor and slowly begins to move, despite the fact that the only way he can do this is by dragging his trailer along the side of both Volvo and caravan. There is a horrible wrenching and scraping noise, but that is immediately drowned by the maniacal scream from Mrs Volvo and a hysterical barrage of vitriolic babble from Mr Volvo. Chloe and I watch the unfolding drama, absolutely agog, as the big trailer inches forwards, wreaking a terrible havoc on the shiny, expensive car and finally meets the leading edge of the caravan. The tractor's irresistible pull drags it through the initial resistance and I stare in wonder, my heart in my mouth, as the big white home on wheels seems to buckle slightly and rear up before giving way with an ear shattering splintering noise. Mr Volvo looks as though he's had a coronary, because nobody should ever be that shade of red and stay healthy, but I think Mrs Volvo has actually passed out. Mr Volvo revives impressively quickly launching into an unspeakable tirade through his open window and as the trailer's rear-end finally clears his door and continues it's inexorable progress along the side of his caravan, he's out like an Exocet missile and doing a little dance in the road as he watches the final cataclysmic raking of his pride and joy. The driver in the car behind the Volvo has recognised that there, but for the imminent grace of God, goes his own caravan and has already taken urgent evasive action, reversing back up the road to where it widens, and to my amazement the tractor driver, free of the dragging effect of the once plush but now wrecked conveyance behind him, makes a break for it and simply carries on up the road with Mr. Volvo in hot pursuit on foot. They disappear round the far bend, the tractor clearly opening a big lead and an eerie quiet descends on the lane.

We decide not to hang around, because there's no telling when Mr Volvo will come back and we'd be pretty useless as material witnesses anyway. All we'd seen is a large trailer full of hay and glimpses of a tractor from our vantage point, we hadn't got a look at the driver and there was no number plate to be seen. I couldn't even reliably state what colour the tractor was. In short, I am busily convincing myself that we wouldn't be much use to anyone and I suspect that Mr Volvo, when he returns, will be very tiresome anyway. There is also the small fact that we've lost over an hour sat here watching the pantomime being played out. Certainly not a wasted hour, I feel, because being a life long fan of Laurel and Hardy I am in fact highly appreciative of a good piece of free slapstick comedy, but nevertheless time is pressing by and we should be getting a move on. We pass the Volvo and caravan slowly and Mrs Volvo, her pride and ego already fatally wounded, simply stares straight ahead through the windscreen, showing no sign that she's even seen us. The great gouges along the side of both car and caravan are bad enough, but the offside front corner of the caravan has had the entire top two feet of it's side panel neatly rolled back exposing the inside, reminding me of the old fashioned corned-beef tins that you had to open with that little key to turn back the lid. I mustn't laugh, I chide myself as we pass but Chloe has no such inhibitions, and I hear the barely suppressed giggle escape her as I select second gear and accelerate away. Bizarrely, we pass the tractor some few miles on, but there is no sign of Mr Volvo. Perhaps he's done a Reginald Perrin and simply walked away from it all, across the fields.

Time's really getting on now, but we eventually join the A55 just south of Rhyl at a little before seven o'clock, and we start to think about looking for a campsite. We stop for a rest in the first lay-by we find, I show Chloe where we've got to and point out the Colwyn Bay area, fifteen miles or so to the west, suggesting that this is going to be a sure fire camping area. We'll head that way and camp at the first site that presents itself, I suggest. Half an hour later I am cursing, because as the sun begins to set, and I pull over to lift the tank bag and turn on Daisy's lights, nothing happens. No lights. Not even a faint glimmer. A quick check confirms the battery is absolutely dead, and I find there's nothing registering on the ammeter when the engine is running. I didn't notice this earlier, as the instruments are tank mounted on Daisy so the tank bag covers them up, and of course being magneto ignition the small detail of a flat battery has no effect on her ability to start and run. Bugger. The thought of riding in bad light on this fairly fast stretch of road is, to say the least, unacceptable so clearly the need to find a camp site has suddenly become fairly urgent and with that thought burning bright, I press on with all haste lest we end up stranded. We carry on west, with Daisy cranked up to nearly eighty in order to make better progress but as the light steadily fails I am getting increasingly uncomfortable with the situation. I finally concede that we are fighting a losing battle, which is now becoming a potentially dangerous one and I decide that we have no other choice but to take the first available turning off the main road, where at least we'll be out of the danger of a tail-ender from fast approaching traffic, and hope to hell that we can get directions in the nearest village to a camp site somewhere near.

Before any turnings come along, we find ourselves approaching a service area where I spy a Travelodge sign. I don't really want the expense, but our predicament is becoming pressing and it's better than risking an accident. As we pull off onto the slip road however, we see a little camping sign pointing up a track to the rear of the parking area. Not quite believing our luck we follow it and sure enough there is indeed a campsite at the end, sprawled around a large farmhouse, where we are received warmly and allowed to check in. We make our way to the tent area, noting as we do that there are not many facilities but luckily we're armed with food and I have a couple of tins, coke for Chloe and bitter for me nestling in the tank bag, alongside the bottle of Newcastle Ale and the tin of Red Bull that are reserved for the big moment of completion. We park Daisy up and Chloe is an immediate blur of activity as she does the honours with the grub whilst I make camp, and half an hour later we're sitting in the twilight watching a huge yellow full moon rise slowly over the fields while we eat. Chloe is delighted to discover that there is a big local bunny population, appearing from the hedgerows as they do, to sit with their ears standing upright as they contemplate whatever it is that rabbits contemplate of an evening. In the distance, high on a rise, we can see a pub, brightly lit and glowing invitingly, so after dinner we set out to find it on foot. This proves to be harder than it looks, and we have to walk along the edge of the A55, behind the crash barrier, stumbling along in the dark until we reach the turning that leads to the pub. A brisk walk later, we're happily ensconced in the snug little bar and poring over the maps that I have brought along. There is a distinct sense of anticipation radiating from Chloe - we'll be riding through Snowdonia National Park tomorrow.

Chloe likes to see where we've been on these forays, and just as she had done in Devon and Cornwall, she wants to know the route travelled and traces her finger slowly across the map as I describe each hop that we have made through the day. But as she moves her digit across Shrewsbury I realize suddenly that buffoonery has occurred again and I stop her progress across the map by exclaiming "Oh God! I don't believe it!" Chloe looks up, startled by the sudden change in my demeanour, as I continue with "Bloody hell, I am such an idiot!" Chloe, having no idea what it is that has so suddenly upset me, asks the inevitable question and I point to the map just below Shrewsbury, where there is a Landmark point highlighted with one of the computer's virtual push-pin labels. This is the one that Chris and I had decided to leave on our homeward leg from Scotland, the one that I was meant to have scheduled into this foray with Chloe. It is the one that I have in fact completely forgotten about until this moment. I cannot believe how stupid I've been, and the thing taunts me from the page as I confess the frightful cock-up to Chloe and admit that we have actually passed within ten miles of it earlier today. We huddle together trying to calculate how far back from our current position it is, but it's not good news because we end up agreeing that it's a good eighty miles away. To double back will put a huge extra leg on our plan; the best part of a day's riding in fact. I have another idea. "OK, let's follow the route round and see if we get closer at any point" and with this Chloe's finger gets into action again whilst I silently curse myself some more for such blatant clownery.

In the end, after trying out various detours from our planned route, the least disruptive course of action is to tack the overlooked Landmark onto the last leg, just before the final stop in the midlands. Instead of taking a direct cross-country route from the Brecon Beacons to the midlands via Hereford, we'll have to dogleg north and skirt the southern tip of Birmingham rather closer than we had planned. This will add a paltry forty miles to the overall distance, as opposed to the next best option of hopping east from Snowdonia and back again, which would add something like eighty miles. With that decision made, it's time to place our call to Chris, waiting patiently at home for the promised progress report and after a lengthy update during which he helpfully points out that I am a twit, Chloe and I return to our deliberations regarding the next day, staying in the little bar until the last bell invites us to make ourselves scarce. I'm ready for bed anyway, after what's been a long but mostly pleasant, and in places amusing day, and we wander happily back down the lane, brave the dark no-man's land behind the crash barrier and find our way back to the farm. It seems as if the entire rabbit population of Wales has migrated to our field, but as we stumble out of the trees they take fright and shoot off in every conceivable direction, much to Chloe's delight. We decide to brave the very rickety-looking shower block before turning in, a decidedly uninspiring experience, and both of us drop off to sleep almost immediately once we've snuggled into our sleeping bags.

Chloe is first up in the morning, and when I manage to regain consciousness at seven o'clock, I am surprised to find that she's not in the tent. I poke my head out onto a misty morning, to find that the bunnies have returned in even more numbers than the previous evening and Chloe is stalking them, ever so slowly. I watch, fascinated for minute as down on all fours, she inches forward, careful to make no sudden movements that will start the mass stampede that we had witnessed last night. Closer and closer she gets, when suddenly the nearest rabbit to her takes fright and legs it, as Chloe breaks cover and runs forward. Within seconds the whole field explodes with activity, and in the blink of an eye there is not a bunny to be seen. Chloe ambles back towards the tent, her cheeks glowing red in the early chill and I don't think I've ever seen her look happier than she does right now. She finally sees me watching, runs over to plant a kiss on my nose and harangue me into getting up and we soon have bacon and scrambled eggs on the go, with lashings of hot tea to wash it all down. Chloe is almost bursting with anticipation, incredibly eager to break camp and set off on our adventures once again, and as she bustles about clearing away the breakfast stuff, firing questions at me about how long it will be to Snowdonia I find that her enthusiasm is infectious enough to get me moving. We're packed up and ready to go within twenty minutes, Daisy fires up first kick, Chloe climbs aboard and gives me a big bear hug from behind and at that moment the sun breaks through the mist to bathe us in it's early golden glory. Suddenly I feel like the luckiest man in the world, and congratulate myself for having bought Daisy, taken up this challenge and indeed encouraged the kids to join in. It's time to put more miles under our wheels and enjoy another day of adventure, and I pull in the clutch, select first, look over my shoulder and ask the unnecessary question "Ready?" the answer makes me laugh as Chloe points to the horizon and quotes from another favourite film of hers.

"Yep" she exclaims "to infinity and beyond!".

We're soon leaving Denbighshire travelling on the empty road west into Conwy, and before long we are bowling along the coastal stretch watching the sun sparkling on the surface of the open sea. The fresh sea air is invigorating and it's just about the perfect start to the day. I have already described what's coming to Chloe, telling her that Daisy is going to sound tremendous as we pass through the string of little tunnels, but before we reach those we have to make a brief detour south, to stop at the next Landmark, which we have already identified as Bodnant Garden. It's not yet open when we get there, so we only stop briefly before doubling back up to the A55 once more and proceeding west again along my favourite bit of the road. Half an hour later, we are having a whale of a time, making plenty of noise in those tunnels, accelerating into each as we approach and then letting Daisy drop onto the over-run for maximum effect as her deep exhaust note bounces around in the enclosed pipes of concrete that cut through headland after headland. Eventually they're behind us and soon we cross the Menai straight, marvelling at the spectacular view afforded by the deep cut between mainland and island, which always looks to me like some exotic picture-postcard millionaire's playground, with the yachts parked in a sparkling clear sea against the backdrop of steep wooded coast in which the odd white building can be seen peeking out over the straight. Wonderful, but we continue without stopping into Anglesey, heading for our next target and wondering what we'll find because this is another Landmark that we have been unable to identify from any of our research. The written clue 'A trough of airmen' gives us a general idea, because the maps clearly show an airfield at the map reference, but we haven't worked out the trough bit, or what it may signify. But of course, that's all part of fun.

Everything's going rather swimmingly I reckon, as we come off the far side of the rather picturesque bridge into Anglesey and begin the straight trek west. Daisy is lapping it up, as has become expected of her, we've made good time along the coast road, already have one Landmark in the bag and it's still early yet. I'm just contemplating the fact that it can only get better, because the day's ride ahead is what we've both been looking forward to the most, when I'm suddenly jerked back to reality as the sound of disaster rings in my ears. Daisy's engine, as if it had overheard my thoughts, has just stopped without warning, and we endure a horrible moment where we go from the entirely satisfactory growl that she emits when cruising along at fifty-five to the depressing, flat descending drone of a suddenly non-functioning power plant. I blip the throttle a couple of times without a response and I'm forced to simply pull in the clutch as we slowly coast to a halt on the hard shoulder, where it becomes immediately apparent what's wrong. There is an overpowering smell of petrol and as I look down in alarm I can see the stuff all over the gearbox and oil tank. We dismount, crouching down for a closer inspection and discover that the petrol pipe from the tank has split just below the tap, allowing the vital liquid to simply ooze away onto the road until Daisy is breathing fresh air.

"Bloody marvellous!" I exclaim, throwing up my hands, but after pulling it off, examining the problem more closely, I can see that all is not lost as there is enough length on the pipe and after a bit of fiddling I manage to cut the thing back and reconnect the unblemished new end to the tap.

Daisy has a reserve tap on the other side of the tank which is good for a few miles, but we're in the middle of nowhere as far as I can see, with no sign of any civilization particularly close by. I discuss the options with Chloe, but this doesn't take long because there are only two. We can continue on this road and trust that there is a petrol station not too far away, or we can take the first available turning that suggests it actually goes somewhere and hope that there is one there. It's not a clear choice at all, so in the end we decide to toss a coin, heads we keep going or tails we turn off. Heads it is, and off we go on reserve, accelerating very cautiously and settling at a paltry thirty miles per hour in an effort to preserve every drop of fuel that we can. Eight miles or so later we have neither seen any petrol stations or attractive looking turn-offs and the inevitable moment arrives when Daisy once more sputters to a halt. We get off again and survey our surroundings, but there is nothing to see but fields and the odd sheep. Neither is there much traffic and really there's nothing for it but to start pushing and hope that salvation comes along. I start the long tedious slog, disheartened even further because the road climbs slowly but surely uphill and makes my task even harder. Chloe brings up the rear carrying the helmets and my jacket but before very long, as Daisy gets heavier and heavier whilst the sun gets hotter and hotter I begin to think about parking her up somewhere and trying to hitch a lift to the nearest place that has fuel. This is not an action that I am prepared to take lightly, because if I do that there is a very real risk that some of our gear or some of Daisy's fittings will be stolen, or worse the whole bike may end up in the back of a van. Equally, for obvious reasons, it is not an option to leave Chloe with the bike whilst I swan off over the horizon, destination unknown. No, on reflection, we'll just have to tough it out.

I needn't have worried as it turns out because before we've progressed more than two hundred yards up the road, which incidentally is enough to nearly kill me, we find a lay-by into which we trudge to have a rest, and discover a little side road hidden behind a grassy bank. There is a family with a caravan having a picnic lunch, but far more interesting is the bright green petrol can sitting under the caravan's steps! A tentative enquiry reveals that yes, it's half full, and yes the chap is quite happy to sell us a few litres so that we can get to the next town. He follows us over the bank with his can, but he obviously wasn't expecting to find anything like Daisy the other side.

"Bloody 'ell" he exclaims, "Was petrol invented when that thing was made?" He chuckles to himself as we reach her, but his face turns to respect as he inspects the pillion pad and turns to Chloe

"And this is your seat is it? All day long you say?" he asks. She assures him that in fact it's very comfortable, not at all as bad as it looks, but he doesn't seem convinced. I have emptied his can into Daisy's tank by now, and after tickling the float bowl to re-fill it I straddle her once more and try a kick. She responds immediately and our saviour lets out a good humoured cheer. I wonder if, when we'd arrived, he'd been getting bored back there with his caravan, and perhaps our arrival was equally good for him as it was for us. He doesn't seem to be in a hurry to return to his lunch after I hand the can back with some money for the fuel. I feel a little awkward just buggering off, but we need to get going, and so after explaining that we still have a long way to go, we mount up, wave goodbye, yell out a "thank you" and rejoin the main carriageway. I look round as we reach the top of the distant rise to see he's still standing in the lay-by looking our way, one hand raised in distant salute.

The obscure clue to the next Landmark turns out to be very easy to solve, once we get there. It's RAF Valley, as proclaimed by a large MOD sign inviting us to not even think about trespassing. We don't, simply getting our photographs and turning round to make our way back to the mainland. I make a big thing with Chloe that its "Snowdonia here we come" and the grin on her face says it all. But first we need to find petrol, which we already thought we'd done just up the road only to find that the forecourt and four pumps we had spied at a junction turn out to belong to an abandoned station that is no longer trading. In fact, no juice has flowed here for years by the look of things. We stop to ask a local but the directions she gives us are so complicated and convoluted that we move on, none the wiser, and try another local further up the road. If anything, this chap's assistance is even less likely to take us to the much needed juice, and after listening to a seemingly endless set of instructions we carry on the way we were, feeling exasperated. Third time lucky, I suggest to Chloe, as we pull over towards yet another fount of local wisdom. This guy tries to send us back to the now defunct station that we have already been to and I have to resist the urge to gibber as I listen politely to the third lot of useless directions in five minutes. What we need to do, I decide, is to study the map and find a bigger town, where surely there will be a plethora of the damned things. Anglesey is only about twelve miles across, I reason, and looking at the map we can't be too far from Holyhead, where the ferries go to and from Ireland. There simply must be a petrol station there, so that's where we'll go. In the end, it's all academic because we find one on the main road within two miles.

Having filled up with juice, and topped Daisy's oil tank off, I turn to Chloe and declare that "Right, *this time* it's *definitely* Snowdonia here we come!" and with that we saddle up and get under way once more, heading back to Conwy where, just across the Menai Straight we turn south to follow the deep rift that is formed by the Irish Sea. We stay on the A487 until we can peel off east on the A4085, the road that will take us through the heart of Snowdonia and we can almost immediately see the stark peaks looming in the distance, beckoning us onwards. I am reminded of our first encounter with mountains in Scotland when Chloe, just like Chris before her, taps urgently on my shoulder and points to the horizon. Like her brother, she has been waiting for this above anything else, and the wait is about to be rewarded. I am struck once again by the closeness of the countryside here, compared to the arms length grandeur of Scotland. Here, the tumbledown woods and hills press right up to the road, and one can simply pull off in any number of places and walk right into it. The roads themselves are absolutely tailor-made for Daisy, allowing a good cruising speed through their winding length, but restrictive enough that most traffic keeps to a sensible speed themselves. We are not jockeying for position, neither do we have anything pressing us from behind and it makes for an almost perfect ride. We enter the National Park area and stop at the first available place we can find, which in this case is a lay-by with a caravan selling teas and snacks, and after ordering a surprisingly good mug of tea each, we survey our surroundings. The view from our current vantage point is grand indeed, positioned as we are on the upper edge of an escarpment that looks across a lush green humpty-bumpty landscape towards mount Snowdon itself. Around it are the lower peaks and the foothills which, I assure Chloe, we are about to ride straight through.

We take our time over the next twenty or so miles, because it would be criminal to do anything else. The wide sweeping landscape gives way to rocky outcrops and the road snakes it's way around the base of Snowdon, following the contours of ancient glacial valleys. The views are simply breathtaking and we find ourselves stopping for a few moments regularly, just to stare in awe at the mighty splendour spreading in every direction. But as we progress through the morning, we notice that with each hour that passes there is an exponential increase in the number of caravans and campers on the roads, and before long the bloody things are becoming a real pain. No sooner do we pass one, having had to sit behind the thing as it crawls around blind bend after blind bend, than there's another, waiting to take up the duty of seriously aggravating everyone else on the road. By the time we reach the far side of the park I have grown to detest the things with an intensity that is surprising; certainly for us they have spoiled what would have been the best ride of the challenge so far. The things should be banned from minor routes during daylight hours, I reckon. Still, we have had a most satisfactory ride all told, Daisy has taken it all in her stride, and despite the plague of caravans we eventually join the A487 again on the other side feeling pretty fresh and deeply contented.

It's well past midday when we finally stop near the boundary of the park's south side. We have one of those Landmarks to get next that require us to detour sideways and then back on ourselves again, making no actual forward progress. As I show Chloe the next leg, twenty miles there and twenty back again, I comment on the fact that if we could do all of these 'as the crow flies' it would be no challenge at all. This one has no direct route to it, and in fact our map shows no roads in its immediate vicinity at all. We're going to have to rely on our instincts and the compass again, even though the last attempt to do that got us well and truly lost around Santa Pod. We have two clear choices of route. We can drop out of the Snowdonia National Park and pick up the bigger roads that go most of the way to our next target, or we can stay within the boundaries and take a less direct route on much smaller roads. Chloe isn't hearing of leaving the Park until we have no choice, and of course, in the spirit of this whole adventure she's absolutely right. No argument from me then, and it's cross country we meander on the wonderful unfenced roads so reminiscent of Cumbria, winding through a number of tiny hamlets and villages at little more than thirty mile per hour. The road follows the lazy meanderings of the river Dovey as we progress, crossing it in places via typically rustic stone bridges, and we stop at one of these crossing points to rest. Chloe is able to splash about in the shallows of the pebble-bedded stream as I just relax for ten minutes, and the real world might as well be a million miles away. Inevitably, we have to press on and finally exit the park just to the northwest of lake Vernwy, the visitor centre of which is our target.

We have swapped the splendour of Snowdonia's peaks for the rolling green of the valleys and lakes, and this one is a joy to ride along. The road hugs the western shore of the lake and is an entirely joyful experience, with Daisy humming along at a steady fifty-five now, the sun glinting off the deep blue of the lake and in the distance is what looks like a dam across the far end of the water. We arrive at the visitor centre, where the first priority for both of us is an ice-cream, which we eat sitting on a grassy bank with the dam-cum-bridge stretching in all it's splendour in front of us. At the visitor centre, we are informed that this beautiful dam was constructed in the late nineteenth century, in order to form a reservoir to feed the growing needs of the population of Liverpool and it's surrounding areas. The original settlement of Llanwddyn was actually submerged by the resulting lake, it's inhabitants being re-housed in a new settlement taking the same name in 1881, all paid for by the Liverpool Corporation. Apparently if the water level drops far enough, the ruins of the old village can still be seen. The dam itself is very typical of the Victorian architecture that is to be seen in many a viaduct around Britain, and with the lake stretching away beyond it the effect is quite charming, so we position Daisy to ensure that our photographs include it as a backdrop. As we finish snapping, I am amazed, and quite taken aback when an American family walking past stop, remove their young toddler from a push chair, and without so much as a by-your-leave proceed to plonk the lad in my seat on Daisy, stretch his arms forward so he can hang on to the handlebars and start to take photographs. Before I have mustered the wits to object they have whipped him off again and are on their way. Some people have the most unbelievably bad manners!

Before long it's time to get going and set out west again. I am incensed that I have to wipe a set of grubby child-sized fingerprints from Daisy's headlight shell, and I wonder again at the blatant gall of that family. We take a different route back to the southern tip of Snowdonia and if the road we had come out here on was delightful for it's gentle meandering by the river, this one is exhilarating for the opposite reason, a wide well kept surface, dipping and rising through the hills through a long set of sweeping bends and not a caravan in site, or any other traffic for that matter. We are soon having a whale of a time, and it seems like no time at all that we find ourselves riding down a tremendously long descent, bordered by a sheer rock cliff on one side and heavy woods on the other, to burst out into bright sunshine at the bottom and the little stone hamlet of Corris, where a steam museum, our next Landmark awaits. There are museums, and there are museums. This one is marvellous for the fact that it's tiny, quaint and friendly. We take our photographs, but it would be rude to leave without ducking in through the tiny door and having a look around, because I find these little pieces of 'living history' fascinating and feel strongly that they should be supported. The best way to do that is with the wallet, so we do. In the cool interior we discover that the railway was constructed to run from the quarries at Aberllefenni to the mid-Wales town of Machynlleth and was commissioned in 1858 before opening for goods traffic as well in 1859. By the 1880s passenger traffic had commenced too until the railway was acquired by the GWR in 1930 and closed to passenger traffic soon after. It was a slow decline thereafter and the last train ran in 1948 before the track was lifted leaving the bed in place. Some of the original Corris locomotives and rolling stock still run on the Talyllyn Railway but the Corris railway is now undergoing restoration by a group of enthusiastic volunteers drawn from the members of the Corris Railway Society. At the time of our visit they are laying track from Maesspoth Junction, a few miles away, going towards Corris itself. Good on 'em, I tell Chloe, and I give her a fiver to shove in the collection box.

With the time pressing on we're off again, heading south for some fifteen miles before another detour inland. But now we get tangled up once again with holiday traffic and the going is inordinately slow and congested. It's a huge shame because the delightful road would be fantastic to ride if I could just give Daisy her legs, but instead we are forced to trundle along amidst a seemingly endless crocodile of the dread caravans, which are out in force. Finally the road eases it's twisting and turning, allowing us a clear view along the centre and we end up having quite good fun weaving in and out of the traffic, waiting our chance to hop past and tucking back in to miss the oncoming caravans. We finally reach the very front of the queue, and suddenly it's clear why everything has backed up so badly as we take our chance and hop past the last vehicles and find a huge and slow moving tractor pulling the inevitable trailer full of hay.

Now we can let Daisy canter along on the suddenly empty highway and it's not long before we turn east once more and cover the last ten miles to the penultimate stop of the day and a very late lunch at the next Landmark, which turns out to be a silver mine. Opposite the entrance it has a nice little café and we are grateful for the chance to eat and contemplate the maps again. Chloe chatters away about the things we've seen and done today, enthusing mightily over the magnificent presence of mount Snowdon, laughing at the Americans and moaning about the caravans. As she rattles on, I realise that this day's riding has probably been the most pleasant of the whole challenge so far in many ways, and I marvel that after nearly eight hours in the saddle I'm still feeling fresh and relaxed. We won't be sorely pressed for the rest of day either, as it's now four thirty and we only have about sixty miles left to do today before camping somewhere near the next Landmark, already identified as Cilgerran Castle, situated three quarters of the way along the piggie's nose. I decide to take a bit of time before we leave again checking Daisy over for any obvious problems, loose nuts or missing bits, although I am not about to go anywhere near that magneto. It ain't broke, even if in the back of my mind I'm waiting for it to do so, I won't make the repeat mistake of fixing it before I have to. I pull out the spanners and a couple of screwdrivers, but less than ten minutes later I am singing the old girl's praises because I can find nothing amiss whatsoever. She isn't even leaking any oil and doesn't seem to have used any since yesterday. To Chloe's amusement I pat her on the tank and happily tell her she's a good girl before declaring that we're ready for the final hop of the day.

Next stop will be Aberaeron, where Daisy will need a drink and I will look for a cash machine, having just spent the last of my ready cash on our late lunch. But as we join the main coastal road we get tangled up in what must pass for rush-hour in Wales with the result that the going gets tedious and slow once more. By the time we finally get to the place it's pushing six o'clock but it seems later because for the first time in days there is a dark band of cloud climbing slowly in the west, and it has snatched away the sun. Chloe remarks that it seems to have got awfully chilly all of a sudden, and she's right. The absence of direct sun has without a doubt had a marked effect on the air temperature and the breeze drifting across from the sea has a distinctly less than a warm feel to it. Never mind, I assure her, there are only thirty odd miles left to do today, although we can actually stop anytime if we feel like it because tomorrow doesn't have to be the day we get home. We'll see how things go. Fuelled up on the outskirts of the town we take a detour into the town to hunt down a cash machine, and we find a delightful town centre brightly decorated with flowers and the like, and remarkably clean looking. This is supposed to be a whistle stop purely for the cash before getting straight on down towards Cilgerran, but as I return from the machine and go to mount Daisy, I find that somebody else has other ideas about a quick getaway.

What we have here is a pedant. A self appointed expert on all things classic bike and dread Custodian of an opinion which, judging by his expression, is the only one that counts. He's a little ferret of a man with an air of little-man syndrome about him, of the sort that you can find in the security hut at the main entrance to any corporation headquarters in the land. He's with two mates, so he's got an audience, and in Daisy he has clearly spotted a perfect opportunity to show off his prowess and expertise and then deliver his opinion. It'll be game set and match and he's not about to pass it up.

"Oh dear, oh dear" he chuckles as he darts across to us and effectively stops me getting on. He crouches down with a theatrical sigh and I study him for a second, then look at his mates, who give me a knowing look. Feeling a bit put out at the sudden intrusion, I return my stare to the gnome, but his attention is all on Daisy as his gaze sweeps her entire length in expert judgment and he makes a series of little "Tsk Tsk" noises with each detail that fails to meet his exacting standards. His mates now have an air of expectation, and it's obvious that they have seen the performance before and are looking forward to the show. I glance at Chloe who pulls a face as if to say "Who on earth is this, and what's his problem?"

I find myself fascinated by the gnome's mannerisms though, and I am stunned that he is prepared to blatantly shove in front of a six-foot-something, leather clad and heavily bearded motorcyclist and carry on the way he currently is. I wait with baited breath for the next act in the performance, and I'm not disappointed as he stands up slowly, completely ignores Chloe and me, and addresses his mates.

"What we have here" he assures his appreciative audience "is a bitsa!" They nod enthusiastically, and he continues, "See? The colour's all wrong for a start, these wuz never that shade of red, oh no, dear me no. And see that carburettor?" He chuckles, as if it's the sorriest thing he's ever clapped eyes on "All wrong, dear me yes, all wrong, should be an SU should that" His mates nod and grin, but he's only just getting into his stride apparently because he's off again "Now then, what about this wheel?" he declares, and in doing so he takes his life in his hands as he all but shoves me aside and bends down as if to grab it. I've had enough of this rivet counting idiot, he's gone too far and I certainly don't take kindly to being shoved, or for that matter impeded in my pursuit of pleasure. Putting on my most pedantic voice I lean forward and address the little squirt

"If you've quite finished with the bullshit, I'd quite like to leave, and you're in my way" You'd think that I'd just assaulted his granny, judging by the way he reacts, jumping backwards and firing back what I suspect is an often used defensive retort.

"There's no need for that! I was only saying!" But now he's out of the way, and I can't be bothered with any more diatribe so I simply give him a look that I hope conveys my displeasure, straddle Daisy's saddle and prepare for the off. She starts on the first kick and I gesture for Chloe to climb aboard, but the gnome manages one last shot as we pull away "I wuz just pointin' out that you've got the wrong wheels on!" he calls after us.

The rest of the ride down towards Cilgerran is enjoyable although there really is a distinct nip in the air all of a sudden. Threading our way along the coast is just as satisfying as our earlier ride on the periphery of Snowdonia, albeit a deeply contrasting experience, and bowling along past the rocky headlands and a sea that is so very clear compared to our own local stuff back in Ramsgate, the miles soon disappear beneath us until it's time to turn inland again at Cardigan Bay, cover the last five to the castle, our final target of the day. Another site that in theory should be steeped in history, the ruins of this early thirteenth century fortress actually seem to have few tales to tell. The family that built the thing had all but died out by the end of the next century, and the place had been left empty as a result. It seems to have stayed that way ever since, slowly crumbling away until all that remained is the few lumps still standing today. However, it does offer one superb feature that in it's own right makes the place worth a visit, and that is the stunning view from it's high position above, and at the very edge of the Teifi Gorge. It's a proper gorge, too, is this, complete with fast running river at the bottom, tumbling crazily along a twisted route, over a stone bed that has been slowly shaped over goodness knows how many centuries. We can see, from our vantage point, a whole series of white water rapids and we can also see a road following the contours of the far bank. I point down at the captivating sight and I suggest to Chloe that we try to find that road and follow the river. I don't need to suggest it twice.

We go down to retrieve the maps, before trudging back to our eerie to try and get a fix on the surroundings. We are able to pick out features that can be identified on the map, and eventually we can see what needs to be done in order to connect up with that road, and with no further ado we're back down to Daisy and setting off once more, looking forward to what promises to be a fully satisfying trundle. We are not disappointed either, finding our way easily to the river bank at the bottom of the gorge, and then following the route, with steep rock on one side of us and rushing white-water on the other. Bloody marvellous, and absolutely the best possible way to end what has been a superb day's riding. I find that I have let Daisy slow right down, until we're barely ticking along at twenty, because it seems criminal to pass this by any faster than we have to. When we reach the little village of Abercych, the road pulls away from the river a bit but Chloe spots a sign that promises a ford, and it seems too good an opportunity to miss so we take the turning back towards the river and pull up for a rest. Chloe soon ditches helmet and gloves and is paddling about at the waters edge as I wonder what to do next. I don't trust the ford, so we'll stay this side of the river for a short distance and cross further down. I want to get to Cenarth, just across the river, in order to find a shop so that we can stock up on provisions for tonight's meal and breakfast.

The shop provides the necessary stuff, but what we also find in Cenarth is a most enchanting and very well appointed campsite. It's just up the road, close to the lovely little village which boasts a nice big pub, next to a superb white-water section of the river tumbling past just twenty feet away. Again, I am struck be the sheer closeness of the wild geography, the ability to walk right up and touch it, explore and experience it, with no fences, gates or signs to stop us. And with this little lot literally a minute's walk from the campsite, I reckon we have found the absolute ideal place to spend the night. Chloe agrees wholeheartedly and we head straight over to the reception building to check-in. At first, it seems as though we are going to be out of luck as we are informed that the place is full. I look out of the windows at the complete lack of people, cars or any other kind of movement and find this hard to believe, but as my gaze takes in the plush drive, the nearest (very up-market) caravans, the swimming pool and the plush-looking clubhouse I realize that this is not about space, but image. The particular image that they don't want to be seen loitering about in their manicured park is that of a leather clad motorcyclist and his almost certainly tear-away daughter. OK, I can understand that to an extent, but equally I have mentally switched into 'stopped for the night' mode and really don't want to leave this rather ideal spot. I decide to try a bit of sleight-of-hand and I go outside again, tell Chloe what's going on and after explaining my thoughts we hatch a fiendish plan.

What the eye don't see, the chef gets away with. I was taught that rather useful piece of information years ago, and it can be true in so many ways. I can see no reason why we shouldn't test this theory out, by the simple means of removing from sight anything that might distress the campsite receptionist, and claiming our slot by stealth instead. We will achieve this remarkable feat by simply going away until the reception shuts, returning in the dark, sneaking Daisy into the very spacious and strangely unpopulated tent area, and obeying the very clear sign, which I have noted by the entrance, which helpfully suggests that 'Late arrivals - if reception closed please report and pay in clubhouse'. I am banking that the staff will have changed by then and I won't be recognised for the 'orrible leathery motorcyclist who had the gall to try and get in earlier. It doesn't even occur to me to consider a plan 'B' as we retire to the pub down the road to wait things out, so sure am I that it will be fine, and in the event this turns out to be an even finer plan than I had thought possible, as we spend a happy hour by the rushing river, me supping a fine ale and Chloe climbing around in the rocks that make up the rapids. But eventually, with the onset of darkness, the time comes when we really need to sort out our spot for the night, get the tent up and the first niggling pangs of hunger remind me that we have the ingredients for a big old stew. I finish the beer and summon Chloe, and we hunker down to discuss the commando-style insertion that we're about to execute on the campsite.

It was a masterful operation, I enthuse to Chloe, as we sit comfortably in the corner of the club house some time later. I had sauntered up the road to do a recce and finding the reception office firmly closed up as expected, we put our plan into action without delay. We managed to slide into the place undetected, pushing Daisy into the entrance, up the short drive and into the well kept tent area where there was just enough light left to get the tent sorted out before total darkness engulfed us. We had the pick of the field, because far from being full there were but three other tents in residence. Chloe soon had the stew on the go and after dinner we showered and dressed appropriately for an evening at the clubhouse, with the only giveaway potentially being my boots but I manage to do them up tight at the top and force my jeans down over the top of them, so they're not too obviously the footwear of Beelzebub himself. The formality of checking in late is completed without a hitch, making us legitimate residents with a ticket to prove it, and we could enjoy an evening of unusual comfort. We make the progress call home, talking Chris through the day's high spots before Chloe takes the telephone and burbles about mountains, rivers, castles and the drama with the petrol. It's a full twenty minutes before I get the chance to talk to Diane and give my own account of what has been a highly satisfactory day. We've picked off six Landmarks on top of yesterday's two, and there are only three to go for the full fifty. Surely, nothing can stop us now?

12. The Final Frontier

Six o'clock. That's the middle of the night in terms of my normal routine at home, or at least it may as well be, but for us today it is time to get up and get going. But there are certain things that must not be hurried, and a camp breakfast is one of them. Sitting by the tent in the early chill, watching the world slowly emerge into colour from the grey dawn whilst scrambled eggs, bacon and tea are prepared is a ritual that I am coming to love. It's a moment and an experience that cannot be reproduced at home, and it has become special for that very reason. To be out in the open in the misty Welsh countryside, just after dawn, is simply fantastic and as on numerous other occasions during the challenge where we have done exactly this, I feel a deep stirring in my soul and have never felt so alive. For Chloe, the magic is different but every bit as satisfying, and I watch her as she plays out her own, now familiar ritual of stalking bunnies, returning with the same happy glow on her face and planting the by now expected kiss. I can't think of a better way to start a day. As we polish off the grub, we talk through the day's ride ahead and although there are only three remaining Landmarks they are well spread out and we'll have to put a solid two hundred and eighty miles behind us if we're to complete the challenge today. Easy, if we weren't deep in the wilds of Wales, but we are, so I reckon this will be quite a challenge in itself.

Once Daisy is all packed up, we push her out onto the road to avoid waking the entire site and after allowing her to warm up we're off on what promises to be a superb ride down to Carmarthen. But as we reach the rapids down the road, where we had spent the early evening, I am left breathless by the utterly captivating sight before us. The gorge at this point runs directly east/west, and the steep rocky sides have captured the early mist between them like a funnel with the sun rising directly behind it. The effect is entirely magical, creating an eerie glow as the morning light struggles to break through the thick white swirls and we simply have to stop to get a photograph of Daisy in front of rapids at the bottom. And our timing is perfect, for by the time I have captured the scene and re-packed the cameras, the moment is gone and the day has arrived. Off we go again, straight across country, heading southeast and following the river all the way down. There is no traffic on the road at all at this early hour and we can allow Daisy to lope along at a steady fifty-five through a magnificent twenty miles of sweeping bends, with woodland on one side and the tumbling white-water cascade on the other. Occasionally a lodge or a Hansel and Gretel type cottage flash by, peeking from the trees, but for the most part it is a long downhill canter through entirely unspoiled countryside. We stop at several places to enjoy the scenery, because it is that good, but eventually we bottom out and leave the tumbling green behind us as the landscape changes to wide open arable farmland, gentle rolling hills, all the way to the distant coast.

The open fields give way to the first signs of human habitation as we approach Carmarthan, finally reaching the point where we must turn east again, for a leg that is going to be as uninspiring as the river valley was exhilarating. We're forced to join the M4 motorway, heading for Cardiff, and our first Landmark. I want to put this forty mile stretch behind us as quickly as possible and slowly wind on the throttle until Daisy is settled at a steady seventy. At least, I'm guessing that it's seventy, because her speedo has reached the limit of it's tolerance again and the needle starts it's wild jumping between ten and ninety mph. A small detail, and anyway it seems no time at all before we're turning off and heading south towards the coast just short of Cardiff, but the first of the day's trials emerges as we coast to the first roundabout. I am jolted awake by the first signs of what will become a major setback to the day's travels. A harsh metallic ringing suddenly issues forth from somewhere below, making a sharp, insistent 'ching-ching-ching' noise that matches the beat of the exhaust and it's startling enough to make me pull over urgently and stop the engine. Chloe has heard it too, and climbing off she has a concerned look on her face as she asks, "What's happened, what was that noise?" What indeed. I have no idea, but it was scary enough that we will have to investigate before going any further. My mind is churning as I crouch down to start prodding around, but the main thought that is pressing itself to the front is "Don't do this to us Daisy, not this close to the finish!"

Whatever it is, it's matched to revs. That much was immediately apparent as we coasted to a halt. I check the obvious things first; a loose chain can bounce around quite alarmingly, making contact with chainguard or casings, but a quick feel around shows both secondary and primary to be well within adjustment. Further investigation fails to show up anything hanging loose that can rattle against spokes or wheels and I can't find anything obvious that would make that noise. I start Daisy but as she ticks over sedately the noise has mysteriously disappeared again. I curse silently. Not another bloody evasive problem surely? I'd nearly gone insane with the sprung hub last week, and I certainly don't need to play hide and seek with another problem like that, not here, not now. I grab the throttle and give it a blip, but as Daisy's engine responds willingly, ching-ching noises remain conspicuous by their total absence. I sit back and consider things, but it's obvious that we are just wasting time and in spite of the fact that I am a little uneasy about both the suddenness and evasive source of the now silent noise I decide that we'll just have to press on and keep an ear out for any further occurrences. Next time I'll keep the engine running and hopefully identify the cause. We continue on our way, heading for the coast at Penarth and the first of this final day's Landmarks, a medieval village. Finding it is no great chore, but neither Chloe nor I have the inclination to go into the place, settling instead for the all important photographs and a quick poke around Daisy once more in an effort to banish my paranoia that something cataclysmic is about to befall us. I can still find nothing out of place, and I tell myself to chill a bit. This doesn't work, because my inner soul is convinced that Daisy's bottom end is about to fall apart.

Chris will be dying to know of progress today, so before we set out for an appointment with the Brecon Beacons, or at least a particular spot nestling somewhere amongst them, we must check in and update him. But this merely leads to more stress, because as I pull the mobile from it's resting place inside our tank-bag, I can't help but notice that it's showing eight missed calls, where none were showing earlier. My heart gives a little jump - it's that feeling one gets when the 'phone at home bursts out in the middle of the night, you just know nothing good will come from the other end. Eight missed calls in such a short time can only mean that either I've suddenly become remarkably popular or that someone is having a drama and wants to spoil my day with it. My immediate concern, of course, is that something has happened at home and I fiddle urgently with the buttons in order to list the time and source of the calls. When the list appears it's a mixture of relief in the first part because none of the calls are from home and then irritation, as I recognise the number at the office where I have been working recently. For them to have called so many times in such a short space of time can only mean one thing I'm sure - captain cock-up has paid a visit in my absence. I decide to ignore it. There are people there that can handle supplier problems, and I know from hard experience that if I make the call I'll just get dragged into whatever it is that's going on and will probably end up having to spend the next hour making 'phone calls and getting right royally peeved. I make the call to Chris at home instead, only to find that he's fielded a call from the office as well and already told them that we're in Wales. Perhaps they'll have taken the hint, I find myself hoping.

Our woes increase immediately we set off again into the busy traffic. The ring-a-ching noise is back with vengeance, and I now know where it's coming from because it is so very obvious all of a sudden that in fact I'm amazed that I didn't make the connection earlier. It's the clutch, ringing out a warning of impending grief, every time it is disengaged. I experiment whilst hopping around in the stop-start traffic, proving beyond doubt that with each action of the clutch lever, the jarring metal ring can be heard, matching the rhythm of the engine with it's own percussion backing track. We continue with the flow, me with my head canted at a silly angle as I look down at the chaincase, and my mind is already busy furnishing my paranoia with the mental image of a host of nasty scenarios, all of which involve a sudden disastrous cessation of forward motion to the accompaniment of a loud and serious metallic clang - which will be the almost inevitable result if I don't do something about the problem. And I have good cause to be paranoid in this instance, having once suffered a serious incident from a very similar set of circumstances back in the days when, as a young and inexperienced rider I had not had the sense to understand or heed the warning signs. The memory of that incident is urgently tapping at the back of my skull right now, as if was only last week.

It was back in the late seventies, my first ever rally on that hard working little Tiger Cub. I had set forth to attend an all British Isle of Wight gathering over the Easter bank holiday weekend that year, and with no previous experience it had seemed like an impossibly long way away. The world seems to have shrunk since those tender teenage years of mine, because later on in life I would consider such a run to be a walk in the local park, but back then it was a grand adventure that would take me further from home than I had ever been under my own steam. Things like breakdown cover were simply extravagances to the likes of me and even if I had considered the idea, which I hadn't if truth were told, I wouldn't have been able to afford it anyway. No, this was a proper unsupported adventure, with the only concession to survival being a real and bulky canvas tent and precious little else. I had just come off the ferry from Poole and was riding the last few miles to the site, feeling like a million dollars because I had made it, when Fate decided to teach me a harsh lesson in why you should never ignore an unexpected noise. To be fair, that little bike made so many strange and eccentric noises anyway, it would have been hard to detect a new and particularly worrying one, but on this occasion the noise I had happily been ignoring in my youthful innocence was that of the clutch slowly coming off. It reached the critical point of no return exactly one mile from the rally site, having finally edged far enough to allow the roller bearings to burst free, dropping the entire clutch drum from it's hitherto solid mounting and jamming the entire drive chain. The back wheel had locked up at fifty, and we had cavorted out of control straight across the long sweeping bend I had just begun to lean into and we had come to a heart stopping, but extremely lucky halt courtesy of a large privet hedge.

As is often the way of things, that first frightening brush with death had not only served to teach me a harsh and important lesson that I would never forget, but also introduced me to a phenomenon that until that incident I had no previous knowledge or experience of - the mutual support and camaraderie of other bikers. Within minutes of the incident I was being scraped from the bush by a tough looking guy with arms like tree trunks, and by the time we had untangled the Cub there were no fewer than five bikes parked up along the road, with me the centre of a jocular group of riders, who, after initial enquiries had ascertained that I was in one piece, set about a critical but good humoured examination of my rather sorry situation. Questions were fired at me in quick succession, as several of the group prodded around and before long the diagnosis of chain case or gearbox problem was pronounced. By now, someone had called the cavalry and an open backed pick-up had appeared, with four or five big guys in the back, who jumped out and joined the happy throng clustered around the sorry little machine. Within minutes they had hoisted it into the back of their truck and invited me to climb up, and we were heading for the rally site with an escort of five or six bikes riding all around us. By the end of the afternoon, having ascertained that this inexperienced teenager had no clue what to do next, they had pulled the chaincase apart, exposed my frightful lack of maintenance, shown me how to put it back together and shamed me into buying a round of beer for their trouble, but they left me with a lasting appreciation of the motorcyclists' creed and I understood there and then that we may be a minority but we stick together and riding a bike means that wherever we may wander, we're never truly on our own.

All good and heart warming, but the important bit of that memory, the bit that is tapping the hardest, is the bit about the wheel locking and cavorting into a hedge. With a twelve year old on the pillion, not to mention the small detail that I'm just too damned old to be doing stuff like that, it's clear that I must investigate things further and do it sooner rather than later. We pull over at the first sensible place and as we stop my spirits take another dent - the 'phone is ringing insistently from it's hideaway inside the tank bag. We push Daisy onto a wide grass border by the road, and whilst removing helmet, gloves and jacket I explain the situation to Chloe. The ringing from the tank continues unabated, and is becoming irritating to say the least so I tell Chloe that as soon as it stops I'll turn the bloody thing off. She's more concerned with the possibility of an imminent, premature curtailing of our adventure however, a fact that is confirmed by her questions

"Can you fix it then?" I mumble something along the lines of bloody well hoping so .

"What happens if you can't?" A good question and 'Hello Mr. Recovery' is the likely option.

"How long will it take?" A lot longer if we don't get on with it is the obvious answer to that one.

Chloe is always game, and not the least bit reticent to get stuck in when it's necessary. She helps me unpack the gear so that we can get to the panniers, and then, once I have pulled out the paltry excuse for a toolkit she's eager to help with the messy bit. As I set to work, she wants to know what the chaincase keeps hidden within it's confines, so I find myself explaining the whole principal of engine, gearbox, and the vital role of the clutch in that relationship. She is hanging on my every word, peering at the gearbox as I explain its function and asking reasonably astute questions. But before we can get to the heart of the matter, the left footrest must come off, followed by the left hand exhaust pipe and silencer. Chloe helps, holding the spanner on one side while I undo the nut on the other and I'm amazed that amidst this potentially Challenge-crushing set back, far from being down hearted she looks as happy as ever and I find that her demeanour lifts my own spirits considerably. In fact, we are having fun it seems, however unlikely that may sound. A few minutes later we are attacking the Allen-screws that hold the chain case cover in place as I enthusiastically declare my love for the simplicity of these old engines. I freely admit that it's a double edged sword, after all if this was a much more modern machine, it's highly unlikely that the problem we are currently investigating would have occurred at all, and we would not find ourselves having to fiddle about with the thing, but for all that there is a perverse pleasure to be had from the fact that we can, and will, fix it.

The cover comes free, and the case gives up its half pint of oil on the grass, making me feel instantly guilty. But I share a giggle with Chloe as we study our now black hands, before turning my attention to the primary drive arrangement, exposed in all its glory. At first, it seems that we are barking up the wrong tree, because it all looks as it should. Chloe voices the opinion that it doesn't *look* broken, but even as she does my eyes settle on the four clutch spring retaining screws, and I draw her attention to the shiny marks on their brass heads. Here, I explain to her, is the source of the 'ching-ching' noise – these screw heads have been rubbing against the cover. I pick the thing up off the grass, and with some Kleenex from the tank-bag I clean the inside of the clutch dome to reveal a perfectly curved groove, about an inch long, worn into the metal. I explain to Chloe that it's not from just one of the screws that has maybe come undone, because all four are showing signs of contact, therefore we have to assume that the whole lot have moved, and I can only think of one thing that will cause that. I grab hold of the outer drum, or chain wheel as it's often called, and we need look no further for our problem. The whole lot is as loose as an MP's morals and is about to do exactly what the little Tiger Cub had done all those years ago. In short, it's about to fall off and we have caught it in the nick of time!

"So can you fix it?" For the first time since starting the job, Chloe's face shows signs of concern.

"Absolutely we can" I assure her, and add that in fact I am mightily relieved that it's this simple. There can be any number of reasons for sudden noises, and although this particular one can be disastrous if not rectified in time, the process of doing so couldn't be simpler. I talk Chloe through things as I work: undo and take out the four clutch spring retainers, remove the springs and the cups, lift off the pressure plate, and voila, the locking nut is exposed. There is a special washer fitted to this nut, which has a small tab that locates into a hole in the clutch centre, whilst it's outer edge is bent over one of the flats on the nut itself. This remarkable design is supposed to prevent the very event that we are fixing. It's plain to see why it has failed, the tab has broken off and is therefore no longer holding the nut in place because it has simply become a bent washer. I can't do anything about the tab but I can do the nut back up as tight as possible, and I explain all this to Chloe before realizing that in fact it's not that simple. The nut is deep inside the clutch, in a round recessed hole, requiring a socket wrench and the only type of spanners I have with us are the normal open-ended type. I try to marry one up, but there is absolutely no way it's going to fit. I curse mightily and sit back, staring at the thing and wondering what on earth we can do. The conclusion doesn't take long - there is no way out of the conundrum that doesn't involve the right tool, so it's clear that we must find the right tool or call those nice recovery people again and hope that they carry standard socket sets on their vans. This is fairly certain, but I don't fancy the hour or so wait, and after thinking for a few minutes, I explain a cunning plan to Chloe.

Ten minutes later, we look a right pair of Charlies I suspect. I am riding Daisy slowly back towards town, with only one footrest, no chaincase cover and a loose exhaust pipe. Chloe is sitting on the back and cradled in her arms is the missing cover, containing nuts, bolts and the other footrest. We are looking for the first place that can lend or sell us the socket-that-fits and luckily we don't have to search for long before we spy an old-fashioned type tool and hardware shop. It's probably called Arkwright's or some such, but that's not important right now for regardless of name it is just what the doctor ordered and we bump up the pavement to park Daisy unceremoniously outside the place. Before we can sort ourselves out and go into the place, the proprietor appears at the door and it's a relief to find that rather than lambaste us for cluttering up his shop-front, he is far more interested in Daisy and has that enthusiast's glint in his eye. His eyes take in the obvious, and I find myself describing the events that had led up to our arrival at his shop with a partially dismantled motorcycle. Two minutes later, we are leaning on his little counter where he has insisted that we should join him in a cup of tea, whilst he scrabbles about in the rear of his storeroom looking for something. A little exclamation of delight precedes his reappearance, and in his hand he is clutching a real gem of a find. "I knew I had this somewhere," he says as he proffers the object towards me "and I reckon it's just the job don't you?" What I am now holding is indeed a superb find. It's a little metal carrier, six or seven inches long, and in it is a neat row of five sockets, held in place by a little tommy-bar that acts as a securing strap and handle. More to the point, the sockets are Whitworth and the largest one looks like it's exactly what we need.

We're on the road again within half an hour and our spirits are high once more. Our encounter with the little shop and its proprietor has been one of those heart warming experiences that leave one in no doubt that human nature can be the noblest of things. The socket had fitted perfectly and the nut now had a stout star washer in place behind it that would hopefully help prevent a repeat of the near disaster. The old boy had insisted that the little set of sockets should stay with

Daisy, and would accept no payment for them or the washer. He had been delighted, he assured us, to help, and he was strangely pleased that he had 'found an appropriate home' for the socket set that he had possessed for more years than he could remember. And he made a mean mug of tea, it has to be said. Eventually we were ready once more, but I had in fact felt a bit churlish to be hurrying off after such generosity and found myself struggling for the right way of saying that we really had to go. Our saviour assured us that he fully understood, having had chapter and verse from Chloe about our adventures while I had worked on the clutch, and brushing off my final attempt to pay at least something for his kindness, he all but shooed us away from the place telling us that we "had no time lose – get going!"

We're soon out of the built up area and back on the open road, the Brecon Beacons beckoning us darkly on the horizon. Our next Landmark is literally on the very edge the range and it's another one that we have simply not been able to identify in advance. The plan is the same as all the others, we'll just have to get there and hope that in front of us is something obvious. It is Chloe who points out to me that we've had mixed success with this strategy, but this time I'm fairly confident because our target is in a place where there is very little else, so it should stand out a mile. She's not convinced. We go as far as Caerphilly on a fairly main 'A' road, but then we branch off and into the smaller roads that meander across the glorious Welsh countryside and Daisy is back in her element once more. Stone walls flash past us on either side for miles as we make a leisurely progress, but as we get closer to the map reference there is less and less evidence of population or civilisation and the landscape is opening up before us to display miles of rolling fields, and not a lot else. But after the mornings trials and stresses it's wonderful to be roaming free once more and I even manage to forget about all those missed calls, with their promise of trouble and yet another opportunity to get frustrated and murderous. The ride from Penarth has been very pleasant, but as we skirt Myrthyr Tydfil from the south things begin to get far more interesting. The geography and roads become very much less predictable, with the beginnings of the Beacons just to the north, and we find ourselves climbing steadily into the foothills, skirting ridges and dipping into the folds, to rise up the other side again amidst a panorama of a rich landscape, mostly green pasture, but dotted with the odd patch of thick woodland and everywhere the scattered evidence of the rocky plateau beneath.

Daisy is having to work hard and I know now, with all the clutch work, that if we hadn't stopped to rectify that loose nut we would have run into serious trouble hereabouts and no mistake, but the scenery is captivating so I ease off the juice somewhat and allow the old girl to proceed at an easier pace anyway. Soon we have reached the higher point of this area and the road flattens out, disappearing off into the distance and surrounded by a sparse and hostile looking plain. Sheep are suddenly the dominant feature, dotting the field of vision as far as the eye can see, and the only other notable sights are the dark bulk of the Beacons to the north and the long straight row of telegraph poles stretching ahead of us to the horizon. We follow this very straight road directly east with Daisy cantering with ease below us, and soon we're on the last five miles or so to our destination - the unknown Landmark. In fact, 'unknown landmark' proves to be a very apt description we decide, after turning off to the little village of Trefil and finding almost nothing there. The computer maps indicate that we are looking for a spot some quarter of a mile out the other side, but this seems unlikely to say the least when we discover that the road stops at the edge of the village. There is a looping track that goes up and over a nearby hill peak, but all that's up there is an old stone outbuilding, unremarkable in every respect and currently serving as home to a few sheep. We trundle back into the village, the centre of which is marked by precious little except for a very small shop, where we stop to check out the clue and seek some more of that priceless 'local knowledge'. The place looks remarkably like a frontier town in a spaghetti western, with it's few huddled buildings and a single dusty road leading out onto the plain. There is even a little dry bush type thing bowling along gently in the wind to complete the deception. What there is not, is anything that could be described as a Landmark of any sort.

I try the shop, and the lady must think I am some kind of raving maniac, waving my strip map around whilst gibbering about temples and lost souls. The clue is exactly that, a temple for lost souls, but it doesn't make me look any saner for the fact that it's written down. I get absolutely nowhere, but we buy some cokes and bars of chocolate before exiting despondently. Outside, we spy a man fiddling with a tractor in the yard adjoining the shop and so we try our luck there. No help at all, nothing, no hint of salvation and no inspirational thoughts whatsoever. Wandering back to Daisy we console ourselves with the sugar intake offered by our purchases at the shop and generally discussing our options, which are very few. We then watch in wonder as four sheep followed by a goose waddle past us up the middle of the road, heading for the plain. A little boy appears, probably no older than five or six years old, all short trousers and scabby knees, and after inspecting Daisy he approaches us and gives us sudden hope as he asks

"Are you finding secret things like the other man yesterday?" This sounds promising.

"We are, yes! Was the other man on a big motorbike like ours?" he was, and the lad banishes any doubt in my mind that the mystery man was a fellow Landmarker when he points at Daisy and adds, "The other man had a Trump as well". A Trump? Close enough, and more importantly it confirms that we must be in the right place, or at least fairly close, even though the 'secret thing', as the lad had described it, was doing a bloody good job staying that way. I am about to ask our potential guide if he saw where the other man stopped, or whether he had seen the him taking photographs, when he pre-empted the questions with another marvellous youthful observation.

"He was funny!" he offered, and then "He kep' going round and round and round and then he sweared into a telly-fone" with that our spy has a good dig around in his left nostril, and having decided that I'm not about to put on a similar show, he loses interest in us and wanders off after the sheep.

The memory is obviously the highlight of the lad's week, but to me it is not good news. Clearly our predecessor had suffered the same problem that we are now faced with, and had engaged in a bad tempered telephone conversation with someone. My guess is that he had called Ken and had clearly not been happy with what he heard if the boy was to be believed. I am going to have to do the same, so without any further mucking around I dig out the numbers and the mobile. I turn it on but get no signal. Cursing under my breath I wander around waving the thing in the air, but there is simply no service anywhere within the confines of the village. I curse some more and look around for a public 'phone box, but that's just a waste of time. I decide to walk a little way out and up towards that hill, and luckily, after about fifty yards, a single bar appears on the signal indicator, but walking further it disappears again so I return to the spot and it comes back. One bar is all we're going to get it seems, and that only if I stand right here, but it's enough to have a bad quality conversation so I dial the number and wait in anticipation. Mrs Ken answers the summons, recognizes my voice almost immediately and after I explain which clue we've failed to solve this time she delivers the answer without any hesitation. It is almost immediately apparent that this isn't going to help us however, because the thing we seek is apparently a Naval Church and I find it highly unlikely that such a place would be buried amidst the foothills of the Brecon Beacons. We compare some of my observations with her notes, and in short order it transpires that we are nowhere near the Landmark at all. In fact, we work out between us that I am currently some thirty-five miles off course, and should in fact be down on the coast at Port Talbot!

A pregnant silence best describes my response to this revelation, but as I stand there trying to work out how I could have got it so wrong I suddenly remember the young lad in the village with his observations from yesterday. Mrs Ken has been very helpful and good natured in my few dealings with her during the challenge so far, and I pick my words with care as I tentatively enquire as to whether any other Landmarkers have had trouble with this one, and suddenly a penny drops.

"Now you mention it, Ken had a call yesterday from a very rude chap who hadn't read the updates to the .... Oh! ... Hang on ..... You've gone to the reference that was misprinted haven't you?" Aha, now we are getting somewhere.

"Have I?" I respond innocently.

"Don't you read the club magazine?" she scolds me good-naturedly "We printed a correction last month!" Marvellous. I explain that we have been mostly out on the road, doing the challenge in fact, and she's quite right, I haven't yet read last month's club magazine. I appeal for a compromise - I really don't want to add a round trip of seventy odd miles of back-tracking to today's already troublesome journey, but Port Talbot is back near Swansea, in the direction that we've spent come from this morning. No wonder matey boy yesterday had been upset as he 'sweared in the telly-fone' but I choose an altogether different tack, and play the Daisy card to great effect. Surely they're not going to make me go all the way back, are they? They are not. Mrs Ken tells me to take the photograph of something where I am, and be sure to make a note for Ken when I submit my entry. After all, it's not my fault is it, and I *am* at the spot originally published. I thank her once again for her help, and indeed understanding, hang up and turn to look for Chloe.

She is kicking stones around by the edge of the village, so I stride back to her and update her on the situation. She reminds me that there was a very clear sign with the village name on the road the other side and we agree to get our photograph there on the way out. Five minutes later I am positioning Daisy just so and as I take the photographs I notice Chloe has wandered back down the road a bit and is giggling. I look where her own gaze is fixed to find a little group of sheep, ears cocked high, examining us from just across the road. Three of them are youngsters, one is a wily old ewe and in a moment of silliness for Chloe's benefit I pipe up with a loud "Baaa!" The response is startling. All three lambs immediately respond in kind, and one of them takes several springy steps towards us before uncertainty, and possibly a dim instinct for survival stop it again. Chloe spontaneously bursts out laughing and I try the same thing again, only louder and longer "Baaaaaaa!" This time all three take steps towards us and reply in a high pitched bawl. The old Ewe is not impressed, and doesn't budge but her youngsters are more than happy to continue what, for all I know, is a deeply philosophical discussion with this pair of two legged strangers. I call Chloe back, but as we get prepared for the road once more we continue our conversation with our new found, if highly improbable friends. Things change dramatically as I start Daisy and in seconds we find ourselves alone, watching the rapidly retreating sheep waddle in their comical way back towards the village. Complete and unadulterated silliness, so it was, but a light moment in this troublesome day for all that.

Twenty minutes later, we are sitting on top of a steep rise, just outside the village of Crucorney in the southeast corner of the Beacons National Park looking out over a fantastic sweeping view. The last ten miles or so have taken us through one of the best motorcycling roads on this leg so far. Amidst the late summer splendour of rolling green hills and distant dark peaks, we've stopped for a last long look back before we finally rejoin bigger roads that will take us through Hereford and on up into Shropshire for the penultimate stop of the whole challenge. We can still take our time too, because despite the setbacks we have actually made better overall progress than I had thought possible and we are easily able to reach the last Landmark today as long as no more time is lost in any incidents like those of the morning, firstly in Penarth with Daisy's clutch and secondly at Trefil and the cock-up with the map reference. We still have some sixty miles to cover to the Shropshire target and from there another eighty to our final spot, but with the time only just past one o'clock I can't see us not achieving it. I realize that I am feeling totally confident about all this, due, in no small part, to the fact that Daisy feels more settled and more solid than she ever has. This revelation had come to me on the long sweeping roads through the Beacons, because as we cruised along at fifty-five or so she had felt so uncannily smooth and untroubled that I had suddenly realised that something quite definite had changed since Penarth. My mind had lazily tried to pinpoint what exactly, and it came to me in the end - the vibration had gone!

I remembered being bothered by the sudden appearance of a vibration when we were on the first stage of the Scottish leg with Chris. I had fiddled about and checked nuts and bolts but hadn't got to the bottom of it and as that adventure had progressed I had simply got used to it after a few days as it had become part of Daisy's general mannerisms. Clearly, if ignoring a sudden noise is asking for trouble, the same logic should be applied to an unexpected vibration because there is now no doubt whatsoever in my mind that the slowly loosening clutch centre had been the cause, and I should have taken it more seriously back then. We live and learn, but as I continue my mental cogitation along these lines another interesting thought occurs to me. With enough miles under the wheels of the same machine, one gets used to its little foibles and those little character traits, and it's easy to become used to its particular behaviour, rightly or wrongly. To suddenly find and rectify even a small thing can dramatically change the feel or manners of the machine in question, and in this case the change is remarkable enough to be extremely pleasing. If Daisy has been a reasonable pleasure to ride through most of the challenge, she is now nothing short of delightful. I find myself lamenting the fact that I hadn't discovered this before now, because all those long days would have been that much more enjoyable. What I can do is enjoy it now, and with the open road waiting patiently for us, stretching away into the wilds of Herefordshire and Shropshire, I prod Chloe from her dreamy contemplation of the horizon, stand up and indicate that it's time to go and enjoy ourselves once more.

It's rather strange, but as you get to a certain point in any enjoyable experience, such as a holiday, time seems to step up a gear and it all goes past too quickly. The inevitable return to the hum-drum of our normal existence seems to accelerate like an express train, the mind begins to re-focus and adjust to the imminent return to banality and the almost certain knowledge that we will face a mountain of rubbish to catch up on, the price for daring to go away in the first place. It's often said that the thing to do is save the best experiences of a holiday until last, and this makes infinite sense, but I find myself wondering what that would be in our case. Scotland was certainly breathtakingly good motorcycling, and maybe that should have been our last foray, but then again Snowdonia and the rest of Wales has been just as satisfying, but in a different way. Devon and Cornwall? Simply marvellous, and what about all those shorter forays into Norfolk, Wiltshire and of course our own back yard in Kent? Well, they've been equally enjoyable, but for very different reasons. No, I decide, it matters not and it's not over yet, because we may be leaving behind us the mountains and valleys of Wales, but we are swapping them for the lush green, and very quaint countryside of England. Daisy is eager, we are relaxed and more than anything else we are approaching the final hurdles, beyond which is the finish line and the moment of completion, achievement and when all's said and done satisfaction.

So we'd better get on with it, I reckon, and firing Daisy up once more, I wait for Chloe to clamber onto her little perch before selecting first gear, give a tweak on the throttle, clutch out and we're off, passing through the last few miles of national park and setting our sites firmly on Hereford. More sweeping roads, rising and dipping as we go, and the barracks town appears in no time at all. Once again we are embroiled in a long line of choking traffic snaking it's way slowly into the centre. We find it nigh on impossible to filter through because there are too many trucks and vans going both ways, and before long I am fighting to keep Daisy ticking over as she begins to overheat. I know it's time to give her a rest when a slight hint of oil smoke begins to drift up from under her tank, leaving a sharp tangy smell in my nostrils and I can also feel the intense heat radiating off her barrels leaving a distinct burning sensation on my calves. We see a big pub up on the left, and although it can only be a hundred or so yards away, it takes nearly five minutes to work our way up to it, but finally we are able to pull off and allow Daisy to cool off. I don't need to kill the engine as we come to halt, the intense heat has effectively stifled her idler jet, vaporizing any fuel long before it can be sucked into the combustion chambers, and she sputters to stop all on her own, letting out a loud 'Phshuth' from the carburettor as she stops. I examine the source of the smoke, which is drifting in little wisps across the car-park now she is completely stationary but it's no big thing, a small amount of oil has seeped from her rocker spindle and where it has dribbled down onto the cylinder head it is bubbling away to atmosphere as if it was in a frying pan.

The heat on my face is fearsome as I peer under the tank, so I reckon we'd better stop for a while and suggest to Chloe that we should maybe get some lunch in the pub. She never needs asking twice when it comes to food and we manage to grab one of the outside tables where we can keep an eye on Daisy. We sit down and I point out the ripples in the air around Daisy's engine, a real heat shimmer. Chloe is already eyeing up the menu which for her is far more interesting. A relaxed lunch follows, as the garden fills up all around us, and after a while the shimmer is hardly discernable at all. I nip over and check by placing a tentative finger on one of the rocker boxes, and although it's still too hot to keep in contact for long, it's no longer the furnace-like intensity it had been only twenty minutes earlier. I wonder idly why she had chosen today to overheat quite so dramatically, because we had suffered many a traffic bottleneck before now, and although she had certainly let her displeasure show by way of a bit of lumpy, uneven running she had never been this bad before. I hope it isn't a sign of things to come. Wandering back to our table, I notice that the endless queue of traffic hasn't abated at all and as I'm not sure how much further we will have to sit in it before we break out onto open roads again, it seems to be a good idea to wait for a while longer and allow Daisy to cool off some more. I sit back down and chat to Chloe and I find that the highlights of her day so far have been the sheep and surprisingly, the fettling of the clutch. She had fun helping apparently, and had enjoyed our encounter with the old boy at the shop. No mention of the ride through the Beacons and all that spectacular scenery at all. Strange girl. What is certain though, is the building sense of anticipation, and it's a feeling we both share. Chloe is eager to know how many miles are left so I send her off to retrieve the maps and we sit there plotting the final stages happily. We reckon it's a hundred and twenty miles, give or take and with the realisation that we are now so close, we suddenly want to get at it once more.

Shropshire has one rather endearing feature, other than some of the best riding to be had anywhere, and that is the place names. It's become a favourite pastime during the challenge, noting the various quaint, eccentric or just damned funny names on the signposts, and the border lands of Herefordshire and Shropshire are easily equal to anywhere else we've travelled in this respect. As we continue our trek north, we are delighted by Moreton on Lugg, giggle at Weobley and positively guffaw when Hope-under-Dinmore slides past on the signs. It constantly fascinates me where these names came from in the first place, but it certainly makes our meandering progress more pleasurable and the time fairly flies by until we find ourselves able to turn off the A49 to complete the last ten miles via Stanton Lacy and Diddlebury to arrive relaxed and happy at the equally wonderfully named Much Wenlock, wherein resides our Landmark. Shipton Hall is a sixteenth century manor house, and if we were inclined to go inside we find that we can't because it's closed. But we will take ten minutes out, because the place is set in the most delightfully rustic little village, absolutely typical of the English rural scene. It's also unbelievably peaceful, with the only noise coming from birds scrabbling about in the big tree under which we currently stand. But soon the urge to get on once more is too much, for this is it, the very last leg of the challenge. Eighty miles, one Landmark and success is ours! We'd better telephone Chris at home, I suggest, and I let Chloe do the honours. She looks at the 'phone and with concern on her face she holds it up to show me that the missed call count has now reached twelve! I assure her that we are not going to play that game, not until we have completed what we came to do, because I have a niggling suspicion that someone wants to spoil my day and if I allow that to happen it will take the shine right off our pending success. It can wait, whatever it is.

Laughably, Chris seems to be even more full of anticipation than we are. He wants to know how long the last leg will take, what time will we be calling and wants assurance that we will 'phone as *soon* as we're there, won't we? He gets all the answers I am able to give, but I have to stress that the estimated time of arrival is obviously just that, an estimate. I have used our previously agreed method of assuming an average speed of thirty odd miles per hour after the odd rest and the fuel stop that we'll have to make soon, and that gives us an expected arrival sometime around six thirty this evening. That's if Daisy has no final surprises for us, but I assure Chris that she has never felt better than right now and that reminds me to tell him that we have found the source of the vibration that had started when he was riding pillion. He is far more interested in me shutting up and getting back on the road and tells me in no uncertain terms to get going without any further delay. It's strange, but I suddenly feel under pressure to perform, and it's the most peculiar feeling heightened I suppose by my own anticipation of the great moment. Chris is right, the best thing to do right now is get going once more, because every mile now edges us closer to victory and after all we've been through, the highs, the lows and the odd, occasionally near-terminal, setbacks it will be a moment that has been well earned. Remembering the very first exclamation that Chloe had used at the start of this last foray, I can't resist using it myself on Chris just before I hang up, and I say it loud enough for Chloe to hear; "Right, OK then we're on our way … To infinity and beyond!"

It's pretty clear almost immediately that an average of thirty may be wishful thinking. The road we find ourselves on is fairly narrow, which in itself is fine, but coupled with the fact that it's twisty with high banks or a thick hedgerow on either side, effectively killing any forward vision, makes cautious riding necessary. But the real problem is the seemingly suicidal drivers that are hurtling in both directions, giving very little consideration to the blind bends and the potential for meeting an equally mad lemming coming the other way. In fact I am appalled at the total absence of road craft on display as we thread our way through the lanes and before long I am seriously looking forward to getting out onto bigger roads. This is what I think is referred to as a 'rat run' – a local shortcut between two popular destinations, and it's scary. We manage to stay in one piece, finally breaking out of the boonies and onto the A458 just west of Bridgenorth. We are in desperate need of a fuel stop so I take the turning into the town in order to hunt down a petrol station. I am glad that I did because hiding along the road is a delightful little town centre and in fact we stop for a short break whilst we have a little poke around the place. Whilst getting fuel it also occurs to me that I haven't put any oil in the clutch casing, after splitting the thing earlier. I had thought that the clutch seemed a bit recalcitrant back in the Hereford traffic and it is now clear to me why that had been.

Back on the main route, the plan is to skirt around the west and south peripheries of Birmingham itself, then cut across country to Royal Leamington Spa, and from there the last fifteen miles or so to the grand finale. It's no kind of hard work either as I note once again how close to the City one can be whilst enjoying some of the best scenery going. The roads have opened up a bit now, we seem to have lost the rat-run syndrome and with our final goal firmly in sight and Daisy feeling better than ever I decide that it's time to let her off the leash a bit. Sweeping along towards Kidderminster I slowly twist the throttle until the burbling exhaust note has climbed to a most satisfactory roaring howl. We pass the seventy mark, indicated by the simple fact the speedo needle is doing it's wild gyrating dance again, and the wind force on my upper body and face tells me that it's time to grin. I grin, probably enough to scare the locals should any look my way, but it's impossible not to really. It's bloody annoying when we reach Kidderminster and have to negotiate a series of roundabouts, but once the other side we can open up once more and I go for the full compliment of flies in my teeth once again. That all comes to a halt with the arrival of Bromsgrove, and now we are threading through the southern brown belt which is a strange mixture of urban built up, a bit of open country, more urban built up, culminating in us getting right royally lost and ending up in solid urban city.

I have no idea how I have done it, but we are now lost, thoroughly embedded in what seems to be largely a collection of little communities all rolled into one bigger one. There are a myriad of what I can only describe as separate little high streets, with their own row of shops and amenities, then more residential streets followed by another little high street. And so it goes, we have clearly lost the ring road and with no obvious direction to take we are going round in circles in suburbia. For some reason, the overwhelming tang of curry spices seems to hang in the air wherever we go here, a not unpleasant aroma by any means, but I have never been in a built up area that possesses such a potent and pervasive signature as right now. Eventually we have to stop and hunt down someone who might help us out of the place. This turns out to be a mistake, because we immediately attract the attention of a local drunk. As he weaves his way unsteadily straight towards us, an unknown purpose clear in his face, I eye him warily and take a step forwards to put myself between him and Chloe. I know from experience that these situations can be extremely unpredictable, but I needn't have worried, this is a happy, if somewhat befuddled, drunkard and he is coming over to be mates with us.

"Whoooaaa lookit you on this booty!" is his opening introduction. I relax a little bit, he doesn't seem to be holding a baseball bat or anything, and seems to be fairly good natured, but I quietly advise Chloe not to engage the guy in conversation. He finally reaches us, via most of the available pavement and a bit of the road.

"Issa Bourneville ainnit?" he declares, confusing plain chocolate with one of Meriden's finest, and as he stops to sway gently before us he seems to have a revelation inside his head, because his face lights up and he raises a finger in the air. I wait for the next Einsteinian proclamation, but instead he scrabbles about in his pockets to produce a can of Special Brew, which he promptly thrusts in my direction.

"'ave a drink!" he says, beaming mightily and displaying a truly scary set of teeth in the process. I curse silently and try to think of the best way of escaping from our new chum without upsetting him, but before I can articulate a response he ups the stakes considerably "Gotta flat jus' there" he says, pointing across the road to a dismal looking boarded up basement "You can stay if y'like, blokes like you is al'as welcome in my flat an' I got more o' this!" he waves the can about in the air. Bugger. This is getting awkward and time is ticking by steadily, but I can't think of an easy way to extricate us from the situation without running the risk of upsetting our admirer. A happy drunk can become a very aggressive drunk in the blink of an eye if handled incorrectly and with Chloe here I have no intention of risking that kind of a scene. But the decision is taken out of my hands when matey's dazed eyes focus on Chloe, still half hidden behind me, and he leans round a bit and tries his persuasion on her.

"You wanna stay in my flat?" he asks.

The unfortunate thing about youngsters, when faced with a situation that horrifies them, is that they tend not to think diplomatically or look for the careful response that a more mature person would probably adopt. Chloe recoils from the sudden attention and says basically what's on her mind.

"No way!" is her immediate response, and she finishes the obvious rebuff off superbly with "Urrgh!" and just in case the message isn't clear enough she retreats behind me and mumbles in an unfortunately audible way "Can we go now Dad?"

This stops chummy in his tracks, and he looks confused. He is clearly, in his own mind, being gregarious, generous and indeed charitable and he's somewhat taken aback by the less than enthusiastic, ungrateful response to his offer. I need to take control of the conversation quickly, before he has time to become affronted, and the best way to do that is to lie through my teeth.

"Hey, that'd be great!" I enthuse, and just to make sure he's is no doubt that we're best buddies, I take the still proffered can of Special Brew, open it and take a swig. While I do this I make a signal behind my back with a wagging finger, hopefully indicating to Chloe that she should not add any more helpful contributions at this stage, and then I play my cards in the hope of a clean exit. I adopt a conspiratorial tone, and press on.

"That's good beer! But I tell you what, if we are going to stop here with you we'll have to go and get a lock for this bike! Can't leave it out here unlocked, so I'd better nip off and get one." He seems to be buying it so I continue, resisting the urge to babble "Can you hold this 'till we get back, we'll only be a couple of minutes" I hold out the beer, hoping to God he'll swallow this rather feeble reasoning, and amazingly he does. In fact he leans forward, adopting a conspiratorial tone of his own, looking surreptitiously around as he speaks.

"Yeah, s'right. Nick anyfing round 'ere they will an' issa nice bike... gotta lock up a nice bike like that 'un."

Marvellous. I signal Chloe that she should get ready for a quick getaway, and before chummy can go off on any tangents I have Daisy started and with Chloe barely seated I pull away with a nod and the assurance "we'll see you back here in a minute!"

A few streets away, I pull up once more and look round at Chloe "Bloody hell, was he one of *your* mates?" I ask her, and I'm rewarded with "Yeah – right!" and a smack on the back of the helmet. We snigger for a while, partially in relief that we've escaped, partially because it was an amusing encounter in retrospect, but now I need to focus back on the fact that we're still no closer to finding our way out of this bloody place. I go for the compass option once more. We need to be heading east, or southeast and so that's what we'll try to do until hopefully we find a bigger road and some signs. It takes us nearly twenty minutes of constant stop-start riding from junction, to traffic lights, to junction and as we struggle with the traffic I can't help but feel that this is not how our big finale is meant to be. I had imagined the last leg would be a glorious ride through open countryside on a road of sweeping bends until finally, there before us would be the lake, where we would pull up at some idyllic viewing point, call Chris, crack open the bottles and declare ourselves victorious. I had not imagined this uninspiring and progressively tedious experience at all, and it was irksome to say the least. Surely we must break out of it soon, I think desperately as we choke on the black fumes of yet another bus, and just to douse my spirits even further Daisy begins to muck about once again. What a complete anti-climax this is turning out to be.

Finally, we find a sign to Warwick and Leamington. "Hurrah! About bloody time too!" I yell over my shoulder at Chloe, and she responds with a little cheer of her own. As we leave the built-up sprawl behind, I am amazed to see a sign that informs me that the borough of Solihull thanks me for driving carefully. Solihull? Good grief, that's way off course and I can't imagine how on earth we have ended up going so badly wrong. But it matters not, for now we have signs that promise Leamington is a mere thirteen miles away, which means that we are only twenty-five or so from glory. But Daisy is not going to let us finish that easily, oh no. She is obstinately refusing to settle down after the snarled-up congestion of the last hour, and has developed a constant misfire that won't go away. I let her stroll along at a very relaxed speed, hoping that she'll cool quickly enough, but after a few miles it is clear that something else is bothering the old girl. We pull up in a lay-by and I check to see how hot her engine is, but there is none of the bubbling and smoke that we had witnessed earlier and the heat doesn't seem to be particularly fierce. I decide to wait for ten minutes or so and allow her to cool off a bit more in the evening air. It's nearly seven o'clock now, and I am beginning to fret a little, remembering that we have no lights and it's clear that we had better start looking out for camping before long lest we get stranded.

The thought of not reaching the final Landmark today, after all we've been through, is galling, but then again it will still be there in the morning, so what the hell. It will mean another night of suspense for young Chris, and Chloe too, but staying alive is probably more important I tell myself. Any doubts regarding the early retirement plan are soon dismissed when we come to set off once more, however. I am so used to Daisy starting immediately with one kick when she's warm that I'm a bit surprised when this time she doesn't. I try again, same result, but the third attempt earns me a shock as she backfires violently and her engine judders to a halt with a loud 'phitt' from the carburettor. Bloody marvellous – less than twenty miles to go and we have this. I prod around checking leads and connections, but in the back of my mind I just know that the bodged points inside the magneto have finally given out once more and I do a passable Victor Meldrew impression, muttering "I don't believe it" as the realisation dawns that it could be quite serious this time if it's broken. I try one more kick, having fiddled about, just on the off chance that I have disturbed something enough to make it all work, but the result is the same. Chloe pipes up with the inevitable; "What's wrong *this* time Dad?" but her face shows genuine interest rather than blind panic or disappointment and I find myself explaining the woeful tale of my stupidity and lack of preventative planning.

We huddle down and remove that dreaded cap once more, as I explain my misgivings about delving around inside the thing again. I can't shake the niggling feeling that this is not actually the cause of Daisy's current sulking at all, and by prodding around I'll break the bloody thing again, just like I had last time. The cap comes free and we peer inside, but just like before everything looks fine. I can see both contacts in place, where they should be, and the one that I had bodge repaired is still attached in its proper place. I nervously poke a finger in there and give the whole assembly a prod, and it wobbles around alarmingly under hardly any pressure at all. Can it be that simple? I dare to believe that it may well be – the little pillar bolt that retains everything (the same little bolt that I had lost the washer for) has come loose again. Any doubt is soon killed when I grasp the thing between thumb and forefinger and wiggle it around, because the entire assembly comes off in my hand. This time, I'm ready for the little washer and I see it make its break for freedom amongst the long grass. I manage to retrieve it, and a few minutes of re-assembly followed by the ministrations of the pliers and it's all done up tight once more. Confidence is high, and a test kick before replacing the cap confirms that all is fine once more as Daisy roars her approval and settles to a steady beat. "Thank Christ for that" I exclaim, but Chloe is even more pleased with the result and issues a little "Yeeeah!" of appreciation. I wonder what else will go wrong, what can possibly happen in the last twenty miles to stop us, and irrationally I have an overwhelming urge to get there just so that I know that we have. But a more pressing concern overshadows these thoughts – we are rapidly running out of light once more!

We manage to get through Leamington but as we head out on the A445 all thoughts of the last Landmark are banished as we race against the sunset hunting feverishly for a place to camp. We seem to be in a general farming area once more and I can't see any obvious place to scuttle for shelter, so we decide to dive off into the lanes in the darkening evening. Finally, I must accept that we have been caught out good and proper and, coming across a large pub standing off the road, I pull in and turn off Daisy's engine. We won't be riding any further tonight. The pub looks inviting in the late dusk, and hopefully, I tell Chloe, they'll be able to help with some ideas as to where we might stay tonight. Inside the news isn't good. There are no camp sites anywhere near, neither are there any B&B's. We can't stop here because the pub has no land to speak of, just the car park, and the landlord isn't too keen anyway. We get ourselves drinks and head outside to consider our options. We don't seem to have any and I curse that our adventure should end like this, in disarray. Captain cock-up has truly staked his claim on us, and no mistake. Thinking hard I can only come up with three options, and in the spirit of our adventure I decide to run them by both Chris and Chloe and see what they think we should do. At least that way a small bonus can be salvaged from the situation and both of the kids will feel that they've indeed been involved in high adventure. We make the call, and soon we're having a three-way debate.

"Right, the options are these. One, we call recovery and get them to take us to a hotel or B&B somewhere. The downside of that is that we'll have to wait quite a while for the man, and we may not be able to get into the first places he takes us. It could be a long and painful evening, and we also have to worry about Daisy overnight." They take this onboard, and prompt me for the next option. "Two then, is that we have a walk along this road and try to find a spot where we can put the tent up. The downside of this one, is that we haven't any facilities if we do that, and we might just get moved on by police or somebody." That one sinks in and I press on with number three. "Three, we don't bother with the tent, we stay here at the pub until chucking out time, and we simply bunker down at the first spot that we can fit two sleeping bags side by side. The downside to this one is obvious" I leave them contemplating the options and go back inside to get some more beer. I'm depressed and peeved that our last day has come to such a shambolic end, but accept that there is nothing that I can reasonably do about it and I suppose that this is all part of the adventure really, we'll just have to get over it. I get the beer and stride back outside with a new purpose.

"We should call the breakdown people," Chloe declares on my return "That's if we can't fix it," she adds.

This stops me in my tracks. Fix it? Bloody hell, why hadn't I actually thought of that? I have made no attempt to carry out even the most rudimentary investigation, and it's not as if I didn't have time over the past few evenings. The problem really could be as simple as a broken wire or dirty pick-ups, and it won't take long to check the obvious. I feel a bit stupid as I place my pint on the ground, and it's only right to give Chloe some credit.

"Why didn't I think of that?"

First things first then, I undo the antiquated strap that holds Daisy's battery, check all the wires out and, finding nothing amiss in there, shove it back on again. Next up are the wires from the dynamo itself and these look fine as far as I can physically follow them. They disappear under the tank though, and I am not about to try and get that off, what with it's nightmare panel and the spaghetti hiding within. I'm an old enough hand to know that sometimes, just by prodding and fiddling with ancient wiring, the desired result can be stumbled across, so before taking the dynamo cap off I start Daisy, peer hopefully at the ammeter and give the throttle a few blips. The needle stays obstinately still. Off with the dynamo cap then, and straight away it's obvious what the problem is when about a quarter of a pint of oily water pours out of the thing!

"Is it meant to do that?" asks Chloe, leaning over my shoulder and peering at the still dribbling dynamo in the barely useful light from the pub's big sign.

"No it's not!"

I am amazed that the thing can have collected so much, and kept it sealed inside the lid. The wires that run from under the tank come down the front frame section and connect to a little block at the top of the dynamo, entering the cap via a slot which is supposed to have a rubber seal. The rubber has long since perished and it's clear that all that rain in Scotland had found the weakness, funnelled down inside and collected amongst the vital gubbins. Chloe gets the Kleenex from the tank bag as I pull out the little spring-loaded carbon brushes to expose the all important copper commutator ring and gaze at the emulsified oily mess that is covering everything. It takes a good ten minutes of dabbing and rubbing, and then I need to start Daisy once more to get the dynamo core spinning so that I can press down on the commutator to clean it's entire circumference. It certainly all looks better than when I had started, but the general impression is still one of dampness. Using my lighter carefully, I play it's flame back and forth across the carbon brushes, and once they are good and warm, therefore in theory dry, I slot them back in place and stand up to start the old girl once more. I blip the throttle, but at first nothing happens and then miraculously I see the first blue sparks appear on the brushes and suddenly the ammeter needle gives a jerk. Bloody marvellous!

Lights on these machines are rarely very good, and with a battery that's as dead as Daisy's there is no ready juice on tap to activate them. But once the dynamo is turning fast enough an amount of juice can get through the system and kick the glow-worms into life. I experiment by turning the things on, and note that at tick-over revs the things barely glow at all, but a hefty twist on the throttle has them flaring up immediately. As long as I can keep the revs high then, we have lights, and that means we can go hunt down a campsite again, or even continue to the next Landmark and look for camping nearby. Either way we're back in the game and we can be pleased with ourselves for not needing to wimp-out on a recovery truck. I congratulate Chloe again for the simple observation that had led me to do what I should have done days ago, and she beams at me with obvious happiness as she mock-scolds me in response "I dunno Dad, what would you do without me?" "I'd be a lot richer!" I shoot back, and with this she giggles and reaches for her helmet and gloves once more. We're ready to go again, and if we managed to get lost in broad daylight out in these lanes, finding our way in the dark will be so much less certain. Who cares, I tell myself, we're very nearly there.

It takes us half an hour of bimbling around in the inky darkness to decide that our quest is hopeless. We stop at a smallish junction and after a short while of peering at the maps in the dim glow of Daisy's headlight, which fail to offer any insight, I declare that the game's up and we'll simply have to camp at the first bit of flat ground we can find. Chloe looks far from impressed with this latest turn of events, and I try to keep her spirits up by gibbering something about adventuring, how this is all part of it and what the hell, Chris and I had camped in far more remote conditions than this up in Cumbria. She isn't buying, and soon it becomes clear why, as she bashfully mumbles that she needs the toilet soon for a 'number two' and no way is she doing that out in the open. I quite agree, not least because it's a fairly antisocial thing to do, but I don't have a ready solution to the dilemma and I stare at the maps again seeking any kind of inspiration. Then the obvious answer to our problems dawns on me, because right down in the corner of my map I notice Newport Pagnell and in a flash of rare inspiration I suddenly know exactly what we should do. I just need to work out where we are exactly, plot a course out of these lanes, do a bit of motorway riding and salvation will be on hand. I check my watch; get a shock to find that it's gone nine o'clock, but I decide that it's fine because hopefully within the hour we'll be ensconced in a comfortable, familiar (at least to me) bar.

Time to fill Chloe in on the plan then, and I tell her of the many, many times during my working life that I have stopped for the night at the Newport Pagnell services, which possesses one of the few lodge type hotels with a bar and restaurant. It's about thirty-five miles I reckon, but if we can find the big roads, the M45 and the M1, we can be there in maybe forty minutes or so. She looks immensely relieved, says "cool" and simply grabs her helmet and gloves expectantly. Right, unanimous decision then, and we set off north in search of Stretton-on-Dunsmore, the nearest town according to the signs and very close to the sought after big roads. Five minutes later we are well on our way, with Daisy galloping along at somewhere above the seventy mark, and it's a matter of only twenty-five minutes or so to reach the promised oasis. We check in with no trouble, waving goodbye to forty-five quid, but it's absolutely worth it after what has been an eventful and at times challenging day. The next problem is Daisy. I have no lock with me, choosing to leave the thing at home for this leg as I had been absolutely sure that we would be camping the whole way. There is no secure parking at these places, and I curse myself for not thinking about this before we came here. I can't just leave her unsecured outside. My only hope is to persuade one of the businesses based here at the services to allow me to park her in the secure service areas that they always have round the back, but first I agree to let Chloe into our room so that she can get a bath or a shower on the go.

We look for our room, and find that it's one of the 'outside' rooms, with their doors opening straight out onto the car park. As we enter, it strikes me that the door is quite wide. Would it be possible, I wonder, to squeeze daisy through the thing and park her in the hallway? It certainly looks that way to me, and although the management may take a dim view of this it seems like a perfect answer to our dilemma. After unpacking her and chucking the stuff in our room, I set off to the nearby services to look for newspapers, and in short order I am back laying the content of two of them out to protect the carpet from any unsightly marks. Next I grab some Kleenex from the bag and kneeling down outside I give Daisy's underside a thorough wipe. Now for the moment of truth, but there are a few people walking around and as I don't really want to be caught in the act of what I'm about to do, I loiter around until the coast looks clear. Right – go! I grab the handlebars, and as quickly as I can shove her up to the door. It's a tight squeeze, and I have to jink the bars a bit to get past the frame, but she's in! I have to breathe in and do the vertical limbo to get past her into the room, but now we can relax properly and that thought reminds me that the bar is still open and should be visited without delay. Luckily Chloe hasn't actually finished running the bath yet and I suggest that she postpones this event until after a drink or two. She readily agrees, as she always does when offered free food or drink, and without any further mucking about we limbo past Daisy once more and head off for a well-deserved nightcap.

Chloe puts in a call to Chris in order to update him, and we all agree that we'll be in no rush in the morning, looking to reach our final, fiftieth Landmark any time after nine o'clock. It seems bizarre after all the anticipation, to have ended up riding past the thing and then have to double back in the morning, but that's the way it goes and that's what we'll have to do. It's only twenty-five miles anyway. Victory this time, *surely*, is guaranteed! Chris assures us he'll be waiting by the telephone from nine onwards, and after that's all agreed he hands over the 'phone to his mum so that I can update her and have a short chat, during which I promise that we'll be home tomorrow, even if it's on a breakdown truck! We stay in the little bar until booting out time, after which dinner comes courtesy of a fast food joint and we settle for chicken, chips, beans and wedges of some description. Having collected that lot we head off for the luxury of a good hot bath, a spot of TV and a comfortable bed. It wasn't how I had envisaged our last night, but from Chloe's perspective it is just wonderful. She spends an impossibly long time in the bath, and is deeply impressed that there is free shampoo, bubble bath and soap for her to use. There's no point telling her that it's all in the price and therefore not really free and I make do with reminding her that there needs to be some left for me! Later on we lie in the darkness, a comfortable bed each, recounting the events of the entire day and all the things that have occurred that seemed to have been sent by fate to stop us, but instead of dwelling on those we end up sniggering at the memory of the happy drunkard. Shortly afterwards I find that I am talking to myself – Chloe is fast asleep. I turn over and drift into a doze, my last thoughts being that despite the setbacks, all in all it had been one of the most enjoyable days of the whole challenge so far, and more to the point, it had all but delivered us to our final destination.

I wake up to an overpowering smell of petrol and have a mild panic. I had entirely forgotten that Daisy's rather antiquated carburettor design tends to be mildly incontinent, and in the enclosed space, with virtually no ventilation, the fumes have nowhere to go. I dress as quickly as I can, and open the large window as far as it will allow, before similarly opening the door to the room. Next thing is to get Daisy out, and I discover that manoeuvring her out of the narrow opening backwards is a lot harder than getting her in had been. The next ten minutes is spent clearing up the newspapers, and then spraying the room with deodorant in a desperate attempt to rid the place of the awful smell. Chloe manages to remain oblivious to all of this frenetic activity, snoring gently, quite undisturbed. I take a shower, leaving the front door partially open still, and by the time I emerge again Chloe is stirring from her slumbers. She comes fully awake, I wave at her, she pulls a face and by way of morning greetings she pronounces "Urrgh, what's that smell?"

While she showers, I spend the time flapping a towel round the room in an effort to move the air around, but even by the time we are ready to leave there is still a distinct tang to the air. We spray a bit more of the smelly stuff around, but there's nothing more can be done and we take the last of our stuff out to Daisy feeling slightly guilty. What I should have done last evening would have been to run Daisy's engine with the petrol turned off, until the large float bowl standing proud and upright next to the carburettor was empty. I am of course stupid, so I hadn't taken this simple step.

I know that the smell will disappear, with any luck before the next guest stays, but I find myself hoping that the cleaners don't go in there before we've breakfasted and made our escape. I needn't have worried. The cleaners are far too busy having a fag and discussing the latest terrible events to be dreamed up by the script writers of last night's soap operas, and don't look like they're in any danger of doing any work for a while. We scuttle into the restaurant, but I can't help feeling slightly guilty about our dark secret, so breakfast is a rushed affair. Chloe is eager to up and get at it too, and it's only fifteen minutes later that we are heading for the door. The cleaners haven't moved but it's a relief to be outside and away, and as Daisy warms up in the morning chill we turn our attention to this, our last leg of the challenge and hopefully the great moment of success. We both agree that we don't want any truck with the motorway, it's absolutely heaving with the morning rat-race of commuters and no fun is to be had fighting with that lot. No, we'll go cross-country and as there is a little service exit here we'll take that and see where it leads before sorting out a proper route to Draycote Water. We climb aboard, and we're off into the misty lanes once more. An hour later, having got ourselves tangled up in the peripheries of Milton Keynes for twenty minutes, we are picking our way through the very last few miles of lanes, searching for our final, much anticipated Landmark.

For the last ten miles however, my mind has been feeding the hungry wolf of paranoia again, nourishing it with visions of potential disaster, a last minute problem to stop us in our tracks so tantalisingly close to our goal. Another puncture perhaps, those points could finally break or a seizure would do it for sure. Irrationally my brain turns every little sound from Daisy's engine into the fear of a sudden cessation of forward momentum and so convinced am I, against all logic, that imminent disaster is going to strike that I even find myself idly wondering whether we could persuade a breakdown driver to take us the few remaining miles, just for the photographs, before the shameful trek south riding shotgun in a pickup truck. Of course I have no grounds whatsoever to really believe any of this, and it's ridiculous to be thinking this way at all, but even though deep down I know I'm just being daft, I can't shake off the feeling. Then suddenly Chloe jerks me out of my morass of misgivings. She's spotted the lake and the anticipation within her is released in a spontaneous, explosive outburst. "Yeeehaa!" I nearly die of heart failure, because this is delivered directly into my left ear, which has been keenly straining to pick up any sudden noises from Daisy, but I recover magnificently as I see her pointed finger and realise that we are finally here. "Yeeehaa" indeed!

We park up by the entrance to the place, and as I dismount I am almost immediately bowled over by Chloe as she flings her arms around me.

"We've done it Dad......we've *done* it!" she exclaims. I am amazed at the sheer exuberance and joy coming off her in palpable waves as she barely pauses for breath.

"Where's the 'phone, we've got to call Chris!"

I dig the thing out, hand it over, and as she dials the number with barely contained excitement I relax and gaze across at the lake. We really have done it, and I switch my gaze to Daisy, sitting there quietly without fuss, just the odd 'tinc' or 'ping' sounding as her engine and exhausts cool off. I feel a sudden pride swelling in me as I look at her, and I consider that as far as I'm concerned she has earned respect and in fact she can blow up now, have as many punctures as she pleases and divest herself of magneto parts at leisure and I won't hold it against her. Yes, *she* has done it and that's that. These thoughts are interrupted as Chloe, face flushed with happiness and pride, shoves the 'phone at me and I turn my attention to sharing the moment with her and Chris. In normal circumstances beer at nine-thirty in the morning would be an abhorrent prospect, but Chris has already opened his and well, why not just this once? We celebrate our achievement in fitting style and just before hanging up the 'phone I call for a toast "To Daisy - and all who sail in her!"

I have mixed emotions on the ride back to our base camp in Cambridge. On the one hand, it's been a great adventure and I have spent more time with the kids than I probably had in the whole of the previous two years, so wrapped up had I been in the business and my professional life. And not just time together, but real personal time talking, planning, laughing, almost crying at times, yarn-telling and most importantly sharing the experiences of the open road. We have certainly come through some challenging times, had overcome many setbacks, suffered exposure to appalling weather, enjoyed the opposite experience of long days in the sun, and we had seen and done things that would stay in the memory for ever. But these happy positive thoughts are tempered by less pleasing ones. What happens now that it's over? What does life have to bring for the next few months, years and God forbid decades? It starts next week, with the kids back at school, my obligation to see a project through that will take me to the other side of the world before the year is out, but what comes after? I decide that all such thoughts can wait. Right now, I want to get home, see my wife, Chris, the dog and I owe Daisy a few hours of attention with a bucket of soapy water and a session with the spanners. I just hope the bloody car starts this time!

Epilogue

October, and as Timmy the RAF Tri-star makes his final descent into Brize Norton back from the Falkland Islands, I find myself replaying in my mind's eye the events of this summer, and I like what I see. I am loath to let go of the freedom that had been discovered out there on the open roads, and I want more than anything else to continue what I've started with the kids. It's clear to me right here, right now, that I must resist at all costs the current pressure to be sucked back into my former existence and I determine at this moment that this will be the last such diversion.

Every story should have an ending, or so I'm told, but that's only true if the end of the story has in fact been reached. For Daisy, the kids and me the Landmark challenge is only the beginning. There are other challenges waiting for us, many more roads out there waiting to be explored, the story is set to continue and perhaps the best way to finish this particular chapter is to look back to where it all started, and compare that to where we are now.

Take a peek into *this* garage. The air may be heavy, but no longer is it due to neglect, that particular atmosphere of neglect that comes from years of inactivity. Peering into the darkness, the shape and outline of an old machine can still be discerned, but this time it's a proud one waiting not for eternity, but simply, patiently, for it's next appointment with the open road, wiling away the short time since it's last canter and ready to put miles beneath it's wheels once more. The dust has had no time to settle, the once-dulled edges are bright and shiny once more and the slick oil waits, not to become thick and useless, but to be warmed once more by an engine that is ready and willing to work. Shards of lazy yellow light may still stab through the murk, leaking around the door and through the odd crack, and they may still highlight the dust motes, swirling gently around in the dark interior but now they cannot settle for this proud example of one of Britain's finest will not rest long enough to allow it. Daisy is a working motorcycle once more, and while her owner is seeking the next challenge, the next adventure, right now she merely dozes.

No, the overwhelming sensation now is one of anticipation.